Cree:
Language of the Plains

nēhiyawēwin:
paskwāwi-pīkiskwēwin

Cree:
Language of the Plains

nēhiyawēwin:
paskwāwi-pīkiskwēwin

by Jean L. Okimāsis

2004

UNIVERSITY OF
REGINA

CANADIAN PLAINS
RESEARCH CENTER

Canadian Plains Research Center
University of Regina
Regina, Saskatchewan S4S 0A2
Canada
Tel: (306) 585-4758
Fax: (306) 585-4699
e-mail: canadian.plains@uregina.ca
http://www.cprc.uregina.ca

National Library of Canada Cataloguing in Publication

Okimasis, Jean L., 1938-
        Cree, language of the Plains / Jean L. Okimasis.

(University of Regina publications ; 13)
Includes bibliographical references.
ISBN 0-88977-155-3

1. Cree language—Textbooks for second language learners—English speakers.
I. University of Regina. Canadian Plains Research Center II. Title. III. Series.

PM987.O38 2004   497'.323   C2004-903448-0

Cover design by Donna Achtzehner, Canadian Plains Research Center
Printed and bound in Canada by Houghton Boston, Saskatoon

We acknowledge the financial support of the Government of Canada through the Book Publishing Industry Development Program (BPIDP) for our publishing activities.

Contents

Foreword to the 2004 Edition

Publishing material can be an exciting and fruitful experience. At least that is my own thought about the last edition. I have learned that although there have been long strides in technology there is nothing like using the ordinary pencil. I appreciate my pen and pencil more now then ever. I feel that I must apologize for the printing errors and the misplacement of asterisks in the Verbs section of the glossary. Because I did the editing I take responsibility and as a result, I have made changes that will, hopefully, simplify the classification of that particular set of verbs. Basically the verb forms of the VTA now coincide using numbers: VTA-1 and VTA-4 use Inverse-1; VTA-2 use Inverse-2; VTA-3 use Inverse-3. The charts also have these numbers for easier indentification.

In this second edition I am adding material that I have been teaching for years and did not write in a form that could be included in the text. So you will find more verb forms; forms that are heard in everyday speech. Some illustrations and diagrams with explanations that were helpful in the classroom are also included this time. Another feature is the inclusion of definitions which were appreciated especially by my Cree-speaking students who had quite a time of it when they were required to put labels on their own Cree vocabulary. And while the non-speakers of Cree appear to understand the structure they also welcome visual illustrations such as charts, diagrams or even my attempts at drawing stick figures on the board while explaining the direction of actions. While there are many new verbs forms and discussions there are also some deletions. The linguistic material in the original Chapter 13 is not included.

At this point I would like to acknowledge Solomon Ratt's contribution to the previous edition. His aptitude in the area of language was apparent when he was a student in a class that I taught one spring. It was this that prompted me to request that he be hired while he finished his degree. I am grateful for that decision as he was always willing to discuss not only the material but he readily gave of his time to edit and to add to other chapters. And now he is on to other endeavors but he has graciously given me permission to take out the material that was too technical for a teaching grammar. Thank you, Solomon and I wish you great success in finishing your doctorate.

Jean L. Okimāsis
June 2004

Preface

What usually goes into a language grammar? What is available to the teachers who are educating children about the Cree language? What is known about the Cree language in terms of its grammatical structure and how it is applied? How can all the material be made available to the educators? What is needed? These are questions that went through my mind as I decided to reorganize and elaborate on the material presented in the first edition of *Cree: Language of the Plains / nēhiyawēwin: paskwāwi-pīkiskwēwin.*

As a result this edition attempts to offer the lay person an overview of more Cree grammar that was not included before but taught in the classroom. Forms of verbs that are commonly used in everyday conversations are introduced: the unspecified actor; the relative clause; the "you and me" set and the proper use of the verb "*ayā-* be."

The discussion on the demonstrative pronouns and their role in Cree sentences is a result of the chapter on the Auxiliary Verb. The verb "to be" is inherent in these pronouns but it had to be explained at least with some examples. After reading parts of *Non-verbal Predication Theory, Typology, Diachrony* by Kees Hengeveld and after some interesting discussions with colleagues I was assured that I should make an attempt to try explaining the function that demonstrative pronouns have in Cree sentences. It is only a beginning but the idea of non-verbal predicates can now be elaborated on by other students of Cree.

As well, a more detailed discussion of the Conjunct mode is included this time. Is it a subordinate or main clause? I am sure students would more than welcome the task of examining texts to see whether verbs in this mode are ever main clauses or not. I hope the information that is presented here will intrigue them enough to do more research on Cree verbs occurring in this mode.

The word "note" appears in many places, which I hope will be helpful. Some of them refer to relevant information that was presented in other chapters; some of them summarize the section above it; others are reminders about rules that were previously introduced. They are meant to assist the teachers and students or even those who read the book to understand the structure of Cree.

And although more verbs and vocabulary have been added I would invite everyone to refer to the dictionary compiled by Arok Wolvengrey, *nēhiyawēwin: itwēwina/Cree: Words.*

I found that we had included too much information in some chapters. So I decided to sort through the topics and present them in separate chapters. That was rather difficult because the subject matter is so intertwined. Because of this some of the examples had verb forms that had not been discussed. I tried to explain some ideas by using hypothetical situations and the mental processes behind the speech. I found that much of how the vocabulary is used depends on context. The use of two words together also can give a totally different meaning. But that in itself would take some research and much discussion with speakers, so I leave it to the teachers, students and the Elders to discuss.

Acknowledgements

In this second edition I again acknowledge those who assisted me in one way or another. In the past, first of all, were the late Anna Crowe, the late Dr. Ahab Spence who both championed the Cree language and both asked me as department heads, in different years, to come to teach with them.

Thank you to the following: Dr. Terry Klokeid, linguist, who gave me feedback on the presentation of the material, Margaret Cote, lecturer of the Saulteaux language, and professors of Cree, Donna Paskemin, Assistant Professor, Doreen Oakes, lecturer, Darren Okemaysim, lecturer. *kinanāskomitināwāw*. For their assistance I thank the late Dr. W. Rubrecht, Elisabeth Kim, Alice Whiteman, Sandra Poncelet-Gardner and Gwen Lafontaine.

I would be amiss if I did not acknowledge my husband Arok; his interest in the Cree language is appreciated and so are the many discussions about all my work and the content in this edition. His patient, and sometimes long linguistic explanations were helpful once he translated them to lay language. Thanks also for taking time out to draw the charts for me so I could display my work the way I want. Kudos, Arok, for the Cree dictionary as it is helpful in our classrooms. I salute you for all your hard work.

Chapter 1: Dialects

There are ten major linguistic groups of Indian languages in Canada, one of which is the Algonkian family. Cree is one of the numerous languages, from Canada and the United States, that make up this Algonkian family. Some other Algonkian languages from Canada are Blackfoot, Ojibway (including Saulteaux), Odawa, and Micmac.

Cree settlements and reservations are scattered throughout Canada from Quebec to the foothills of Alberta. Residents in a few settlements in northern British Columbia also speak Cree.

There are five major variants, or dialects, of Cree within this area:

1. Plains Cree (Y): Southern Saskatchewan and central Alberta.
2. Woodlands Cree (Th): Northern Saskatchewan and some areas of Manitoba.
3. Swampy Cree (N): Manitoba and Northern Ontario and east-central Saskatchewan.
4. Moose Cree (L): Moose Factory and Hudson Bay area.
5. Atikamēk Cree (R) Quebec.

The dialect, Atikamēk Cree, spoken in Quebec, is quite different from the others, and Montagnais and Naskapi are also closely related languages with many similarities.

The following three dialects are spoken in Saskatchewan:

• The "*th*": Woodlands Cree is spoken in various northern communities such as Peter Ballantyne, LaRonge, Stanley Mission and South End. The people who speak this dialect in northern Manitoba have been referred to as the "Rock Cree."

• The "*n*": Swampy Cree is spoken in the northern community of Cumberland House. The people of the Red Earth reserve also speak this dialect.

• The third dialect is the "*y*": Plains Cree. This dialect can be further divided to represent the Northern Plains Cree and the Southern Plains Cree. They both use the "*y*" but there is one particular vowel sound difference. For example, in the word for "a girl" Northern Plains people will use an "*ī*" — *iskwīsis* and the Southern Plains group will use an "*ē*" — *iskwēsis*.

The Southern Plains dialect is spoken in communities located within an area ranging from White Bear reserve in the southeast corner to the northwest community of Onion Lake plus the community of Nekaneet in the southwest corner of the province. In addition to these reserves the following also speak the Southern Plains "*y*" dialect: Ochapahwace, Piapot, Thunderchild, Red Pheasant, Muskeg Lake, Beardy's and Sandy Lake, James Smith and others.

The Northern Plains "*y*" dialect is spoken by those living in White Fish, Sturgeon Lake, Meadow Lake, Canoe Lake. These are only a few of the many Northern Plains "*y*" dialect-speaking communities.

As well, there are many in the province who speak 'Michif' a language which is a mixture of French and the "*y*" dialect of Cree. In this book however, only the Southern "*y*" dialect is discussed.

Chapter 2: Spelling and Sound System

Fourteen letters of the Roman alphabet are used to represent the sounds of the Cree language, compared to the twenty-six letters used for the English language. These letters represent seventeen distinct sounds.

The ten consonants are *c, h, k, m, n, p, s, t, w,* and *y.* Most consonants are pronounced similar to their English counterparts but there are four that need special attention. These four are the *c, k, p* and *t.*

Consonants: c, k, p, and t

c: pronounced like the "ts" in cats.

cēskwa	wait
acāhkos	star
anohc	now, today

k: pronounced as a cross between a "g" in "gill" and "k" in "kill" but it is never the hard "k" sound in a word such as "kick."

kīspin	if
akihcikē	count
kotak	another

p: a cross between the "p" in "pit" and the "b" in "bit" when it is in the beginning and in the middle. It has a softer aspirated sound when it is at the end of a word.

pēhin	wait for me
api	sit
sīsīp	a duck

t: is pronounced like the "t" in "stanza." In other words it is a cross between the "t" in "tin" and the "d" in "dim."

tāpwē	true, truly, really!
āta	although
ātiht	some

Vowels

Four symbols are used to accommodate the long and short vowel sounds of Cree. A special diacritical symbol is used to differentiate the long vowel sound from the short vowel sound. The short vowel sounds are not specially marked and they are spoken quickly.

Short vowels are *a, i,* and *o.*

a: pronounced like the first "a" in "appeal."

awas	go away
āstam	come
ōta	here

i: pronounced like the "i" in "if."

iskwēw	a woman
otina	take it
ēkosi	there, that's it.

o: pronounced like the initial "o" in "oppose."

otin	take it
kotak	another
nēwo	four

NOTE: The English vowel symbol "u" is not used for writing Cree because it can be mistakenly pronounced as the "u" in words such as: "use," "unicorn" or "unique."

Long vowels are enunciated slowly. Speakers sometimes hear degrees of the length of these vowel sounds. Unless it is definitely a short sound one must use a macron. Long vowels are written like the regular vowels but with a diacritical mark called a macron. It can be a line or a circumflex over the vowel but never an accent which is used for indicating stress patterns. This diacritical marking is important when reading and writing Cree in the Roman orthography because a non-speaker of Cree is guided by these symbols. Otherwise, they would have a difficult time to distinguish long from the short sounds. Furthermore, leaving the macron out could result in a word with an entirely different meaning as the following examples illustrate. There are many such pairs in Cree.

asam	feed him/her/it	askihk	a pail
asām	a snowshoe	askīhk	on the land/earth

Long vowels are: *ā, ī, ō,* and *ē.*

ā: pronounced like the "a" in "fa" as in "do, ray, me, fa, so, la, ti, do."

āstam	come
tānisi	hello, how are you? how?
tāniwā	where is he/she/it?

ī: pronounced like the "i" in "machine."

mīpit	a tooth
apisīs	a little
cī	a question indicator

ō: pronounced like the "o" in "sole."

ōta	here
pōna	put it in the fire
kāsōw	he/she hides

ē: pronounced like the "e" in "berry" or the "a" in the word "acorn."

ēkosi	there, that's it
mēkwāc	now (at the present time)
kīwē	go home

NOTE: It is recommended that if you are a speaker learning how to write your language and find that you are hearing some sounds that are not as long as others but longer than the short vowels then a macron should be placed over the vowel.

Pronunciation

Those who are not speakers of Cree quite often place the stress on the second last syllable because they are following the English system. They might also place the stress on the long vowels of Cree, especially if the second last syllable contains a long vowel. However, that still wouldn't necessarily be the correct pronunciation. Instead of the accent mark *in the examples below italics are used to indicate the stressed syllable.*

To determine which syllable is accented or stressed, one works from the right to the left on a word. Consider the following three-syllable words.

1. In the following words the stress occurs on the third syllable from the right:

mīciwin	food	*mī* ci win
sōniyāw	money	*sō* ni yāw
tānisi	how, hello	*tā* ni si
kikosis	your (sg.) son	*ki* ko sis

2. In these four-syllable words below we again note that the stress falls on the third syllable from the right:

kimiwasin	It is drizzling.	ki *mi* wa sin
tāniwēhā	Where are they?	tā *ni* wē hā
kipimohtān	You (sg.) walk	ki *pi* moh tān

3. These five-syllable words not only show that the stress falls on the third syllable from the right, but that a secondary stress falls on the second syllable to the left of this (note the italicized letters indicating this):

ātayōhkēwin	a legend/story	*ā* ta *yōh* kē win
nitawēyihta	want it	*ni* ta *wē* yih ta
oskinīkiskwēw	a young girl	*os* ki *nī* kis kwēw
pimācihowin	culture	*pi* mā *ci* ho win

4. Two-syllable words, however, do not follow this format. Instead, the stress is on the last syllable:

ōta	here	ō *ta*
api	sit	a *pi*

Chapter 3: Minimal Pairs and Minimal Sets

This unusual aspect of Cree was mentioned in the last chapter where the long vowels were discussed. A minimal pair is two words that are identical in spelling except for one sound. They are spelled with the same letters except for the fact that the vowel in one word has a macron which changes the sound and therefore the meaning of the word. Here are only a few examples.

sākahikan	a lake	kisitēw	It is hot.
sakahikan	a nail (for building)	kīsitēw	It is cooked.
niyānan	five	tāniwā	Where is s/he?
niyanān	us	tāniwē	Where is it?
miyaw	a body	wīcēwākan	a partner/friend
miyāw	S/he is given s.t.	wīcēwāhkan	accompany him/her (later)

There may also be a change in the use of consonants which again results in a different sound and meaning of words. For instance:

yōtin	It is windy.	kōna	snow
nōtin	Fight him/her.	pōna	Put it in the fire.
ōma	this	sōniyāw	money
ōta	here	mōniyāw	a non-Indian
tahkipēstāw	It is cold rain falling.	nāpēw	a man
pahkipēstāw	Large drops of rain are falling.	nātēw	He/she fetches him/her/it

Minimal sets are sets of three or more words rather than pairs that differ in only one important sound and therefore have different meanings. Examples:

nīsta	me too/also	nīpit	my tooth
kīsta	you too/also	kīpit	your tooth
wīsta	him/her too/also	wīpit	his/her tooth
pihko	soot/ashes	maci	evil/bad (preverb)
mihko	blood	māci	begin (preverb)
sihko	spit (imperative)	mācī	hunt big game

Chapter 4: Nouns: An Overview

In Cree, like English, there are nouns, pronouns, verbs and adverbs. This chapter will discuss nouns and how they can undergo a process of compounding with verbs or other nouns to form new nouns or verbs. As will be shown pluralizing nouns in Cree is another matter which has its own set of rules. The term "diminutive" as it applies to Cree nouns will also be explained.

Nouns are words which refer to things like animals, birds, fish, people, parts of the anatomy, clothing, insects, land forms, machines, utensils, plants and stars, sun and the moon. In Cree, nouns are classified either as animate or inanimate.

Animate nouns usually refer to living things, such as animals, birds, people, plants, fish, insects. Stones or rocks, celestial bodies, sun, moon, stars, northern lights are also in this category. In addition, however, some items of clothing, some utensils, some body parts and some machines are also animate.

It can be said then that animate nouns are words that refer not only to things that are living but also to terms that refer to some items that are not. Some of these words are important to the cultural beliefs of the Cree people. Examples of animate nouns:

mōswa	a moose	iskwēw	a woman
piyēsīs	a bird	niska	a goose
nāpēw	a man	pīsim	the sun
kinosēw	a fish	kihiw	an eagle

Some non-living objects that are classified as animate are:

ospwākan	a pipe	mitās	a pair of trousers
maskasiy	a nail (finger or toe)	asiniy	a rock/stone
astis	a mitten/glove	asikan	a sock/stocking
tāpiskākan	a scarf/necktie	ēmihkwān	a spoon
tēwēhikan	a drum	mistikwaskihk	a drum
sēhkēpayīs	a car	mitohtōsim	a breast/teat

Inanimate nouns include most utensils, most machines, most clothing and buildings, all of which are not living objects. However, there are also some living, such as body parts, that are considered to be inanimate nouns. Examples of inanimate nouns:

mohkomān	a knife	pimihākan	an aeroplane
astotin	a hat/cap	oyākan	a dish
masinahikan	a book	tēhtapiwin	a chair/bench
maskisin	a shoe	tāpiskākan	a collar/a horse-collar

Here are a few living objects that are classified as inanimate:

miskīsik	an eye	misit	a foot
miskāt	a leg	micihciy	a hand
mitēh	a heart	wāpakwaniy	a flower

Compounds

Cree is one of a number of languages that are considered "Incorporating" languages. Simply put this is a process where certain words can be put together to make new words. Another term for this process is compounding. However, neither term actually describes adequately this process. It is virtually a short cut or perhaps just another way of saying what you want to say. Examples of combination of a verb and a noun follow.

Putting on clothing using separate words:

postiska astotin.	(literally) put it on (VTI) a hat	Put on a hat.
postiskaw asikan.	(literally) put it on (VTA) a sock	Put on a sock.

Compounding or combining a part of the above verbs with a noun or part of a noun results in a new verb which will virtually have the same meaning.

Note the incorporation:

post + noun + ē   = VAI
post + astotin + ē   = postastotinē – put on a hat
post + asikan + ē   = postasikanē – put on sock[s]

Notice that "*post*" is part of the verb *postiska* and *postiskaw* and that it also appears as part of the new words:

postastisē   put mitts on
postasākē   put a coat on
postitāsē   put pants on
poscitāsē   put pants on
postaskisinē   put shoes on
postayiwinisē   put clothes on

One might argue that it is assumed that the translation of the above would be "put your … on" and it would be right if his/her mittens etc. were right in front of him/her. But if you don't want to have the children scrapping over mittens then one can be more specific by saying the following:

postiska kitastotin.   (literally) put it on (VTI) your hat   Put on your hat.
postikaw kitasikan.   (literally) put it on (VTA) your sock   Put on your sock.

Taking clothing off (undressing):

kēcikoska   take it off (VTI)
kēcikoskaw   take it off (VTA)
kēt + noun + ē   = VAI
kēc + noun + ē   = VAI
eg. kēt + asikan + ē   = kētasikanē (take off your socks)
kētastisē   take off your mitt
kētasākē   take your coat off
kētitāsē   take off your pants
kēcitāsē   take off your pants
kētaskisinē   take off your shoes
kētayiwinisē   take off your clothes (undress)
kētastotinē   take off your hat

NOTE: Use *kēc-* before a short "i," or *kēt-* before a short "a."

Colours Plus Nouns

Combining colours with nouns to make new words is also a unique structure because, in Cree, colours are verbs. So one should be familiar with the difference in meaning of the following structures:

kaskitēwāw   "It is black."
kaskitēwāw ōma miskotākay…   "This coat is black."
kaskitēwasākay ōma   "This is a black coat."

Notice the portion "*kaskitē-*" of the verb above appears to be the part that means "black." One will find that this part will occur with other nouns to mean "black" or "dark." The following examples appear to follow this rule.

Color + noun combinations:

kaskitēwaskisin   a black shoe
sīpīhkopapakiwayān   a blue shirt
mihkwasākay   a red coat

wāposāwipakwahtēhon	a yellow belt
osāwitās	an orange pair of pants
nīpāmāyātastotin	a purple hat
wāpistikwān	white hair (literally – a white head)

The fact that Cree is a highly derivational language becomes most apparent in the way new nouns can be formed either by adding a suffix to a verb, particle, or another noun or even by joining parts of two verbs. With the verb form, either the first person imperative or the third person independent is used.

Consider the following:

1. Abstract nouns ...win/itowin/owin

kisēwātisi + win	kisēwātisiwin
be kind	kindness
nēhiyawē + win	nēhiyawēwin
speak Cree	Cree (language)
ākayāsimo + win	ākayāsimowin
speak English	English (language)
māsīh +itowin	māsīhitowin
wrestle him/her	wrestling
sākih + itowin	sākihitowin
love her/him	love
kihcēyihtam + owin	kihcēyihtamowin
s/he has respect for it	respect

2. Concrete nouns/substance ...win

mīci + win	mīciwin
eat it	food
pwātisimo + win	pwātisimowin
dance (the grass dance)	Grass Dance (Siouan)
āhkosi + win	āhkosiwin
be sick	sickness/illness
tēhtapi + win	tēhtapiwin
sit on top of something	a chair

3. Tools and Instruments ...kan

kitohcikē + kan	kitohcikan
make music	a musical instrument
cīkahikē + kan	cīkahikan
chop	an axe
pimihā + kan	pimihākan
fly	an aeroplane
tipahikē + kan	tipahikan
measure	a measurement (eg. yard, time)

4. Artifical objects ... ihkān, ... ohkān

pīsim + ohkān	pīsimohkān
moon/sun	a clock
mohcowi + ohkān	mohcohkān
be foolish	a clown
awāsis + ihkān	awāsisihkān
a child	a doll
pimiy + ihkān	pimihkān
oil/grease	pemmican

Chapter 5: Diminutives

The term "diminutive" is used here to refer to nouns for items or objects that are smaller than the norm. This is represented by a sound change and the addition of suffixes. In some cases, adding a suffix is not enough so the "t" is replaced by "c." So, unlike English which uses entirely different words for objects smaller or younger than the mature version, (for instance, man–boy; cat–kitten; woman–girl), Cree uses suffixes. English also uses adjectives to show this concept as in: a box–a little box. As the following rules indicate a number of changes occur to the Cree nouns when the suffixes are added.

1. Add "-isis" or more often "-is" to most nouns:

Noun	Diminutive Noun
minōs	minōsis
a cat	a little cat/kitten
oyākan	oyākanis
a dish	a small dish
sīsīp	sīsīpisis
a duck	a little duck/duckling

2. If the noun contains "t," all are changed to "c," in addition to adding the suffix "is."

Noun	Diminutive Noun
mistikowat	miscikowacis
a box	a little box
mistikwān	miscikwānis
a head	a little head
astotin	ascocinis
a hat/cap	a little hat
tēhtapiwin	cēhcapiwinis
a chair	a little chair
iskwāhtēm	iskwāhcēmis
a door	a small door

3. When the word ends in a vowel and a "w" drop the "w" and add "sis." If the vowel is short make it long then add "s" or "sis."

Noun	Diminutive Noun
nāpēw	nāpēsis
a man	a boy
iskwēw	iskwēsis
a woman	a girl
pihēw	pihēsis
a grouse	a little grouse (prairie chicken)
āmōw	āmōsis
a bee	a little bee
pikiw	pikīs
gum	a bit of gum

4. For some nouns, the diminutive ending is "osis," after changing any "t"s to "c"s.

Noun	Diminutive Noun
atim	acimosis
a dog	a little dog/puppy
mistatim	miscacimosis
a horse	a little horse/pony

5. For some nouns, the diminutive suffix is "os."

Noun	Diminutive Noun
sikāk	sikākos
a skunk	a little skunk
kinēpik	kinēpikos
a snake	a little snake

Since all diminutives end in "s" simply add "ak" to any animate diminutive and "a" to any inanimate diminutive to form the plural diminutive noun.

Larger Objects

Diminutives have already been explained as words that refer to the smaller version of mature or regular sized objects. Larger than regular size articles can also be referred to. However, this is accomplished by using prenouns or prefixes that indicate the idea of augmentation. In the words below the prenouns/prefixes: *misi-*; *misti-*; *mahki-*; and *kihci-* are incorporated with the nouns. You will find that the use of these prenouns sometimes results in a new word altogether. So instead of saying: *misikitiw atim*; *misāw astotin*; *misāw mōhkomān*; *misikitiw sikāk*; one can say it with one word.

For the time being the changes will not be discussed because there are some nouns included in this list that require a more detailed explanation of the word formation. Those words are marked by asterisks.

a dog	atim	misi-atim	a big dog
		mis-ātim	a big dog
		misatim	a horse
		mistatim	a horse
a hat/cap	astotin	mis-āstotin	a large/big hat
muskeg	maskēk	misi-maskēk	a large muskeg
a berry	mīnis	*mahkiminakāw	a large patch of berries
a knife	mohkomān	misi-mōhkomān	a big knife
		*misti-mōhkomān	a big knife
		mistihkomān	a big knife
		kihci-mōhkomān	a big knife, an American
a moose	mōswa	misi-mōswa	a large moose
		misti-mōswa	a large moose
a rabbit	wāpos	*mistāpos	a big rabbit/jackrabbit
a man	nāpēw	*mistāpēw	a big/tall man
a goose	niska	misi-niska	a big goose
a pipe	ospwākan	mis-ōspwākan	a big pipe
		kihc-ōspwākan	a sacred pipe
a skunk	sikāk	misi-sikāk	a big skunk
a belly	matay	mahkatay	a big belly
an ear	mihtawakay	mahkihtawakay	a big/large ear
a nose	mikot	mahkikot	a big nose
a thigh	mipwām	mahkipwām	a large thigh
an eye	miskīsik	*mahkacāp	one who has a big eyes
a foot	misit	mahkisit	a big foot
a mouth	mitōn	mahkitōn	a big mouth
buttocks	misōkan	*mahkisōkan	a big derriere

NOTE: Body parts use "*mahki-*" to mean large. And some nouns use more than one prenoun.

Chapter 6: Word Order and Preverbs

In an ordinary English sentence the word order is either: subject–verb or subject–verb–object. "My child is singing." is not usually expressed as "Singing is my child." and the sentence "The dog chased the cat." is not the same as "The cat chased the dog." Judging from these sentences English word order is rigid. In the Cree examples below word order is not as strict. In 1a below, where the subject *nicawāsimis* precedes the verb *nipāw*, word order is the same as the English subject–verb. But in Cree *nicawāsimis* can be placed before or after *nipāw* without greatly affecting the meaning of the sentence. In example 1b. verb–subject construction, *nipāw* (verb) before *nicawāsimis* (subject) is possible.

1a. nicawāsimis nipāw.

My child	is sleeping
subject	verb

1b. nipāw nicawāsimis.

He/she is sleeping	my child
verb	subject

2a. niwāpamāw atim.

I	see	a dog.
subject	verb	object

2b. atim niwāpamāw.

a dog	I	see.
object	subject	verb

3a. kiwāpamāw cī sīsīp?

Do you	see	the duck?
subject	verb	object

3b. sīsīp cī kiwāpamāw?

The duck	do you	see?
object	subject	verb

The Cree sentences above are all correct.

As the previous examples reveal word order in Cree, for the most part, can be "free," that is, "subject," "verb," and "subject," "verb," "object" can be moved about. However, there are certain instances where the word order is "bound." The following are a few examples where certain phrases occur in a particular order. (Sentences marked with an asterisk are ungrammatical.)

1. The question indicator "cī" is usually placed in the second position.

(subject –) verb – object in:

a. kiwāpamāw cī sīsīp? Do you (sg.) see the duck?

and object - (subject -) verb in:

b. sīsīp cī kiwāpamāw? Duck do you see?

The subject, verb, and object have been moved about without affecting the meaning, but the "*cī*" question indicator has retained its position in both interrogative sentences. Now consider the examples below.

c. *cī kiwāpamāw sīsīp

d. *kiwāpamāw sīsīp cī?;

Because placing the "cī" in positions other than the second position results in a string of words that do not make sense, "*cī*" must always be placed in the second position. Questions of this type are known as "polarity questions" and simply require a "yes" or "no" answer.

2. The other "question" words, or interrogative pronouns, also occur in a particular order most of the time. These pronouns are commonly known as the "tān" words and represent the who, what, when, where and why in Cree. The following examples show that the "tān" words are placed at the beginning of the question:

a. tāniwā ana atim…	Where is that dog?
b. tāniwē anima masinahikan…	Where is that book?
c. *ana tāniwā atim…	That where dog.
d. *ana atim tāniwā…	That dog where.

c and d are both ungrammatical and thus would not be acceptable as properly spoken Cree. When one answers with more information than yes or no the person is answering a "content question."

NOTE: It is most important to remember that "cī" and the "tān-" words are never used together to ask a question. "tān-" words are used occasionally in positions other than the first in a sentence. Because it is not a frequent usage it will not be dealt with here.

3. The demonstrative pronouns are yet another instance where Cree is bound. Placing a demonstrative pronoun before or after a noun can alter the meaning of the phrase but only when it is being used in isolation with a noun.

a. nāpēw ana…	That is a man.
b. ana nāpēw…	That man.

The demonstrative pronoun "ana" must be placed after the noun to get the English statement "That is a man" and before the noun to say "that man." All demonstrative pronouns are arranged in this manner depending on the intent of the speaker. There is one instance, however, where the demonstrative pronoun can come before the noun and still have the copular verb "is" in the statement: This is in answer to a "cī" question where the answer is in the negative;

a. nāpēw cī ana?	Is that a man?
b. namōya, namōya ana nāpēw; iskwēw ana.	No, that is not a man; that is a woman.

NOTE: Here "ana" is only in front of "nāpēw" by chance or choice for emphasis. It follows "namōya" and that is what is important.

4. The construction of longer phrases using preverbs is yet another area where arrangement of words or parts of words must follow a rigid pattern.

Consider these four examples:

a. ninēhiyawān.	I speak Cree.
b. ninōhtē-nēhiyawān.	I want to speak Cree.
c. ninōhtē-nihtā-nēhiyawān.	I want to speak Cree well.
d. nikī-nōhtē-nihtā-nēhiyawān.	I wanted to speak Cree well.

Notice the "ni+" – the person indicator for "I" – is always placed at the beginning of this verb phrase; placed anywhere else the phrase would not make sense. The preverb "nōhtē-" and any other preverb, must always be placed before the verb stem. Furthermore some preverbs must precede other preverbs to get the intended meaning as shown in c. and d. above. The tense indicator "kī-" (for past tense), and any other tense indicator are also preverbs, and must always be placed immediately after the person indicator. So, what we have for all sentence structures is this rigid arrangement for verbs in the Independent mode:

Person +	Tense -	Preverb -	Verb Stem +	Suffix

NOTE: A (-) hyphen is required after the past and the future tenses and after the preverb. And a (+) plus indicates direct attachment without hyphen.

Chapter 8:
Interrogative, Indefinite, Demonstrative Pronouns

In English the word "pronoun" is a grammatical term referring to any class of relationship or single words which assume the function of nouns. I, you, her, him, they, it, ours, who, which, myself, anybody, others, are all pronouns.

The Cree language also has pronouns and, like English, they can be classified into different types. "I, you" are termed personal pronouns and "who, which" are called interrogative pronouns. In effect, Cree has five types of pronouns: personal, inclusive, interrogative, indefinite, demonstrative pronouns. While the personal and inclusive pronouns were discussed in the previous chapter this chapter focusses on the interrogative, indefinite and demonstrative pronouns. The obviative form is also included here.

Interrogative Pronouns

These particular words ask a question. They are one of two main kinds of question indicators. The other is the word "*ci*" which was mentioned in Chapter 6 and the interrogative pronouns discussed here. There are those that are used with animate nouns and those that are used with inanimate nouns. Some are used to ask general questions. Most of the time they occur at the beginning of a sentence. Here is a list of some of those that are used to ask general questions.

awīna	who (singular)	kīkwāy	what (singular)
awīniki	who (plural)	kīkwāya	what (plural)

Examples:

1. awīna ana kā-wāpamat?
   Who is it that you see?
2. awīniki aniki kā-kī-mētawēcik cīki wāskahikanihk?
   Who were those that were playing near the house?
3. kīkwāy ē-nitawēyihtaman?
   What do you want?
4. kīkwāya anihi?
   What are those?

The words below are not influenced by gender or classification and can also be used to ask general questions. They are equivalent to English questions such as why, where, when, what kind, how much, and how many. One can easily recognize these because most of them begin with the syllable "*tān-*".

tānisi?	How?
tānispīhk?	When?
tānēhki?	Why?
tāniyikohk?	How much? (quantity)
tānimayikohk?	How much? (quantity)
tānitahto?	How many? (numbers)
tānitahtwāw?	How many times?
tānitē?	Where?
tānitowahk?	What kind?

1. tānisi anima kā-kī-isi-itōtaman?   How did you do that?
2. tānēhki otākosīhk wīpac kā-kī-kīwēyan?   Why did you go home early yesterday?
3. tānispīhk kē-kīwēyan anohc?   When will you go home today?
4. tānitahto aniki iskwēsisak kā-mētawēcik wayawītimihk?
   Literal: How many little girls are there that are playing outside?
            How many little girls are playing outside?

5. tāniyikohk anima ē-itakihtēk?   How much does that cost?

6. tānitahtwāw ōma kā-kī-kiyokawacik?   How many times did you visit them?

7. tānitē anima kā-wī-itohtēyan?   Where is it that you are intending to go?

8. tānitowahk ana oyākana kā-kī-atāwēt?   What kind of dishes did she buy?

NOTE: Most of the time these pronouns are placed at the beginning of sentences.

Those interrogative pronouns that refer specifically to animate or inanimate nouns are listed below. Each form agrees in classification and number with the noun it modifies. The following chart summarizes which interrogative is to be used for an animate or in inanimate noun.

Number	Animate	Inanimate	English
Singular	tāniwā	tāniwē	Where is he/she/it?
	tāna	tānima	Which one?
	awīna	—	Who?
	kīkwāy	kīkwāy	What?
Plural	tāniwēhkāk	tāniwēhā	Where are they?
	tāniki	tānihi	Which ones?
	awīniki	—	Who?
	kīkwāyak	kīkwāya	What?

Examples:

1) tāniwā?   Where is he/she or it? (animate singular)

2) tāniwēhkāk?   Where are they? (animate plural)

3) tāniwā kitōtēm anohc?   Where is your friend today?

4) tāniwēhkāk kitastisak?   Where are your mitts?

5) tāniwā Bobby mēkwāc?   Where is Bobby right now?

6) tāniwēhkāk Bobby ēkwa otōtēma?   Whe are Bobby and his friends?

7) tāniwē?   Where is it? (inanimate singular)

8) tāniwēhā?   Where are they? (inanimate plural)

9) tāniwē minihkwācikan?   Where is the cup?

10) tāniwēhā nimaskisina?   Where are my shoes?

11) tāniwē anima masinahikan kā-kī-atāwēyan?   Where is that book that you bought?

12) tāna?   Which one? (animate singular)

13) tāniki?   Which ones? (animate plural)

14) tāna ana askihk kā-nōhtē-āpacihat?   Which pail do you want to use?

15) tānima?   Which one? (inanimate singular)

16) tānihi?   Which ones? (inanimate plural)

17) tānima masinahikan kā-nitawēyihtaman?   Which book is it that you want?

18) tānihi ē-nōhtē-atāwēyan?   Which ones do you want to buy?

Indefinite Pronouns

The following chart includes terms that refer to a person or thing without indicating who or what is being spoken about yet there is the idea that there is something or someone concrete there. Again, there are singular and plural forms. Some of the examples below show some interesting ways to express the same idea. In addition to the animate and inanimate categories there are the obviative forms. The obviative forms are explained, in the next section, with examples.

Number	Animate	Inanimate	English
Singular	awiyak	—	Someone
	kīkway	kīkway	Something
	nam āwiyak	—	Nobody
	—	nama kīkway	Nothing
	pikw āwiyak	—	Everyone/anyone
	—	piko kīkway	Everything/anything
Plural	awiyakak	—	Some people
	kīkwayak	kīkwaya	Some things
	kahkiyaw awiyak	—	Everybody
	—	kahkiyaw kīkwaya	Everything/all things

Here are some examples:

1a. nikī-wāpamāw awiyak nētē ē-pa-pāmohtēt.
   I saw somebody walking (around) over there.

1b. kiki-nakiskawāw cī awiyak ēkotē ē-papimohtēt?
   Did you meet someone (as s/he was) walking there?

2a. kīkway cī kikī-atāwēstamawin?
   Did you buy something for me?

2b. kīkway cī ē-nōhtē-atāwēyan? mitās ahpō astotin?
   Are you wanting to buy something? a pants or hat?

3a. nam āwiyak nikī-nakiskawāw.
   I met nobody/no one.

3b. namōya nikī-nakiskawāw awiyak.
   I did not meet anyone.

4a. nama kīkway ēkota.
   There is nothing there.

4b. namōya kīkway kikī-atāwēstamātin.
   I did not buy you anything.

4c. nama kīkway ēkota niya.
   There is nothing there for me. (literal)
   It's none of my business. (colloquialism)

5a. pikw āwiyak ēkotē kī-takosinwak tipiskohk.
   Everybody arrived there last night.

6a. piko kīkway māna awa ē-nōhtē-atāwēt.
   This one is always wanting to buy everything.

7a. awiyakak ōki kā-pē-ayācik.
   There are some people coming.

8a. māka mīna awa nanātohk kīkwaya ē-nitawēyihtahk.
   As usual this one wants all sorts of things.

9a. kahkiyaw awiyak kākikē ta-kī-kakwē-wīcihāt wīc-āyisiyinīma.
   Everyone should always try to give a helping hand to his fellowman.

10a kahkiyaw kīkway māna nikosis ē-kocihtāt.
   My son is always trying (his hand at) everything.

Obviative Form of the Indefinite Pronouns

In addition to the above pronouns there is the obviative form. Recall that the 3's and 3'p in the conjugation of verbs indicates "obviative." It means that a third person is acting on another third person or thing. Notice that these words all end in an "*a*" rather than "*ak*." This is the clue that these are the obviative forms. The examples show how these are applied.

Obviative	awiya	—	somebody/anyone
	nam āwiya	—	nobody
	pikw āwiya	—	everybody
	kahkiyaw awiya	—	everybody

Examples:

1a. namōya wiya kī-wāpamēw awiya.
   S/he did not see anyone.
   3s   →   3's

1b. awiya cī John ē-kī-wīsāmikot?
   3's   ←   3s
   Was John invited by someone?

1c. awiyak cī kī-wīsāmēw Johna?
   3s   →   3's
   Did somebody invite John? (Did anyone invite John?)

2a. nam āwiya kī-wīsāmikow.
   S/he was not invited by anyone.
   3s   ←   3's

3a. pikw āwiya kī-atamiskawēw.
   S/he greeted everyone.
   3s   →   3's

4a. kahkiyaw awiya kihcēyimikow.
   S/he is highly thought of by everyone.
   3s   ←   3's

Demonstrative Pronouns

Demonstrative pronouns, as the name indicates, demonstrate; in this case it is the location of an object, animate or inanimate. These particular forms of pronouns are the "pointing words." They, too, must agree in number and classification with the nouns they modify. The distance between the speaker and object also determines which pronoun to use. Many combinations of these particular particles occur in spoken Cree, each of which gives a more precise meaning. Only an elementary example is given at this time however. The chart below gives only a basic explanation about which pronouns to use for animate nouns and which to use for inanimate nouns:

Number	Animate	Inanimate	English
Singular	awa	ōma	This
	ana	anima	That
	nāha	nēma	That yonder
Pural	ōki	ōhi	These
	aniki	anihi	Those
	nēki	nēhi	Those yonder

Caution should be used in the word order of these demonstrative pronouns. "awa atim" is different from "atim awa." "atim awa" means – "This is a dog." and "awa atim" – means "This dog." When a demonstrative pronoun is placed before the noun there is no verb in the translation: "ana atim" – That dog (there); "nāha atim" – that dog (over there). When a noun precedes a demonstrative pronoun then we must include the verb "to be" in the translation: "atim ana" – That is a dog (there); "atim ana nāha" – That is a dog over there. The verb "to be" is understood in this sort of expression. This also applies to the plural forms.

Chapter 10: Verbs: An Overview

These are words that express action or state be it physical, mental or emotional. They are words that express natural happenings such as weather, seasons, days of the week. They also refer to a state of being such as colors, hardness, softness or they can describe geographic conditions (eg. It is hilly, steep, mountainous, flat etc.). The Cree language uses these as complete sentences whereas in English they are very often adjectives. Of course verbs also express actions.

A basic division in Cree verb forms is between the Intransitive and the Transitive which are defined here to help clarify the concept of word order referred to in Chapter 5. For the same reason, diagrams are also included. In Cree, verbs are classified according to whether the action is being transferred to someone or something (transitive) or whether there is no action transferred at all (intransitive).

Intransitive Verbs

Those verbs that express an action by an animate noun but is not transferred to anyone or anything are called Animate Intransitive verbs (VAI). States, conditions, happenings, occurrences are also verb forms and they are referred to as Inanimate Intransitive verbs (VII).

Transitive Verbs

Those verbs that express actions which affect, or are stimulated by animate nouns are referred to as Transitive Animate verbs (VTA). Those verbs that express actions which affect or are stimulated by inanimate nouns are called Transitive Inanimate verbs (VTI).

One can identify these verbs by asking a couple of questions.

a) Is there a transfer of action to someone or something?

> If the answer is 'no' then the verb is "Intransitive."

> If the answer is "yes" then the verb is "Transitive" and the next question will be:

b) Who or what is being affected? One needs to know whether the person or thing being affected is classified as animate or inanimate.

> If the answer to this question is 'animate' then the verb is "Transitive Animate."

> If the answer is "inanimate" then the verb is "Transitive Inanimate."

Reviewing the following diagrams will perhaps help to visualize this concept of transfer of action. Note that (S) Subject is the doer; the (V) Verb is the action; and the (O) Object is the one being affected by the action. The symbol Ø indicates no object.

a) Intransitive Verbs — Sentence Structure

	S	V →	Ø
Animate Intransitive →	animate	does not transfer action to anyone or anything	no object
Inanimate Intransitive →	inanimate	does not transfer action to anyone or anything	no object

b) Transitive Verbs — Sentence Structure

	S	V →	O
Transitive Animate →	animate	transfers action to someone or something	animate object
Transitive Inanimate →	animate	transfers action to something	inanimate object

NOTE: The *subject* is animate for VAI, VTA, VTI; the *subject* is inanimate only for the VII. The subjects usually come in the guise of pronouns such as I, me, you, it (singular and plural), he, she, we (inclusive and exclusive), they.

The Transitive and Intransitive verbs have unusual features that are more noticeable when compared to those in English. For instance, unlike Cree, the English verb "eat" can be both a) *transitive* as in: I eat fish. and b) *intransitive* as in: I eat. Notice that the verb form does not change in either sentence.

	a)	I	eat	fish.		b)	I	eat.	
		S	V	O			S	V	Ø

In Cree however, there are three forms for the verb "eat": one form (*mīciso*) is intransitive and the other two are transitive (*mīci* and *mōw*). Because there is no object involved and the verb defines only the act of eating "*mīciso*" is therefore an intransitive verb. The transitive verb stems "*mīci*" – eat (something inanimate) and "*mōw*" eat (something animate), however, need objects. To use these two correctly one needs to know the classification of the object being eaten. For example: "I eat fish." and "I eat meat." in English show no difference in the verb; in Cree on the other hand, one needs to know the classification of "fish" and "meat" to be able to utter, or compose a proper sentence:

I eat meat.	I eat fish.
*nimīcison wiyās.	*nimīcison kinosēw.
*nimōwāw wiyās.	*nimīcin kinosēw.
nimīcin wiyās.	nimōwāw kinosēw.

The structures with an (*) asterisk are all impossible combinations.

According to the diagrams above the verb "eat" in Cree falls into three categories:

a) mīciso – eat – is the animate intransitive verb (VAI);
b) mīci – eat (food classified as inanimate) – is the transitive inanimate verb (VTI);
c) mōw – eat (food classified as animate) – is the transitive animate verb (VTA).

Conjugation

The process of verb conjugation, one that verbs in all languages go through, can reflect and include all of the notions mentioned above. In order to understand how Cree operates the following comparison with English and French conjugation may be helpful. Although most verbs follow a basic conjugation pattern, as in the following, Cree has some unique features.

NOTE: For French: m = male; f = female; for English: m = male; f = female; n = neutral (it); for Cree: only one term is used to refer to male/female/it.

French		Cree		English	
être (to be)		ayā (to be)		to be	
1s	je suis	1s	nitayān	1s	I am
2s	tu es	2s	kitayān	2s	you are
3sm	il est	3s	ayāw	3sm	he is
3sf	elle est			3sf	she is
				3sn	it is
	—	3's	ayāyiwa		—
1p	nous sommes	1p	nitayānān	1p	we are
		21	kitayānāw		
2p	vous êtes	2p	kitayānāwāw	2p	you are
3pm	ils sont	3p	ayāwak	3p	they are
3pf	elles sont				
	—	3'p	ayāyiwa		—

Observe that the first three person indicators 1s, 2s, and 3s in both the French and English of the verb "to be" have no noticeable connection. Only a fluent speaker of these languages would know that these are forms of the verb "to be" "suis, es and est" are all the same verb as are "am, are, and is." In Cree, however, the verb stem "*ayā*" remains constant throughout the conjugation. Each verb in Cree works in this manner.

NOTE: The Cree verb "to be" is never used as an auxiliary verb. It is used only to indicate location as in "I am at (place)…" Refer to Chapter 27 for a more detailed explanation of this verb.

The concept of conjugation plays an important part in any language. In Cree there are nine forms which fit into the pattern. The pattern above for Cree follows the table set out by the personal pronouns which indicate who is doing the action. Consider the chart below:

1s	niya	I, me	1p	niyanān	We (exclusive)
			21	kiyānaw	We (inclusive)
2s	kiya	You (sg.)	2p	kiyawāw	You (plural)
3s	wiya	he, she, it	3p	wiyawāw	They
3's	his (e.g.: friend)		3'p		Their (e.g.: friend/s)

It is important to know what the numbers (1s, 2s, 3s, 3's, 1p, 2p, 3p and 3'p) stand for because every verb (VAI, VTI and VTA) follows this numbering system.

1s	indicates	the first person singular (I, me)
2s	indicates	the second person singular (you)
3s	indicates	the third person singular (he, she, it)
3's	indicates	the obviative singular (e.g.: his friend/s)
1p	indicates	the first person plural (exclusive we)
21	indicates	the first person plural (inclusive we)
2p	indicates	the second person plural (you – pl)
3p	indicates	the third person plural (they)
3'p	indicates	the obviative plural (e.g.: their friend/s)

The explanation following the three sentences below may help to understand 1p and 21:

a) sēmāk ēkwa niyanān niwī-ati-kīwānān.   We are going home right away (us).

b) sēmāk ēkwa nika-ati-kīwānān.   We will be on our way home right away.

c) sēmāk ēkwa kika-ati-kīwānaw.   We will be on our way home right away.

The speaker in a) and b) is informing someone that he and another party are going home. In effect, he is saying "We (not you) are going home." The speaker is excluding the person or persons to whom he is speaking. This is why the first person plural "we" is labeled as exclusive (1p).

In c) however, the speaker is informing another person or persons that "We (including you), will be on our way home right away." Therefore the first person plural "we" is known as inclusive (21).

The English language does not have special endings or forms to show the differences between these two situations. Cree, however, has suffixes which help to differentiate – 1p – we, exclusive from – 21 – we, inclusive. As you will note each verb form shows these different suffixes.

Obviative

Another note is required to explain the 3's and 3'p forms of the conjugation pattern. 3's is the third person obviative singular and 3'p its plural counterpart. Exactly who is doing the action here is often confusing. The 3s and 3p forms are also third person indicators. 3s is the third person singular (he, she, it) and 3p is its plural counterpart (they).

The obviative forms become clear when we keep in mind that the actor of 3's is a singular relative, friend, dog or any other possession of 3s and 3p. It follows then that actor of 3'p are relatives, friends, dogs or any other possessions of 3s or 3p. The translation of the 3's conjugation is therefore: "His (3) friend/s is/are doing the action." and the 3'p translates to "Their (3p) friend/s is/are doing the action." The sentences below are examples of how this works:

a) ohtāwiya kī-itohtēyiwa ōtēnāhk otākosīhk.	His/her father went to town yesterday.
b) Betty ohtāwiya wī-itohtēyiwa ōtēnāhk.	Betty's father intends to go to town.
c) John otōtēma wī-pē-kiyokēyiwa mwēstas.	John's friend(s) is coming to visit later.
d) kī-pē-kiyokēyiwa otōtēmiwāwa anohc.	Their friend(s) came to visit today.
e) ēkotē anihi otōtēmiwāwa atoskēyiwa.	Their friend(s) work there.

NOTE: The suffix for 3's and 3'p are always exactly the same.

Modes

Every verb can occur in a number of modes. These modes are various patterns of the inflections of verbs. Most of these inflections affect the VII, VAI, VTI and VTA however there is one exception: The VII do not have the imperative mode. The following are descriptions of these patterns.

Imperative Mode: This mode refers to verbs that occur in the form of orders, commands, invitations or requests. There are two kinds:

a) Immediate Imperative are orders, commands, invitations/requests that are to be done right away. In other words it means that when one is giving an order or command to someone it is expected that the action be done immediately.

b) Delayed Imperative on the other hand means that the action is to occur at a future or later time.

Immediate Imperative	Delayed Imperative
(a) kāsīhkwē (sēmāk)	(a) kāsīhkwēhkan (mwēstas)
Wash your face. (immediately)	Wash your face. (later)
(b) kāsīhkwēk (sēmāk)	(b) kāsīhkwēhkēk (mwēstas)
Wash your faces. (immediately)	Wash your faces. (later)
(c) mīcisotān (sēmāk)	(c) mīcisohkahk (mwēstas)
Let's eat. (immediately)	Let's eat. (later)

It is not necessary to use the words "*sēmāk*" and "*mwēstas*" because the suffixes on the commands themselves are understood to mean now and later. When they are used it is usually for emphasis or when it is used in context.

NOTE: Remember the Imperative mode does not apply to VII.

Independent Mode: This is the same as what has been referred to as the indicative mode. Verbs in the Independent mode take the person prefixes *ni-*; *ki-*: as in *nipimipahtān* – I run; *kimīcison* – You (sg) eat. This form makes a statement which can be in the present, past or future tense.

Conjunct mode: This is the same as what is sometimes referred to as the subjunctive mode. All verbs occurring in this mode begin with the prefix *ē-*…; there are no person markers. Here are examples: *ē-apiyān*: as I am sitting; *ē-nipāyān*: as I am sleeping. Verbs in this mode quite often, but not always, represent a subordinate clause as they can also represent a principal clause. All verbs can occur in this mode and in the present, past or future tense.

3s	takohtēci	3s	if/when s/he arrives ____	
3's	takohtēyici	3's	if/when his/her ____ arrives ____	
1p	takohtēyāhki	1p	if/when we (excl) arrive ____	
21	takohtēyahko	21	if/when we (incl) arrive ____	
2p	takohtēyēko	2p	if/when you (pl) arrive ____	
3p	takohtētwāwi	3p	if /when they arrive ____	
3'p	takohtēyici	3'p	if/when their ____ arrives ____	

NOTE: It is important to know that 1p can end in an "i" or an "o" while 21 and 2p remain with the "o" ending. It is possible that this is a regional preference. Here are several sentences that show how this future conditional form of verbs is applied:

1. takohtēci wīpac kika-ati-sipwēhtānaw.

If he/she arrives soon, we'll leave (go).

2. takohtēyani ici ōta sēmāk kika-nitawi-wāpamānaw kōhkominaw.

When you arrive here we will go and see our grandmother right away.

3. takohtētwāwi ēkospīhk piko nika-māci-kīsiswāw pahkwēsikan.

I'll start cooking the bannock only when they arrive.

4. itohtēyāni atāwēwikamikohk, kīkwāy ē-nitawēyihtaman.

If /when I go to the store what do you want?

5. nōhtēkwasiyani anita kikāh-kawisimon.

If you get sleepy you (sg) can sleep there.

6. mācikōtitān kīspoyici ocawāsimisa ka-pōni-mātoyiwa.

You will see that when her child is full it will stop crying.

Notice the verb stems above did not change at all. *takohtē*; *itohtē*; *nōhtēkwasi*; *kīspo* remain as they are in the 2s imperative form and are placed before the suffixes.

Connective "t" Rule

Verb stems beginning with a vowel need a connective "t" between the person indicator and the verb stem for the following persons: 1, 2s, 1p, 21, and 2p; or put in another way, for only the first and second person indicators and never the third person indicators. However, this "t-connection" rule *applies only in the present tense of the independent mode*. Some verbs that follow this rule are: api – sit; ākayāsimo – speak English.

Independent Mode   "V-initial" = (verb stem begins with a vowel)

1s	nit _____ n	
2s	kit _____ n	
3s	_____ w	
3's	_____ yiwa	
1p	nit _____ nān	
21	kit _____ naw	
2p	kit _____ nāwāw	
3p	_____ wak	
3'p	_____ yiwa	

Example: VAI – "api – sit"

1s	nitapin	1s	I sit	
2s	kitapin	2s	You (singular) sit	
3s	Ø apiw	3s	He/she/it sits	
3's	Ø apiyiwa	3's	His/her _____ sits	
1p	nitapinān	1p	We sit (exclusive)	
21	kitapinaw	21	We sit (inclusive)	

2p	kitapināwāw		2p	You (plural) sit
3p	Ø apiwak		3p	They sit
3'p	Ø apiyiwa		3'p	Their _____ sits.

NOTE: -1a. niapin ōta.*
       -1b. nitapin ōta. I sit here.
       1a. above is ungrammatical.

NOTE: Other verb classes which will be introduced later must also follow this rule.

The "ē to ā" Rule

The "ē to ā" rule is applied only to those stems ending in "ē" and in: 1s, 2s, 1p, 21 and 2p of the independent mode only, but in all tenses of that mode.

Example: VAI – "nēhiyawē – speak Cree"

1s	ninēhiyawān		1s	I speak Cree
2s	kinēhiyawān		2s	You (singular) speak Cree
3s	nēhiyawēw		3s	He/she speaks Cree
3's	nēhiyawēyiwa		3's	His/her _____ speaks Cree
1p	ninēhiyawānān		1p	We (exclusive) speak Cree
21	kinēhiyawānaw		21	We (inclusive) speak Cree
2p	kinēhiyawānāwāw		2p	You (plural) speak Cree
3p	nēhiyawēwak		3p	They speak Cree
3'p	nēhiyawēyiwa		3'p	Their _____ (pl) speaks Cree.

Application of both "ē to ā" rule and the "t" rule

Furthermore, verb stems, which end in "ē" and begin with a vowel, require both the "t" connector and "ē to ā" rules; only in the independent mode, present tense and never in the Conjunct mode. Some of these verb stems are: atoskē – work; itohtē – go; and ayamihcikē – read.

As an example here is the verb "*atoskē* – work" in all three modes:

Immediate Imperative Mode

Example: VAI – "atoskē – work"

2s	atoskē	work (you singular)
2p	atoskēk	work (you plural)
21	atoskētān	Let's work. (including yourself)

Independent Mode

Example: VAI – "atoskē – work"

1s	nitatoskān		1s	I work
2s	kitatoskān		2s	You work
3s	atoskēw		3s	He/she/it works
3's	atoskēyiwa		3's	His _____ works
1p	nitatoskānān		1p	We (exclusive) work
21	kitatoskānaw		21	We (inclusive) work
2p	kitatoskānāwāw		2p	You (plural) work
3p	atoskēwak		3p	They work
3'p	atoskēyiwa		3'p	Their _____ works.

Conjunct Mode – Present tense

1s	ē-atoskēyān		1s	I am working
2s	ē-atoskēyan		2s	You are working
3s	ē-atoskēt		3s	He is working
3's	ē-atoskēyit		3's	His _____ is working

1p	ē-atoskēyāhk	1p	We (exclusive) are working
21	ē-atoskēyahk	21	We (inclusive) are working
2p	ē-atoskēyēk	2p	You (plural) are working
3p	ē-atoskēcik	3p	They are working
3'p	ē-atoskēyit	3'p	Their _____ is working.

NOTE: The "*ē* to *ā*" rule is not appplied to the Conjunct mode. It only occurs with the "*ni-*" and "*ki-*" prefixes of the independent mode.

Past tense refers to an event or action which has been completed or which occurred before the time of speaking. To express simple past tense in the independent mode, the tense indicator "*kī-*" is inserted between the person indicator and the rest of the verb. This is the only change in the form of the verb. The person indicators, the verb stem and its endings remain the way they are written in the present tense. Note the placement of the tense marker in the following chart for VAIs for past tense, independent mode.

VAI – Independent mode, past tense

1s	nikī-_____n		1p	nikī-_____nān	
			21	kikī-_____naw	
2s	kikī-_____n		2p	kikī-_____nāwāw	
3s	kī-_____w		3p	kī-_____wak	
3'	kī-_____yiwa		3'p	kī-_____yiwa	

Example: VAI – "atoskē – work"

1s	nikī-atoskān		1p	nikī-atoskānān (exclusive)	
			21	kikī-atoskānaw (inclusive)	
2s	kikī-atoskān		2p	kikī-atoskānāwāw	
3s	kī-atoskēw		3p	kī-atoskēwak	
3's	kī-atoskēyiwa		3'p	kī-atoskēyiwa	

NOTE: The "*ē* to *ā*" rule is applied but not the "*t*" connector because it is now in a tense other than the present and there is a hyphen separating the vowels.

These sentences are examples of VAIs in the past tense:

1. āsay niya ni*kī*-mīcison.   I ate already.
2. ki*kī*-atoskān kiya otākosīhk.   You worked yesterday.

Similarly the definite future tense is indicated by the insertion of the future tense indicators. "*ka-*" is used for the first and second person singular and plural. "*ta-*" is used for the third person singular and plural plus in the obviative. The future tense refers to situations or events which are going to or will occur after the time of speaking.

Future Definite:

1s	nika-_____n		1p	nika-_____nān	
			21	kika-_____naw	
2s	kika-_____n		2p	kika-_____nāwāw	
3s	ta-_____w		3p	ta-_____wak	
3's	ta-_____yiwa		3'p	ta-_____yiwa	

Example: VAI – "kīwē – go home"

1s	nika-kīwān		1p	nika-kīwānān	
			21	kika-kīwānaw	
2s	kika-kīwān		2p	kika-kīwānāwāw	
3s	ta-kīwēw		3p	ta-kīwēwak	
3'	ta-kīwēyiwa		3'p	ta-kīwēyiwa	

Examples:

1. wīpac nika-kīwān.   I will go home soon.
2. kika-nēhiyawān.   You will speak Cree.
3. ta-mīcisowak āpihtā-kīsikāyiki.   They will eat at noon.

The future intentional tense differs from the above in that it implies that the speaker has decided to act on his intention of doing an action. This can be translated as "I intend to…" or "I am going to…"

VAI – Future Intentional tense:

1s	niwī-_____n	1p	niwī-_____nān
		21	kiwī-_____naw
2s	kiwī-_____n	2p	kiwī-_____nāwāw
3s	wī-_____w	3p	wī-_____wak
3'	wī-_____yiwa	3'p	wī-_____yiwa

Example: VAI – "sipwēhtē – leave"

1s	niwī-sipwēhtān	1p	niwī-sipwēhtānān
		21	kiwī-sipwēhtānaw
2s	kiwī-sipwēhtān	2p	kiwī-sipwēhtānāwāw
3s	wī-sipwēhtēw	3p	wī-sipwēhtēwak
3's	wī-sipwēhtēyiwa	3'p	wī-sipwēhtēyiwa

Examples:

1. niwī-kīwān ēkwa.   I am going home now.
2. kiwī-māci-atoskān cī?   Are you going to start working?
3. anohc awa wī-sipwēhtēw.   He/she is leaving today. or He/she intends to leave today.

NOTE: Keep in mind that verbs in: a) the imperative mode are orders, b) the independent mode are statements, c) the conjunct mode are most often subordinate clauses.

Hyphens

Here is the basic verb structure for verbs in the Independent mode:

Person +	Tense -	Preverb -	Verb Stem	+ Ending

NOTE: A (-) hyphen is required after a tense marker and after the preverb. And a (+) plus indicates direct attachment without hyphen. Preverbs were discussed in Chapter 6.

Examples:

1) nikanawāpamāw māna ana.   I usually watch that one.
2) nikī-sēsāwipahtān kīkisēp.   I jogged this morning.
3) nikī-*kakwē*-kawisimon wīpac tipiskohk. I tried to go to bed early last night.
4) ni*nōhtē*-mīcison ēkwa.   I want to eat now.

The basic structure for verbs in the Conjunct mode is:

ē -	Tense -	Preverb -	Verb Stem	+ Ending

NOTE: A(-) hyphen is required after "*ē*"; after the marker; and after the preverb. And a (+) plus indicates direct attachment without hyphen.

Examples:

1) ē-atoskēt awa mēkwāc.   S/he, this one, is working at the moment.
2) ē-kī-osāmihkwāmit ana anohc.   S/he, that one, slept in today.
3) ē-kīsi-mīcisoyān nikī-sipwēhtānān.   When I finished eating we left.
4) ē-kī-*nōhtē*-mētawēt ana wayawītimihk. S/he, that one, wanted to play outside.

Chapter 12: Other Animate Intransitive Verbs

Colour terms that modify animate nouns are considered Animate Intransitive verbs. Because all colours are in the form of verbs they must agree with the noun they modify in which case they will either be VAI or VII-2. In this chapter only the VAI will be introduced. Examples of these verbs in the Independent, Conjunct and Future Conditional modes are shown here. As well, since animate nouns are either singular or plural then the verbs must also be in the singular and the plural form.

VAI – Independent mode – Colours

Singular

wāpiskisiw	It is white.
kaskitēsiw	It is black.
kaskitēwinākosiw	It appears black.
mihkosiw	It is red.
sīpihkosiw	It is blue.
askihtakosiw	It is green.
wāposāwisiw	It is yellow.
osāwisiw	It is orange.
nīpāmāyātisiw	It is purple.
wāpinākosiw	It appears white.

Examples: VAI – "mihkosi – be red"; kaskitēsi – be black"; "wāpiskisi – be white"; "wāposāwisi – be yellow"

1) mihkosiw astis.	The mitt is red.
2) kaskitēsiw mitās.	The pants is black.
3) wāpiskisiw asikan.	The sock is white.
4) wāposāwisiw tāpiskākan.	The necktie is yellow.

Plural

wāpiskisiwak	They are white.
kaskitēsiwak	They are black.
kaskitēwinākosiwak	They appear black.
mihkosiwak	They are red.
sīpihkosiwak	They are blue.
askihtakosiwak	They are green.
wāposāwisiwak	They are yellow.
osāwisiwak	They are orange.
nīpāmāyātisiwak	They are purple.
wāpinākosiwak	They appear white

Examples: VAI – "mihkosi – be red"; "kaskitēsi – be black"; "wāpiskisi – be white"; "wāposāwisi – be yellow"

1) mihkosiwak astisak.	The mitts are red.
2) kaskitēsiwak mitāsak.	The pants/trousers (pl) are black.
3) wāpiskisiwak asikanak.	The socks are white.
4) wāposāwisiwak tāpiskākanak.	The neckties are yellow.

NOTE: The identifying suffix for VAI - Colours: 1) "*siw*" for stems ending in a vowel; 2) "*isiw*" for stems ending in a consonant; 3) "*ak*" is the plural suffix for both nouns and verbs in the indicative mode.

VAI – Conjunct – Colours

Singular

ē-wāpiskisit	as it is white
ē-kaskitēsit	as it is black
ē-kaskitēwinākosit	as it appears black
ē-mihkosit	as it is red
ē-sīpihkosit	as it is blue
ē-askihtakosit	as it is green
ē-wāposāwisit	as it is yellow
ē-osāwisit	as it is orange
ē-nīpāmāyātisit	as it is purple
ē-wāpinākosit	as it appears white

Plural

ē-wāpiskisicik	as they are white
ē-kaskitēsicik	as they are black
ē-kaskitēwinākosicik	as they appear black
ē-mihkosicik	as they are red
ē-sīpihkosicik	as they are blue
ē-askihtakosicik	as they are green
ē-wāposāwisicik	as they are yellow
ē-osāwisicik	as they are orange
ē-nīpāmāyātisicik	as they are purple
ē-wāpinākosicik	as they appear white

VAI – Future Conditional – VAI – "if and when"

Singular

wāpiskisici	if/when it is white
kaskitēsici	if/when it is black
kaskitēwinākosici	if/when it appears black
mihkosici	if/when it is red
sīpihkosici	if/when it is blue
askihtakosici	if/when it is green
wāposāwisici	if/when it is yellow
osāwisici	if/when it is orange
nīpāmāyātisici	if/when it is purple
wāpinākosici	if/when it appears white

Plural

wāpiskisitwāwi	if/when they are white
kaskitēsitwāwi	if/when they are black
kaskitēwinākositwāwi	if/when they are appear black
mihkositwāwi	if/when they are red
sīpihkositwāwi	if/when they are blue
askihtakositwāwi	if/when they are green
wāposāwisitwāwi	if/when they are yellow
osāwisitwāwi	if/when they are orange
nīpāmāyātisitwāwi	if/when they are purple
wāpinākositwāwi	if/when they are appear white

VAI – Obviative of Conjunct – Colours

Singular

ē-wāpiskisiyit	as his/her/its _____ is white
ē-kaskitēsiyit	as his/her/its _____ is black
ē-kaskitēwinākosiyit	as his/her/its _____ appear/s black
ē-mihkosiyit	as his/her/its _____ is red
ē-sīpihkosiyit	as his/her/its _____ is blue
ē-askihtakosiyit	as his/her/its _____ is green
ē-wāposāwisiyit	as his/her/its _____ is yellow
ē-osāwisiyit	as his/her/its _____ is orange
ē-nīpāmāyātisiyit	as his/her/its _____ is purple
ē-wāpinākosiyit	as his/her/its _____ appear/s white

Plural

ē-wāpiskisiyit	as their _____ are white
ē-kaskitēsiyit	as their _____ are black
ē-kaskitēwinākosiyit	as their _____ appear/s black
ē-mihkosiyit	as their _____ are red
ē-sīpihkosiyit	as their _____ are blue
ē-askihtakosiyit	as their _____ are green
ē-wāposāwisiyit	as their _____ are yellow
ē-osāwisiyit	as their _____ are orange
ē-nīpāmāyātisiyit	as their _____ are purple
ē-wāpinākosiyit	as their _____ appear/s white

Observe that the charts above are identical for Cree but it is the English translation which is important to observe.

NOTE: Obviative is an action by the second of two distinct third persons or it is a reference to a third person's possession. Whether it is singular or plural is known only by the context of the situation or the speaker has personal knowledge. That is why there is only one form for singular and plural. This is the case for both the Obviative of the conjunct and Obviative of the Future conditional form.

Obviative of Future Conditional

Singular

wāpiskisiyici	if/when his/her _____ is white
kaskitēsiyici	if/when his/her _____ is black
kaskitēwinākosiyici	if/when his/her _____ appears black
mihkosiyici	if/when his/her _____ is red
sīpihkosiyici	if/when his/her _____ is blue
askihtakosiyici	if/when his/her _____ is green
wāposāwisiyici	if/when his/her _____ is yellow
osāwisiyici	if/when his/her _____ is orange
nīpāmāyātisiyici	if/when his/her _____ is purple
wāpinākosiyici	if/when his/her _____ appears white

Plural

wāpiskisiyici	if/when their _____ are white
kaskitēsiyici	if/when their _____ are black
kaskitēwinākosiyici	if/when their _____ appear black
mihkosiyici	if/when their _____ are red
sīpihkosiyici	if/when their _____ are blue

askihtakosiyici	if/when their ____ are green
wāposāwisiyici	if/when their ____ are yellow
osāwisiyici	if/when their ____ are orange
nīpāmāyātisiyici	if/when their ____ are purple
wāpinākosiyici	if/when their ____ are appear white

Examples of questions about colours:

When asking about the colour of an object or clothing that is animate one would use the VAI "*itasināso* – be coloured so" either in the Independent or conjunct mode. It depends on whether you are talking about "a pair of mitts" or perhaps some item belonging to a third person other than the one you are speaking to.

a) Indicative Mode:

tānisi itasināsow awa mitās?   What colour is this pair of trousers/pants?

b) Conjunct Mode:

tānisi awa ē-itasināsot mitās?   What colour is this pair of pants?

More examples:

Q	tānisi awa ē-itasināsot astis?	What colour is this mitt?
A	wāposāwisiw ana ēwako astis.	
Q	tānisi ōki itasināsowak astisak?	What colour are these mitts?
A	wāposāwisiwak aniki ēwakonik astisak	
Q	tānisi ē-itasināsot awa mitās?	What colour is this pants?
A	ē-wāposāwisit ana ēwako mitās.	
Q	tānisi ōki ē-itasināsocik mitāsak?	What colour are these pants?
A	ē-wāposāwisicik aniki ēwakonik mitāsak.	

Questions using "cī"

a) mihkosiw cī awa astis?	Is this mitten red?
b) wāpiskisiwak cī ōki asikanak?	Are these socks white?
c) ē-mihkosit cī awa astis?	Is this mitten red?
d) ē-sīpihkosicik cī ōki asikanak?	Are these socks blue?

NOTE: Changing colour terms from Independent to Conjunct to Future Conditionals one follows the steps and rules below.

a) Independent mode to conjunct form of *mihkosiw* – It is red.
   i) add "*ē*" to beginning and hyphenate; → ē-mihkosiw
   ii) drop final consonant; → ē-mihkosi
   iii) then add a "*t*" at the end. → ē-mihkosit

b) Conjunct form to future conditional:
   i) drop "*ē*" → mihkosit
   ii) change "*t*" to "*c*" → mihkosic
   iii) then add "*i*" → mihkosici

eg. ē-mihkosit … mihkosici   ē-sīpihkosit … sīpihkosici.

It is more difficult to give examples for Future Conditional form for colours without explaining the context but here is a scenario that may help to understand its use.

Supposing someone was going to a different country and you are asking this person to bring a certain garment or scarf for you. You might want only a specific color otherwise the person doesn't have to bother purchasing it.

wāpamaci kīsowahpison ē-mihkosit atāwēstamawihkan. *mihkosici* oti piko!

If you see a red scarf buy it for me.   Only *if* it is red!

Chapter 13: Requests, Permissions, Questions, Answers and Negation

Modals

The appearance of the definite future tense indicator "*ka-*" or "*ta-*" together with the past tense indicator "*kī-*" in the same verbal clause introduces simple requests as questions or possibility in non-questions. Notice that the use of the words "can or could" in some of the examples asks someone to do something or is asking for permission to do something rather than referring to ability.

A. Can/may *I* sit here?

    1a) nika-apin cī ōta.
    2b) niwī-apin cī ōta.
    3c) nikī-apin cī ōta.
    4d) nika-kī-apin cī ōta.

Of the four examples above, only 4d) corresponds with A.

    1a) is "Will I sit here?";
    2b) is "Do I intend to sit here?";
    3c) is "Did I sit here?"

The first two really do not sound appropriate; the third might be used in a certain context but it is not a translation of the English sentence above. Here is another example:

B. Can/could *you(sg)* write your name here?

    1a) kika-masinahēn cī ōta kiwīhowin.
    2b) kiwī-masinahēn cī ōta kiwīhowin.
    3c) kikī-masinahēn cī ōta kiwīhowin.
    4d) kika-kī-masinahēn cī ōta kiwīhowin.

As in the example above only 4d) corresponds with the English.

    1a) is asking "Will you write your name here?"
    2b) is asking "Do you intend to write your name here?"
    3c) is asking "Did you write your name here?"

All of these are legitimate questions referring to one's signing his/her name but they do not translate the English sentence. Now study this next example:

C. Can/could *s/he* use your book?

    1a) ta-āpacihtāw cī kimasinahikan.
    2b) wī-āpacihtāw cī kimasinahikan.
    3c) kī-āpacihtāw cī kimasinahikan.
    4d) ta-kī-āpacihtāw cī kimasinahikan.

Once again, only 4d) is acceptable for C.

    1a) asks "Will he…"
    2b) asks "Does he intend to…"
    3c) asks "Did he…"

But only 4d) asks "Can/could he…" The conclusion then is that "*ka-kī-*" is the form one would use to ask whether one "Can/could do … something?"

Verb classes, VAI, VTA, VTI, must use the combined "*ka-kī-*" when making simple requests such as those in the above examples. The conjugation patterns do not change but "*ka-kī-*" or "*ta-kī-*" must be used after the person indicator (if there is one) for the independent mode. The examples in D. below show that there is no hyphen after the person indicator.

NOTE: All verb classes except the VII -1 and VII- 2, can occur in the modal form.

D. Permission or ability.

Examples:

1a. kika-kī-pē-wīcihin cī wāpahki.

Can you (sg) come help me tomorrow?

1b. kika-kaskihtān cī ta-pē-wīcihiyan wāpahki.

Will you (sg) be able to come and help me tomorrow?

2a. nika-kī-āpacihtān cī kimōhkomān.

Can/may I use your knife?

2b. kētahtawē nika-kaskihtān ta-āpacihtāyān kimōhkomān.

I will eventually be able to use your knife.

Notice the difference between sentences 1a and 1b; 2a and 2b. Both 1a and 2a use "*ka-kī-*" for "Can/could…" while 1b and 2b use the verb "*kaskihtā - be able to*" with the future definite pre-verb "*ka-*" to make a request or to make a statement about ability. All these sentences say something about "being able to" yet there is a difference. In short, "*ka-kī-*" and "*ta-kī-*" are the Cree counterpart to the English modals "can," "may," "could," "would," "might" and "should."

NOTE: Both 1b and 2b refer to the "ability to" rather than a "request or permission" to do something.

"Yes" and "No" Answers

As was explained, the question indicator "*cī*" requires a "yes" or "no" answer. Note in the examples above that the "*cī*" is always in the second position in the sentence. Whether the verb is a VAI, VII, VTA, or VTI does not make a difference.

To answer "yes" to a "*cī*" question one would use "*āha*" – which is "yes" – plus the rest of the interrogative statement where the "*cī*" is dropped and the person indicator is changed to suit the number of the speaker or speakers. For example:

A) kinihtā-nēhiyawān cī. āha, ninihtā-nēhiyawān.

Can you (sg) speak Cree well? Yes, I can speak Cree well.

B) kinihtā-nēhiyawānāwāw cī. āha, ninihtā-nēhiyawānān.

Can you (pl) speak Cree well? Yes, we (excl) can speak Cree well.

C) nihtā-nēhiyawēw cī. āha, nihtā-nēhiyawēw.

Does he/she speak Cree well? Yes, he/she speaks Cree well.

D) nihtā-nēhiyawēwak cī. āha, nihtā-nēhiyawēwak.

Do they speak Cree well? Yes, they speak Cree well.

Notice that the question in:

A) is in the second person singular (2s) form and that the answer is in the first person singular (1s) form,

B) is in the 2p form (plural) and the answer is in the 1p form (plural).

C) is in the 3s form (singular) so the answer remains in the 3s form (singular).

D) is in the 3p form (plural) so the answer remains in the 3p form (plural).

To simplify this let Q = question and A = answer:

- if Q is in 1s … A is in 2s

- if Q is in 1p … A is in 2p

- if Q is in 2s … A is in 1s

- if Q is in 2p … A is 1p

- if Q is in 3s, 3's, 21, 3p or 3'p … In this case, "A" will correspond with these person indicators.

In other words, change the person indicators in the answer only if the question is in the form of the 1st and 2nd persons except 21. All other forms keep the same person indicator in the answer as it is in the question.

To answer in the negative follow the same procedures as the above except that one uses "*namōya*" – once for "no" and a second time to negate the verb:

kinōhtē-mētawān cī.   namōya, namōya ninōhtē-mētawān.
Do you want to play?   No, I don't want to go play.

This long way of answering in the negative is used to make a point or to answer a written question that requires a complete statement. Although it is cumbersome one will sometimes hear it in the instances above. More often than not however, the answer is a simple "no" – "*mwāc, mōya, namōya*" and other times there are more specific answers that require the additional particle "*ohci.*" This is exemplified in the sentences below.

Any one of the following may be used by itself: "*mwāc, mōya, namōya.*" Or they can be used with "*ohci.*" When this occurs then "*ohci*" is placed between the person indicator and the rest of the verb in its Independent mode. Or it can occur as a collapsed form "*ōh*" and placed in the same position as "*ohci.*" Either one is acceptable for expressing, "I/we have not …" however, in the case of "*-ōh*" an explanation is needed.

Notice that in the examples below there is "*nitohci-*" and then there is "*nōh-.*" "*nōh-*" is the collapsed form of "*ni*" and "*ohci*" in "*nitohci-.*" Both of these forms occur in a sentence with the term *mōy* or *mwāc.*

1) Bill: kinōhtē-wāpamāw cī?   Do you want to see him/her?
    Jim: mōya   No.
2) Bill: kikī-wāpamāw cī nitōtēm?   Did you see my friend?
    Jim: mōy nitohci-wāpamāw.   I have not seen him/her.
3) Bill: kikī-wāpamāw cī nitōtēm?   Did you see my friend?
    Jim: mwāc nōh-wāpamāw.   I have not seen him/her.
4) Bill: kikī-wāpamāw cī cāniy?   Did you see Johnny?
    Jim: mwāc nōhci-wāpamāw.   I have not seen him.

NOTE: An important detail regarding the use of "*ohci-*" must be addressed here. All the information about past tense so far has been about the preverb "*kī-*" which translates to the *simple past tense*: "I did not …" But with the use of "*ohci-*" the translation changes to the *perfect aspect*, "I have not …"

Negating Imperatives, Future Conditional forms and Conjunct Mode

Previously, the imperative mode was explained as the form of a verb that gives orders. However, the form that tells someone not to do something, negative imperative mode, has not been introduced. When giving this kind of order one can use one of the forms of negation marker "*ēkāwiya.*" Notice that the regular imperative mode structure does not change.

Example: VAI - "*pasikō* – get up"

Imperative Mode		Negative Imperative Mode	
2s pasikō	Get up.	2s ēkāwiya pasikō	Don't get up.
2p pasikōk	Get up.	2p ēkāwiya pasikōk	Don't get up.
21 pasikōtān	Let's get up.	21 ēkāwiya pasikōtān	Let's not get up.

NOTE: The variants *ēkā*, *kāya* and *kāwiya* can also be used to negate any verb in the imperative.

One of these variant forms, *ēkā* is also used to negate the conjunct mode and the future conditional forms of verbs. It is placed before the verb.

The conjunct mode uses the word "*ēkā*" to indicate the idea of negation, as in situations that indicate "being unable" or "not wanting" or "not having done something." A few sentences follow to show the various translations resulting from the use of "*ēkā*" with verbs in the conjunct mode.

Conjunct mode:

1. ēkā awa ē-nōhtē-mīcit anihi sīwāsa. This one does not want to eat those candies.
   S/he does not want to eat those candies.

2. ēkā cī ana ē-kaskihtāt ta-atoskēt? Is s/he not able to work?
   Is s/he unable to work?

3. ēkā cī ē-kī-kisīpēkinikēyan You didn't do laundry yesterday?
   otākosīhk?

Future conditionals:

1. ēkā takohtēci wīpac, If he/she does not arrive soon, we will leave.
   kika-ati-sipwēhtānaw.

2. ēkā kimiwahki wāpahki, If it doesn't rain tomorrow we will go and swim.
   kika-nitawi-pakāsimonaw.

NOTE: In summary:

a) *ēkāwiya, kāya, kāwiya* negate verbs in the *imperative mode*.

b) *namōya, mōya* negate verbs in the *independent mode*.

c) *ēkā* negates verbs in the *conjunct mode*.

d) *ēkā* also negates verbs in their *future conditional form*.

Chapter 14: Weather Terms – VII-1

Inanimate intransitive verbs are not conjugated but can be expressed in the past, present and future tenses. Natural happenings or states: i) weather, ii) days of the week, iii) seasons are referred to as VII-1. Vocabulary referring to state such as hardness, softness, colour are examples of VII-2.

Only the VII-1 weather conditions in the Independent, Conjunct, Future conditional form and obviative form of the Conjunct mode and of the Future conditional form are in this chapter. But explanations and application of tense is also included here; as well the negation of statements is explained. Also included here is an explanation of how one asks questions using the question indicator "*ci*" which has been previously introduced.

The next chapter includes: seasons, months, weekdays and clock time. And Chapter 16 looks at the VII-2 terms referring to state and colours.

As the translations show one Cree word makes a complete statement.

Independent Mode

wāsēskwan.	It is sunny/clear.	yīkwaskwan.	It is cloudy.
mispon.	It is snowing	yīkowan.	It is foggy.
yōtin.	It is windy.	misi-yōtin.	It is very windy
sōhkiyowēw.	It is a strong wind.	kimiwan.	It is raining.
sīkipēstāw.	It is pouring (rain).	kimiwasin.	It is drizzling.
kaskaniwipēscāsin.	It is misty.	kaskaniwipēstāw.	It is drizzling.
pīwan.	It is drifting.	āhkwatin.	It is freezing.
kīsikāw.	It is daytime.	nīpāyāstēw.	It is moonlight.
kisināw.	It is cold weather.	tahkāyāw.	It is cold weather.
tipiskāw.	It is dark/night.	kīsapwēyāw.	It is hot.
saskan.	It is melting/chinook		
pahkipēstāw.	There are large drops of rain.		
wīpāci-kīsikāw.	It is a nasty day/weather.		
tihkitēw.	It is melting.(also inanimate objects)		
kisāstēw.	It is hot. (summer weather not objects)		
kisitēw.	It is hot. (weather or inanimate objects)		

Conjunct Mode

The conjunct mode of all Cree verbs is used extensively both as a principle clause but mainly as a subordinate clause. Preverbs can be used to make changes to their meaning. Be aware that this structure is the basis for the change to the future conditional forms of verbs.

ē-kaskaniwipēstāk	as it is drizzling	ē-kaskaniwipēscāsik	as it is misty
ē-mispok	as it is snowing	ē-pīwahk	as it is drifting
ē-yōtik	as it is windy	ē-sōhkiyowēk	as it is very windy
ē-wāsēskwahk	as it is clear/	ē-kimiwasik	as it is drizzling
ē-yīkwaskwahk	as it is cloudy	ē-yīkowahk	as it is foggy
ē-āhkwatik	as it is freezing	ē-saskahk	as it is a chinook
ē-tihkitēk	as it is melting	ē-kisitēk	as it is hot
ē-kisāstēk	as it is hot	ē-kisināk.	as it is cold
ē-tahkāyāk	as it is cold	ē-kīsapwēyāk	as it is warm
ē-wāpahk	as it is morning	ē-kīsikāk	as it is day
ē-tipiskāk	as it is dark/	ē-nīpāyāstēk	as it is moonlight
ē-otākosik	as it is evening	ē-sīkipēstāk	as it is pouring rain
ē-tipiskāk	as it is dark	ē-pahkipēstāk	as it is showering
ē-wīpāci-kīsikāk	as it is a nasty	ē-kōnipēstāk	as it is sleeting

Here are examples of sentences using VII-1.

1. ē-ati-tipiskāk anima kā-kī-pōni-atoskēyāhk.
   It was beginning to get dark when we quit working.
2. ē-māci-pahkipēstāk nikī-pīhtokwēyāmonān.
   We fled indoors when drops of rain started to fall.
   (As drops of rain began to fall we fled indoors.)
3. ēkā itohtēk ēkotē, ē-wīpāci-kīsikāk ōma.
   Don't go over there, it's a nasty day.

Future Conditional Form – "If and When"

The future conditional verb form is a rather complex idea because the future tense preverbs are not necessary. Instead there are changes to the form of a verb in the conjunct mode. In other words the future conditional form necessitates changes to a verb's structure in order to convey the idea that "If or When something happens" then a a state or course of action will result.

The examples in the next section will show that one can use the conditional forms as presented, without the additional terms "ispīhk," "ici," "nici" or "kīspin." These examples will also indicate that the use of these words is often dictated by the context of the situation.

The change to a VII-1 in the conjunct mode is basically the format that can be applied to the other verb classes. The change is not complicated; one simply drops the "ē-" from the conjunct form of any verb then add an "i" to the end of the word. Here are the same verbs from the list.

kaskaniwipēstāki	if/when it drizzles
kaskaniwipēscāsiki	if/when it is misty
mispoki	if/when it snows
pīwahki	if/when it is drifting
yōtiki	if/when it is windy
sōhkiyowēki	if/when it is very windy
wāsēskwahki	if/when it is clear/sunny
kimiwasiki	if/when it is drizzling
yīkwaskwahki	if/when it is cloudy
yīkowahki	if/when it is foggy
āhkwatiki	if/when it freezes
saskahki	if/when it is a chinook
tihkitēki	if/when it melts
kisitēki	if/when it is hot
kisāstēki	if/when it is hot
kisināki	if/when it is cold
tahkāyāki	if/when it is cold
kīsapwēyāki	if/when it is warm
wāpahki	if/when it is morning
kīsikāki	if/when it is day
tipiskāki	if/when it is dark/night
nīpāyāstēki	if/when it is moonlight
otākosiki	if/when it is evening
sīkipēstāki	if/when it is pouring rain
tipiskāki	if/when it is dark/tonight
pahkipēstāki	if/when it showers
wīpāci-kīsikāki	if/when it is a nasty day
kōnipēstāki	if/when there is sleet

NOTE: The difference in the translation of these two forms is as follows: The Conjunct Mode is in the form, "as it is…" which suggests that it is a subordinate clause whereas the Future conditional form contains the word "if" which also refers to the idea of "when." A "supposition" such as this requires the conditional form of a verb. This may sound simple when referring to English but it isn't when expressing this same idea in Cree.

First of all, it is important to note that the verb structure for "when" things happen in the future and "if" things happen are the same. Second, in Cree, even when "if" is not used as a separate word it is already contained within the structure of a conditional verb form. So, sometimes, depending on the context one doesn't have to worry about using "*kīspin.*" Third, if one wants to say "When this happens or that happens … then something else happens or another action will be taken" the word "when" may or may not be used.

Consider these sentences:

    a) kisāstēki anohc nika-nitawi-pakāsimonān.

        If it is hot today we will go and swim.

    b) kīspin kisāstēki anohc nika-nitawi-pakāsimonān.

        If it is hot today we will go and swim.

It is obvious from this example that "*kisāstēki*" and "*kīspin kisāstēki*" mean the same so "*kīspin*" is optional.

Now take a look at this next set:

    a) kīsapwēyāki nika-nitawi-sēsāwipahtān.

        If it is warm I will go and jog.

    b) ispīhk kīsapwēyāki nika-nitawi-sēsāwipahtān.

        When it is warm I will go and jog. (at that time)

    c) kīsapwēyāki *ici* nika-nitawi-sēsāwipahtān.

        If it is warm then I will go and jog. (or)

        If it is warm, I will go and jog at that time. (but still at a later time)

Even though the structure of the weather word remains the same throughout the sentences above, sentence a) does not mean the same as b) and c), but sentences b) and c) mean the same because they are referring to a time in the future or later but definitely after the present.

Note the extra terms used to make this difference in b) and c). In these instances, they should be used otherwise the "time" of the action will not be specified because "*ispīhk*" literally means "when" while the particle "*ici*" denotes "at that time; afterward; then; that is the time." These particles mark the "time clause." But these two terms cannot be used together to mean "when."

Here are more examples:

    1. kīspin māci-mispoki nika-kīwānān wīpac.

        If it starts snowing we will go home soon.

    2. ispīhk māci-mispoki nika-pē-kīwān.

        I will come home WHEN it begins snowing.

    3. kīspin kimiwahki nika-pīhtokwēyāmon.

        If it rains I will flee indoors.

    4. māci-kimiwahki *ici* kika-pīhtokwēyāmonaw (incl).

        WHEN it starts raining we (incl) will flee indoors.

In sentences 1 and 3 there seems to have been a reference to the possibility of snow or rain. But the point is that "*kīspin*" is not necessary especially in 3.

Sentence 2 suggests that someone is being told to come home because it looks like it might snow. This answer may mean that coming home will happen only WHEN it begins to snow.

Sentence 4 implies that though there is a strong possibility of rain and it appears that it will start raining shortly "we will flee indoors" only at that time, when it begins to rain. Both refer to a "time" for action; it is not just a possibility.

Remember that *kīspin* is a personal preference but *ispīhk* should be used. That is in 1 and 3 *kīspin* is optional while *ispīhk* and *ici* in 2 and 4 are obligatory. It depends a lot on the message a person wants to convey.

Another consideration is that one may want to use "*ici*" or "*nici*," instead of "*ispīhk*."

NOTE: The most obvious change here is the absence of the "*ē-*" and the presence of the suffix "*i*" which is attached to the conjunct mode of the verb stems.

Obviative Form of the Conjunct Mode

The forms above and on the previous page may be used when involving everyone except the third person singular or plural (he/she/it or they and his/her/its). But when one is referring to an action of either the third person singular or plural and a future happening or activity, the obviative suffix is added to the inanimate intransitive verbs.

ē-kaskaniwipēstāyik	as it is drizzling	ē-kaskaniwipēscāsiyik	as it is misty
ē-misponiyik	as it is snowing	ē-pīwaniyik	as it is drifting
ē-yōtiniyik	as it is windy	ē-sōhkiyowēyik	as it is very windy
ē-wāsēskwaniyik	as it is clear/sunny	ē-kimiwasiniyik	as it is drizzling
ē-yīkwaskwaniyik	as it is cloudy	ē-yīkowaniyik	as it is foggy
ē-āhkwatiniyik	as it is freezing	ē-saskaniyik	as it is a chinook
ē-tihkitēyik	as it is melting	ē-kisitēyik	as it is hot
ē-kisāstēyik	as it is hot	ē-kisināyik	as it is cold
ē-tahkāyāyik	as it is cold	ē-kīsapwēyāyik	as it is warm
ē-wāpaniyik	as it is morning	ē-kīsikāyik	as it is day
ē-tipiskāyik	as it is dark/night	ē-nīpāyāstēyik	as it is moonlight
ē-otākosiniyik	as it is evening	ē-sīkipēstāyik	as it is pouring rain
ē-tipiskāyik	as it is dark (tonight)	ē-pahkipēstāyik	as it is showering
ē-wīpaci-kīsikāyik	as it is a nasty day	ē-kōnipēstāyik	as it is sleeting

NOTE: This form quite often occurs with another verb which is introduced as a relative clause by the preverb "*kā-*." Relative clauses are introduced in a separate chapter.

In the examples below the conjunct forms are italicized while 3s and 3p in the translation are italicized and underlined. This is the suffix which identifies an action by a third person. In the case of VII-1 the word "it" is used to indicate an inanimate actor.

Examples:
1. *ē-wīpaci-kīsikāy<u>ik</u>* mōy awa kī-mētawēw wayawītimihk.
   As <u>it</u> was a nasty day <u>s/he</u>, this one, *did not play* outside.
2. *ē-niso-kīsikāy<u>ik</u>* kī-pē-takohtēw.
   <u>S/he</u> arrived on *Tuesday*. (Literally: *When <u>it</u> was Tuesday <u>s/he</u> arrived.*)
3. *ē-misponiy<u>ik</u>* awa namōya kī-pē-kīwēw.
   <u>S/he</u>, this one, did not come home *when it snowed.*
4. *ē-kisāstēy<u>ik</u>* ōki kiskinwahamawākanak kī-nitawi-pakāsimowak otākosīhk.
   As it was nice/hot yesterday these <u>(they)</u> students went and swam.

The obviative form of VII-1 is used when the weather condition, season, day of the week or colour has something to do with the 3s (s/he/it) or 3p (they/them). Both Cree and English third person/s are italicized and underlined only so that the reader can see that the suffix modifies the 3s and 3p actors.

NOTE: This form quite often occurs with another verb which is introduced as a relative clause by the preverb "*kā-*." Relative clauses are introduced in a separate chapter.

Obviative of Future Conditional

kaskaniwipēstāyiki	if/when it drizzles…
misponiyiki	if/when it snows…
yōtiniyiki	if/when it is windy…
wāsēskwaniyiki	if/when it is clear/sunny…
yīkwaskwaniyiki	if/when it is cloudy…
āhkwatiniyiki	if/when it freezes…
saskaniyiki	if/when it is a chinook…
tihkitēyiki	if/when it melts…
kisitēyiki	if/when it is hot…
kisāstēyiki	if/when it is hot…
kisināyiki	if/when it is cold…
tahkāyāyiki	if/when it is cold…
kīsapwēyāyiki	if/when it is warm…
wāpaniyiki	if/when it is morning…
kīsikāyiki	if/when it is day…
tipiskāyiki	if/when it is dark/night…
nīpāyāstēyiki	if/when it is moonlight…
otākosiniyiki	if/when it is evening…
sīkipēstāyiki	if/when it is pouring rain…
tipiskāyiki	if/when it is dark/tonight…
pahkipēstāyiki	if/when it showers…
wīpāci-kīsikāyiki	if/when it is a nasty day…
pīwaniyiki	if/when it is drifting…
sōhkiyowēyiki	if/when it is very windy…
kimiwasiniyiki	if/when it is drizzling…
yīkowaniyiki	if/when it is foggy…
kōnipēstāyiki	if/when there is sleet…
kaskaniwipēscāsiniyiki	if/when it is misty…

This form is used when one is referring to an action by a third person, singular or plural, if or when this condition occurs.

Examples:

a) *wīpāci-kīsikāyiki* namōya ta-mētawēw awa wayawītimihk.
   If it is a nasty day s/he, this one, will not play outside.

b) *nīso-kīsikāyiki* māskōc ta-pē-takosinwak.
   Perhaps they will arrive on *Tuesday*. (Literally: *When it is Tuesday* perhaps *they* will arrive.)

c) *misponiyiki* namōya ka-pē-kīwēw.
   He/she will not come home *if it snows*.

d) kiskinwahamawākanak ta-nitawi-pakāsimowak *kisāstēyiki* wāpahki.
   The students (they) will go and swim tomorrow *if it is nice/hot*.

Tenses for VII-1

The concept of past, future and intentional tense has been mentioned in a previous chapter but here are extra examples for VII-1. The different tenses for these VII-1 are expressed by simply placing the preverbs before the verb. The past tense preverb is italicized in the examples below:

1) Use of past tense indicator:

    a) *kī*-yōtin.   It was windy.

    b) *kī*-mispon.   It snowed.

    c) *kī*-miyo-kīsikāw.   It was a fine day.

The possible conditions may be written with the *future tense* indicator/preverb "*kita-*" (will) — but the word "*māskōc*" (perhaps) should be used. The use of "*māskōc*" indicates a possibility. The "*kī*" is quite often dropped and only "*ta-*" is used. However, the intentional tense indicator "*wī-*" — "It's going to" (literally, "it intends to") — is more often used because one never knows for sure what the weather will be like. For example:

1) Use of future tense indicator:

    a) māskōc *ta*-kimiwan.   Perhaps it will rain.

    b) māskōc *ta*-mispon.   Perhaps it will snow.

2) Use of future intentional tense indicator:

    a) *wī*-kimiwan.   It is going to rain.

    b) *wī*-āhkwatin anohc.   It is going to freeze today.

To expand and change the nature of the action of the present conditions, past and future tenses, certain preverbs and adverbs may be used. *māci-, pōni-, kihci-, misi-, sōhki-, miyo-* and *māyi-* are such words which could alter the meaning of statements pertaining to weather conditions. *kihci-, misi-* and *sōhki-*, mean "hard or very," while *miyo-* means "nice or good," and *māyi-* means "bad or not nice." *māci-* means "beginning" and *pōni-* "stop, quit."

a) kī-misi-mispon anima ēkospīhk.

    It really snowed hard that time. (or)

    There was a lot of snow that time.

b) nānitaw ētikwē anima ē-āpihtā-tipiskāk kā-kī-pōni-kimiwahk.

    It was about midnight when it quit raining.

Notice the sequence of the tense indicators, preverbs and verb stems above. They are separated by hyphens. The tense indicator always comes before all other preverbs.

One word of caution is that the use of preverbs does not apply to all these weather conditions. Sometimes there are entirely different statements for altered weather conditions. For instance when referring to windy conditions one can use preverbs, but to describe some of these conditions an entirely different term is used. As an example, "*kipihciyowēw*" – "It suddenly stopped being windy." does not have the term "*yōtin*" within its configuration. But having said that, only those painstakingly studying these forms may realize that there is a verb root, "-*yow-*" which indicates that the word does have something to do with wind. It can be quite difficult for a nonspeaker to recognize this. But the point remains that preverbs are not always necessary for all of the weather words.

Negating Inanimate Intransitive Verbs

Any statement that is in the *independent mode* may be changed from an affirmative statement to a negative statement by placing *namōya* (no/not) before the verb. *namōya* or one of its variant forms, *mōy, mōya* can be used in this manner even if the verb is in the past or future tense. Consider the following inanimate intransitive verbs showing both the affirmative and negative statements:

Affirmative – kimiwan mēkwāc.	It is raining right now.
Negative – mōya kimiwan mēkwāc.	It is not raining right now.
Affirmative – kisāstēw anohc.	It is hot today.
Negative – namōya kisāstēw anohc.	It is not hot today.
Affirmative – kī-kimiwan otākosīhk.	It rained yesterday.
Negative – namōya kī-kimiwan otākosīhk.	It did not rain yesterday.

Affirmative – wī-tahkāyāw wāpahki.   It is going to be cold tomorrow.
Negative – namōya wī-tahkāyāw wāpahki.   It is not going to be cold tomorrow.

NOTE: Consider the following summary on how to negate verbs in different modes:

    a) *ēkāwiya, kāya, kāwiya* negate verbs in the *imperative mode*.
    b) *namōya, mōya* negate verbs in the *independent mode*.
    c) *ēkā* negates verbs in the *conjunct mode*.
    d) *ēkā* also negates verbs in their *future conditional form*.

Inanimate Intransitive Verbs and "*cī*"

The position of the question indicator "*cī*" has been referred to previously. It is always in the second position in a sentence. Similarily, Inanimate Intransitive verbs or weather statements can be changed into questions simply by placing "*cī*" after the verb in a sentence such as in the following examples:

wāsēskwan cī?	Is it sunny? (clear)
yōtin cī?	Is it windy?
kimiwan cī ?	Is it raining?

But even when the past or future preverbs or any other preverbs are used, the weather statements plus the tense indicator/preverb are still considered the first word because they are connected by hyphens. Therefore "*cī*" will be placed in the second position. As an example:

kī-kimiwan cī?	Did it rain?
kī-wāsēskwan cī?	Was it sunny?
wī-miyo-kīsikāw cī?	Is it going to be a nice day?
wī-māyi-kīsikāw cī?	Is it going to storm?

Additional examples will help to show that "*cī*" usually follows the first word in a sentence. Consider the following sentences regarding the weather:

kēyāpic cī kimiwan?	Is it still raining?
kimiwan cī kēyāpic?	Is it still raining?
kī-māyi-kīsikāw cī otākosīhk?	Was it an unpleasant day yesterday?
otākosīhk cī kī-māyi-kīsikāw?	Was it an unpleasant day yesterday?

Chapter 15: Seasons, Months, Weekdays and Time

Words referring to the passage of time are also inanimate intransitive verbs because time is a happening. The Cree use the natural happenings around them to tell these occurrences. This chapter includes these VII-1 terms for seasons, months and the adapted terminology to accommodate the European custom of days of the week and "clock" time.

Seasons

Most Cree people are in agreement with the following terms for the seasons of the year but there are additional terms that are regional preferences. They can be used interchangeably without really making a difference in meaning. Seasons and months never occur in the Imperative mode. However, the following modes are applicable.

Independent Mode

pipon	It is winter.
sīkwan	It is spring.
miyoskamin	It is spring.
nīpin	It is summer.
takwākin	It is fall.
mikiskāw	It is late fall.

a) pipon ōma mēkwāc kitaskīnāhk.

   It is winter in our land right now.

b) ēkota ohci ta-miyoskamin.

   From there it will be spring.

Conjunct Mode

ē-pipohk	As it is winter____
ē-sīkwahk	As it is spring____
ē-miyoskamik	As it is spring____
ē-nīpihk	As it is summer____
ē-takwākik	As it is fall____
ē-mikiskāk	As it is late fall____

a) mahti postastotinē mōy ōma ē-nīpihk.

   Put your hat on it's not summer.

b) ē-mikiskāk ōma ēkwa ēkosi niwī-nitawi-mācīnān.

   It is late fall now so we are going to go and hunt.

Future Conditional

pipohki	if/when it is winter____
sīkwahki	if/when it is spring____
miyoskamiki	if/when it is spring____
nīpihki	if/when it is summer____
takwākihki	if/when it is fall____
mikiskāki	if/when it is late fall____

a) nīpihki ici kika-nitawi-wāpamānawak kiwāhkōmākaninawak.

   When it is summer we will go and see our relatives.

Obviative of the Conjunct

ē-piponiyik	as it is winter s/he/it____
ē-sīkwaniyik	as it is spring s/he/it____
ē-miyoskamiyik	As it is spring s/he/it____
ē-nīpiniyik	As it is summer s/he/it____

ē-takwākiniyik	As it is fall s/he/it____
ē-mikiskāyik	As it is late fall s/he/it____

NOTE: This form quite often occurs with another verb which is introduced as a relative clause by the preverb "*kā-*." Relative clauses are introduced in a separate chapter.

Obviative of Future Conditional

piponiyiki	When it is winter s/he/it____
sīkwaniyiki	When it is spring s/he/it____
miyoskamiyiki	When it is spring s/he/it____
nīpiniyiki	When it is summer s/he/it____
takwākiniyiki	When it is fall s/he/it____
mikiskāyiki	When it is late fall s/he/it____

a) piponiyiki awa wī-pē-kīwēyiwa otānisa.

This one's daughter is coming home when it is winter. (or)

His/her daughter is coming home this winter.

Perhaps the following illustration will help clarify the significance of obviative suffixes.

b)   okosisiwāw*a*   miyoskamin*iyiki* kāwi ka-nitawi-atoskē*yiwa*.

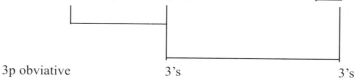

3p obviative	3's	3's

Their son will go back to work when it is spring.

(Their son will go back to work this coming spring.)

NOTE: In the two examples above somebody's son or daughter is going to do the action at a certain time. Thus there are three obviative suffixes visible: one on the possessive form okosisiwāw*a*, another on the time, *miyoskaminiyiki*; then on the verb *ka-nitawi-atoskēyiwa*.

c) ē-mikiskāyik ēkwa ōma ēkosi okosisa ka-nitawi-mācīyiwa.

It is late fall now so his/her sons will go and hunt.

Reference to "last or this past" season

Four of the six season terms have a unique suffix to express the idea of the last season or this past season. That is, rather than using the past tense "*kī-*" the suffix "*ohk*" is attached to the word for the following season terms.

piponohk	Last winter or this past winter.
sīkwanohk	Last spring or this past spring.
nīpinohk	Last summer or this past summer.
takwākohk	Last fall or this past fall.

a) takwākohk ana aspin kā-kī-sipwēhtēt.

It was last fall that s/he left. (It was this past fall that s/he went away.)

b) nīpinohk macī aniki kā-kī-wāpamāyahkik.

Was it not last summer that we saw them?

Months

First Nations people relied on celestial bodies to determine passage of time. Each moon signified a certain phase in the growth of animal and plant life. They lived accordingly. Here is a list of the moons and months of the year:

kisē-pīsim	The Great Moon (January)
mikisiwi-pīsim	The Eagle Moon (February)

niski-pīsim	The Goose Moon (March)
ayīki-pīsim	The Frog Moon (April)
sākipakāwi-pīsim	The Budding Moon (May)
pāskāwihowi-pīsim	The Hatching Moon (June)
paskowi-pīsim	The Moulting Moon (July)
ohpahowi-pīsim	The Flying Up Moon (August)
nōcihitowi-pīsim/takwāki-pīsim	The Mating Moon/Autumn Moon (September)
pimahāwi-pīsim	The Migrating Moon (October)
iyikopiwi-pīsim	The Frost Moon (November)
pawācakinasīsi-pīsim	The Frost Exploding Trees Moon (December)

Below are examples of some questions and answers.

Q. tāna ēwako pīsim mēkwāc.

What month is it? (literally: Which moon is that?)

A. ayīki-pīsim awa mēkwāc.

It is April now. (literally: It is presently the Frog Moon.)

Q. tāniyikohk ē-akimiht awa pīsim.

What is the date? (literally: How much is this moon counted?)

A. niyānanosāp akimāw awa ayīki-pīsim.

It is April fifteenth. It is the fifteenth of April. (literally: The Frog Moon is counted fifteen.)

Days of the Week

The concept of days of the week was introduced by the Europeans and the Cree do not attempt to translate them, instead Monday is the first day, Tuesday the second day, and so on. This is the simplest way to talk about the days of the week in Cree. One will hear other terms which may be regional preferences but it appears everyone knows of the alternate names for the weekdays so there is no problem.

VII-1 Independent Mode

pēyako-kīsikāw.	It is Monday.
nīso-kīsikāw.	It is Tuesday.
nisto-kīsikāw.	It is Wednesday.
nēwo-kīsikāw.	It is Thursday.
niyānano-kīsikāw.	It is Friday.
nikotwāso-kīsikāw.	It is Saturday.
ayamihēwi-kīsikāw.	It is Sunday.

Some weekdays that are referred to by a different term are listed below: They refer to events that occurred on that particular day in that community.

Monday:	pōn-āyamihēwi-kīsikāw	literally – Sunday (prayer day) has ended.
Wednesday:	āpihtāwipayin	literally – It has reached the half way point.
Friday:	pahkwēsikani-kīsikāw	literally – Flour day – In some localities flour was distributed on Friday.
Saturday:	mātinawē-kīsikāw	Distribution day – This term was used for Friday or Saturday depending on when "rations" were distributed on a particular reserve.

VII-1 Conjunct Mode

ē-pēyako-kīsikāk	as it is Monday_____
ē-nīso-kīsikāk	as it is Tuesday_____
ē-nisto-kīsikāk	as it is Wednesday_____

ē-nēwo-kīsikā*k*	as it is Thursday____
ē-niyānano-kīsikā*k*	as it is Friday____
ē-nikotwāso-kīsikā*k*	as it is Saturday____
ē-ayamihēwi-kīsikā*k*	as it is Sunday____

NOTE: This form quite often occurs with another verb which is introduced as a relative clause by the preverb "*kā-*." Relative clauses are introduced in a separate chapter.

Future Conditional Form for Weekdays

The future conditional form has been explained to mean "when/if..." referring to a happening in the future. The following changes occur to the independent mode, of the weekday terms, to form the future conditional.

a) the "*w*" in *kīsikāw* is removed and
b) the suffix "*ki*" is added.

The list below shows this transformation. Note that the translation is also altered. For example:

pēyako-kīsikāki	when/if it is Monday____
nīso-kīsikāki	when/if it is Tuesday____
nisto-kīsikāki	when/if it is Wednesday____
nēwo-kīsikāki	when/if it is Thursday____
niyānano-kīsikāki	when/if it is Friday____
nikotwāso-kīsikāki	when/if it is Saturday____
ayamihēwi-kīsikāki	when/if it is Sunday____

For a better translation of the future conditional form the underlined words below may be used.

- pēyako-kīsikāki – If/when it is Monday or When Monday comes, e.g.. on Monday.
- nēwo-kīsikāki – If/when it is Thursday or When Thursday comes, e.g.. on Thursday.

Example:
nēwo-kīsikāki nika-itohtānān sākahikanihk.
We will go to the lake when Thursday comes.

This is the literal translation and perhaps not standard English. The following would represent a standard English sentence:

We will go to the lake on Thursday.

VII-1 Obviative of Conjunct

ē-pēyako-kīsikāyik	as it is Monday
ē-nīso-kīsikāyik	as it is Tuesday
ē-nisto-kīsikāyik	as it is Wednesday
ē-nēwo-kīsikāyik	as it is Thursday
ē-niyānano-kīsikāyik	as it is Friday
ē-nikotwāso-kīsikāyik	as it is Saturday
ē-ayamihēwi-kīsikāyik	as it is Sunday

This is an example of how the Conjunct obviative form is used:

a) ē-ayamihēwi-kīsikāyik māna nōhkominān nipē-kiyokākonān.
When it is Sunday our grandmother usually comes to visit us.

b) ē-niyānano-kīsikāyik ōma anohc, wīpac ta-kī-takosihk.
As it is Friday today, s/he should be arriving soon.

NOTE: This form quite often occurs with another verb which is introduced as a relative clause by the preverb "*kā-*." Relative clauses are discussed in a separate chapter.

Obviative of Future Conditional

pēyako-kīsikāyik*i*	if/when it is Monday
nīso-kīsikāyik*i*	if/when it is Tuesday
nisto-kīsikāyiki	if/when it is Wednesday
nēwo-kīsikāyiki	if/when it is Thursday
niyānano-kīsikāyiki	if/when it is Friday
nikotwāso-kīsikāyiki	if/when it is Saturday
ayamihēwi-kīsikāyiki	if/when it is Sunday

Let's take the sentence above a) and use it in the future conditional obviative form to observe the change in meaning.

> ayamihēwi-kīsikāyiki kīhtwām nōhkominān nika-pē-kiyokākonān.
>
> When *it is* Sunday our grandmother will come to visit us again.
>
> (Our grandmother will come visit us again on Sunday.)

Remember: VII-1 translate as "*It is…*" The word "*It…* in this case refers to a (inanimate) third person's action affecting another third person or persons.

Time – Hours and Minutes

Expressing time in terms of hours and minutes is as exact as interpretation will permit. The Cree have adapted their word *tipahikan* – a measurement, to denote "hour." *cipahikanis*, which is the diminutive for *tipahikan*, is used to mean "minute." There is no term for "seconds." The diagram below might help to understand how Cree people tell time according to a "clock" – *pīsimohkān*.

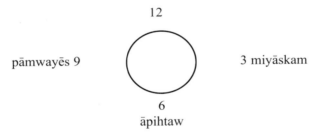

The following vocabulary is used to tell time:

miyāskam	He/she/it has past something. (Independent form)
miyāskahki	If/when it/she/he has past something (Future Conditional form)
ē-miyāskahk	as it passes… (Conjunct form)
ispayin	literally: It goes/runs. (Independent form)
ispayiki	if/when it happens. (Future Conditional form)
ē-ispayik	as it becomes/goes/runs. (Conjunct form)
tipahikan	hour
cipahikanis	a minute, a diminutive of "*tipahikan*"
pāmwayēs	before
mēkwāc	present/right now
mīna	and
mīna apisīs	and a bit
mīna āpihtaw	and/plus half

Examples:

1. niyānan tipahikan ispayin mēkwāc. It is five o'clock right now.
2. nīso tipahikan ispayin mēkwāc. It is two o'clock right now.

1. nisto tipahikan mīna āpihtaw ispayin.   It is three-thirty.
2. kēkā-mitātaht tipahikan mīna āpihtaw ispayin.   It is nine-thirty.

To express time after the hour the word "*miyāskam*" is used in this way:

1. niyānan cipahikanis miyāskam   It is five minutes after four. (literally: Five minutes
nēwo tipahikan.   have passed four o'clock.)
2. niyānanosāp cipahikanis miyāskam   It is fifteen minutes after seven.
tēpakohp tipahikan.

When expressing time before the hour one uses the word "*pāmwayēs*":

1. mitātaht cipahikanis pāmwayēs   It is ten minutes before three.
nisto tipahikan.
2. nīsitanaw cipahikanis pāmwayēs   It is twenty minutes before ten.
mitātaht tipahikan.

When referring to time that has not yet happened the terms or the future conditional form "*miyāskahki*" "*ispayiki*" are used along with verbs which are in the future tense. These statements can be recognized by words such as *ici* – at that time, *kīspin* – if, or *ispīhk* – when. For example:

1. nika-kīwān anohc ispīhk nēwo tipahikan ispayiki.

    I will go home today when it is four o'clock.

2. kīspin niyānan tipahikan ispayiki pāmwayēs takohtēci kika-wīcētin.

    If it is five o'clock before she arrives I will go with you.

3. nēwo cipahikanis miyāskahki nīso tipahikan kika-sipwēhtānaw ici.

    We will leave when it is four minutes after two.

The following is a summary of how verbs are negated in the different modes:

a) *ēkāwiya, kāya, kāwiya* negate verbs in the *imperative mode*.
b) *namōya, mōya* negate verbs in the *independent mode*.
c) *ēkā* negates verbs in the *conjunct mode*.
d) *ēkā* also negates verbs in their *future conditional form*.

Chapter 16: VII-2 Terms – State and Colour

There is another set of Inanimate Intransitive verbs, many of which are equivalent to English adjectival clauses, stating a condition or the state of inanimate nouns. For instance when a cup falls off the table one might say, "*minihkwācikan pahkihtin…*" This is a very simple example but it makes the point that the cup, which is an inanimate noun, fell, which is an action. Because they are modifying nouns, which can be singular or plural, the verb must agree with the noun in number. In this instance the verbs will occur in singular and plural forms as necessary. Since the nouns are inanimate the verb is Inanimate Intransitive.

They occur in the same modes and forms as the VII-1: Independent, Conjunct; Future conditional; Obviative of Conjunct, Obviative of Future conditionals but not in the Imperative mode. Tense and negation can also be applied.

Some examples of state are:

VII-2 Independent mode

Singular		Plural	
miywāsin	It is nice.	miywāsinwa	They are nice.
pīkopayin	It is broken.	pīkopayinwa	They are broken.
miyopayin	It works/runs well.	miyopayinwa	They work/run well.
āhkwatin	It is frozen.	āhkwatinwa	They are frozen.
māyātan	It is ugly.	māyātanwa	They are ugly.
pahkihtin	It falls.	pahkihtinwa	They fall.

The following examples show that the singular verb agrees with the singular noun and that the plural verb form is used when the noun is plural:

a) miywāsin anima astotin. That hat is nice.
b) miywāsin*wa* anihi miskotāka*ya*. Those coats are nice.
c) āhkwatin*wa* ēkwa sākahika*na*. The lakes are frozen now.
d) papakāsin anima masinahikanēkin. That paper is thin.

Sentences a) and d) refer to singular objects while b) and c) refer to plural objects.

VII-2 Conjunct mode

Singular		Plural	
ē-miywāsik	as it is nice.	ē-miywāsiki	as they are nice.
ē-pīkopayik	as it is broken.	ē-pīkopayiki	as they are broken.
ē-miyopayik	as it is running well.	ē-miyopayiki	as they are working well.
ē-āhkwatik	as it is frozen.	ē-āhkwatiki	as they are frozen.
ē-māyātahk	as it is ugly.	ē-māyātahki	as they are ugly.

Examples:

a) mētoni anihi maskisina ē-miywāsiki.
   Those shoes are really nice.

b) ē-miywāsik mīna anima astotin.
   That hat is also nice.

c) ē-māyātahk māka wiya anima miskotākay, ēkā atāwē.
   But that dress is ugly, don't buy it.

d) wahwā, nipiy anima askihkohk kā-astēk ē-āhkwatik.
   Oh my, that water in the pail is frozen.

VII-2 Future Conditional form

Singular

| miywāsiniyiki | if/when it is nice |
| pīkopayiniyiki | if/when it is broken |

miyopayiniyiki   if/when it is working well
āhkwatiniyiki   if/when it is frozen
māyātaniyiki   if/when it is ugly)

Examples:

a) miywāsiniyiki māskōc ta-pē-kiyokēwak.

     Perhaps when it is nice (weather) they will come visit.

b) mācikōtitān ka-pē-pīhtokwēw pīkopayiniyiki omēcawākanis.

     You'll see, s/he will come inside when his/her toy is broken.

Plural

miywāsiniyikwāwi   if/when they are nice
pīkopayiniyikwāwi   if/when they are broken
miyopayiniyikwāwi   if/when they are working well
āhkwatiniyikwāwi   if/when they are frozen
māyātaniyikwāwi   if/when they are ugly

NOTE: This form quite often occurs with another verb which is introduced as a relative clause by the preverb "*kā-*." Relative clauses are introduced in a separate chapter.

VII-2 Obviative form of the Conjunct mode

Singular

ē-miywāsiniyik   as his/her/it _____ is nice.
ē-pīkopayiniyik   as his/her/it _____ is broken.
ē-miyopayiniyik   as his/her/it _____ works/runs well.
ē-āhkwatiniyik   as his/her/it _____ is frozen.
ē-māyātaniyik   as his/her/it _____ is ugly.

Plural

ē-miywāsiniyiki   as his/her/their _____ are nice.
ē-pīkopayiniyiki   as his/her/their _____ are broken.
ē-miyopayiniyiki   as his/her/their _____ are running well.
ē-āhkwatiniyiki   as his/her/their _____ are frozen.
ē-māyātaniyiki   as his/her/their _____ are ugly.

Examples:

a) mētoni anihi omaskisina ē-miywāsiniyiki.

     His/her shoes are really nice.

b) ē-miywāsiniyik mīna anima otastotin.

     His/her cap/hat is also nice.

c) ē-māyātaniyik māka wiya anima oskotākay.

     But her dress is ugly.

d) kī-wēpinam anihi mōhkomāna ē-pīkopayiniyiki.

     (Because) those knives were broken s/he threw them away.

Negating the VII-2

Negation does not always entail the usage of *namōya* or *ēkāwiya*. For example the list above includes a word for "It is nice." and one for "It is ugly." These can be used to express the opposite of "nice" or "ugly," if one choses to do so. As a matter of fact it would be the preferred form. Below is a summary of how to negate verbs in the different modes:

a) *ēkāwiya, kāya, kāwiya* negate verbs in the *imperative mode*.

b) *namōya, mōya* negate verbs in the *independent mode*.

c) *ēkā* negates verbs in the *conjunct mode*.

d) *ēkā* also negates verbs in their *future conditional form*.

Colours

Colours modifying inanimate nouns are also considered VII-2. They are presented here in the independent, conjunct, future conditional, and the obviative forms. In the examples below a) is singular and b) is plural. Notice the *italicized* letters on the nouns and verbs only to indicate their plural forms.

VII-2 Independent

a) wāpiskāw anima astotin.	That hat is white.
b) wāpiskāwa anihi astotina.	Those hats are white.
a) mihkwāw anima papakiwayān.	That shirt is red.
b) mihkwāwa anihi papakiwayāna.	Those shirts are red.
a) sīpihkwāw anima nāpēwasākay.	That coat (men's) is blue.
b) sīpihkwāwa anihi nāpēwasākaya.	Those coats (men's) are blue.
a) kaskitēwāw anima astotin.	The hat is black.
b) kaskitēwāwa anihi astotina.	The hats are black.
a) osāwāw miskotākay.	The coat is orange.
b) osāwāwa miskotākaya.	The coats are orange.

NOTE: For the VII-2 subject verb agreement the following changes occur: an "-a" is added to the singular for the Independent plural VII-2; an "-a" is also added to the singular for a plural inanimate noun.

VII-2 Conjunct

One may refer to the chapter on VAI for additional colour terms. Only five colours are presented here in their singular and plural forms.

Singular		Plural	
ē-wāpiskāk	as it is white	ē-wāpiskāki	as they are white
ē-mihkwāk	as it is red	ē-mihkwāki	as they are red
ē-sīpihkwāk	as it is blue	ē-sīpihkwāki	as they are blue
ē-kaskitēwāk	as it is black	ē-kaskitēwāki	as they are black
ē-osāwāk	as it is orange	ē-osāwāki	as they are orange

a) ē-wāpiskāk astotin nikī-wāpahtēn.	I saw a hat that was white. (I saw a white hat.)
b) ē-wāpiskāki astotina nikī-wāpahtēn.	I saw hats that were white. (I saw white hats.)
a) ē-mihkwāk papakiwayān nimiywēyihtēn.	I like a shirt that is red. (I like a red shirt.)
b) ē-mihkwāki papakiwayāna nimiywēyihtēn.	I like shirts that are red. (I like red shirts.)
a) ē-sīpihkwāk nāpēwasākay niwī-kaskiwātēn.	I am going to sew a man's coat that is blue. (I am going to sew a blue-colored man's coat.)
b) ē-sīpihkwāki nāpēwasākaya niwī-kaskiwātēn.	I am going to sew men's coats that are blue. (I am going to sew blue-colored men's coats.)
a) ē-kaskitēwāk astotin nikī-atāwān.	I bought a hat that is black. (I bought a black hat.)

b) ē-kaskitēwāk*i* maskisin*a* mīna nikī-atāwān.　　I also bought shoes that are black.
　　　　　　　　　　　　　　　　　　　　　　　　　(I also bought black shoes.)

a) ē-osāwāk miskotākay nikī-wāpahtēn.　　I saw a coat that is orange.
　　　　　　　　　　　　　　　　　　　　I an orange-coloured coat.

b) ē-osāwāk*i* miskotākay*a* nikī-wāpahtēn.　　I saw coats that are orange.
　　　　　　　　　　　　　　　　　　　　　I saw orange-coloured coats.

NOTE: To change from independent to conjunct mode the following occurs: suffix "*ē-*" is placed before the independent mode form and replace "*-w*" with "*-k*" at end of colour term. This is the singular form. To form the plural conjunct add "*-i*" to the singular conjunct. This form quite often occurs with another verb which is introduced as a relative clause by the preverb "*kā-*." Relative clauses are introduced in a separate chapter.

VII-2 Future Conditional

Singular

wāpiskāk*i*	if/when it is white
mihkwāk*i*	if/when it is red
sīpihkwāk*i*	if/when it is blue
kaskitēwāk*i*	if/when it is black
osāwāk*i*	if/when it is orange

NOTE: The singular future conditional was formed by deleting the prefix "*ē-*" from the conjunct then adding the suffix "*-i*."

Examples:

a) wāpiskāki askiy kika-kiskēyihtēn ē-pipohk.
　　When the land is white you will know it is winter.

b) ēkā atāwēstamawihkan miskotākay wāwis oti osāwāki.
　　Don't buy a coat for me especially if it is orange.

Plural

wāpiskāk*wāwi*	if/when they are white
mihkwāk*wāwi*	if/when they are red
sīpihkwāk*wāwi*	if/when they are blue
kaskitēwāk*wāwi*	if/when they are black
osāwāk*wāwi*	if/when they are orange

NOTE: The plural form of the future conditional was formed by deleting the prefix "*ē-*" from the conjunct then adding the suffix "*-wāwi*."

VII-2 Obviative of the Conjunct

Singular		*Plural*	
ē-wāpiskāyik	as his/her ____ is white	ē-wāpiskāyiki	as his/her ____ are white
ē-mihkwāyik	as his/her ____ is red	ē-mihkwāyiki	as his/her ____ are red
ē-sīpihkwāyik	as his/her ____ is blue	ē-sīpihkwāyiki	as his/her ____ are blue
ē-kaskitēwāyik	as his/her ____ is black	ē-kaskitēwāyiki	as his/her ____ are black
ē-osāwāyik	as his/her ____ is orange	ē-osāwāyiki	as his/her____ are orange

NOTE: For the VII-2, the "*-k*" on the conjunct mode of the colour term is replaced by "*-yik*" to form the singular obviative of the conjunct. The "*-i*" is added to the singular obviative of the conjunct to form the plural obviative of the conjunct.

VII-2 Obviative of Future Conditionals

Singular

wāpiskāyiki	if/when his/her ____ is white
mihkwāyiki	if/when his/her ____ is red

sīpihkwāyik*i*	if/when his/her _____ is blue
kaskitēwāyik*i*	if/when his/her _____ is black
osāwāyik*i*	if/when his/her _____ is orange
Plural	
wāpiskāyik*wāwi*	if/when his/her _____ are white
mihkwāyik*wāwi*	if/when his/her _____ are red
sīpihkwāyik*wāwi*	if/when his/her _____ are blue
kaskitēwāyik*wāwi*	if/when his/her _____ are black
osāwāyik*wāwi*	if/when his/her _____ are orange

NOTE: For the VII-2, "-*k*" on the future conditional of the colour term is replaced by "-*yiki*" to form the singular obviative of the future conditional. The "-*i*" is deleted from the singular obviative of the future conditional then an additional suffix "-*wāwi*" is added to form the plural obviative of the future conditional.

NOTE: How to apply Negation to the different mode forms:

a) *ēkāwiya, kāya, kāwiya* negate verbs in the *imperative mode*.

b) *namōya, mōya* negate verbs in the *independent mode*.

c) *ēkā* negates verbs in the *conjunct mode*.

d) *ēkā* also negates verbs in their *future conditional form*.

Chapter 17: Transitive Inanimate Verbs

There are two main categories known as transitive verbs. Unlike the intransitive verbs introduced previously, these verbs describe action that is transferred to a direct object. The sentence structure includes Subject, Verb and Object; the object is an animate or inanimate noun. This chapter introduces the Transitive Inanimate verbs.

Transitive Inanimate Verbs – VTI-1

Transitive inanimate verbs fall into three categories, each depending on the ending of the verb stem. "*atoskāta*," "*ayā*," and "*mīci*" are all VTIs. Each of them, because of their endings, fall into a different classification: the VTI-1 all end in "*a*" as in "*atoskāta* – work at it"; the VTI-2 all end in "*ā*" as in "*ayā* – have it." Both VTI-2 and VTI-3 verbs follow the same conjugation pattern as the animate intransitive verbs (VAI) which were introduced in Chapter 11. The VTI -1 verbs however, follow a different conjugation pattern.

Immediate Imperative Mode

The main format to remember for these verbs is: the spelling of the VTI-1 verb stem *does not include* the short "*-a.*" This is because the suffix for 2p begins with an "*-a*" and the suffix for 21 begins with an "*-ē*" so the verb stem cannot end in a consistent vowel. If the vowel is left on the stem then the resulting word would be incorrect. So just *drop* the short "*-a*" at the end of the stem before inserting it into the chart.

VTI-1 Immediate Imperative

2s	_____ a
2p	_____ amok
21	_____ ētān

Example: Immediate Imperative mode: "atoskāta" – work at it

2s	atoskāta	Work on it.
2p	atoskātamok	Work on it.
21	atoskātētān	Let's work on it.

Here are some of the many VTI-1 verb stems which can be conjugated using the paradigm above:

atoskāta	work on it	itōta	do it
postiska	put it on	tahkoskāta	step on it
kēcikoska	take it off	masinaha	write it
kisīpēkina	wash it	kiskēyihta	know it
kīsisa	cook it	otina	take it
nisitohta	understand it	yahkowēpaha	push/shove it forward

The verbs representing the five senses of seeing, touching, hearing, smelling, and tasting are also classified as VTI-1:

wāpahta	see it	nitohta	listen to it
kanawāpahta	look at it	kocispita	taste it
mīskona	feel it	paswāta	smell it
sāmina	touch it	miyāhta	smell it
pēhta	hear it	māmitonēyihta	think about it

NOTE: All VTI-1 stems end in a consonant because one *drops* the short "*a.*" The command in 2s will be the identifying sign to tell you that the verb is a VTI-1.

Delayed Imperative Mode

Transitive Inanimate-1 verbs also have the delayed imperative mode. Here is the chart with the necessary suffixes:

VTI-1 Delayed Imperative

2s _____ mohkan
2p _____ mohkēk
21 _____ mohkahk

Example: Delayed Imperative mode VTI-1 "nitohta – listen to it"

2s	nitohtamohkan	Listen to it later.
2p	nitohtamohkēk	Listen to it later.
21	nitohtamohkahk	Let's listen to it later.

Examples:

a) mwēstas mahti nitohtamohkan anima kitohcikan, ē-kiyokēcik ōki mēkwāc.
    Listen to that radio later, these ones are visiting right now.

b) kwayas nitohtamohkēk māci-pīkiskwēci ana kēhtē-aya.
    Really listen when that Elder begins speaking.

c) nitohtamohkahk anima kitohcikan ita awāsisak kā-kī-nikamocik.
    Let's listen to that tape where the children were singing.

Negative imperatives:

a) ēkāwiya mahti nitohta anima kitohcikan mēkwāc ōki ē-kiyokēcik.
    Don't listen to the radio while as these ones are visiting.

b) kāwiya ēkosi itōtamok, pōnihtāk anima sēmāk.
    Don't do that, quit it right now!

c) kāya nānitaw itwē!
    Don't say anything!

Negating Transitive Verbs

The explanation in Chapter 13 regarding negation of verbs and information about "yes" and "no" answers has been copied here as a review as the process is the same for VTI-1.

In addition to using *ēkāwiya*, the variants *ēkā, kāya and kāwiya* can also be used to negate any verb in the imperative. One of these variant forms, *ēkā* is used to negate the conjunct mode and the future conditional forms of verbs. It is placed before the verb. The conjunct mode uses the word "*ēkā*" to indicate the idea of negation, as in situations that indicate "being unable" or "not wanting" or "not having done something."

To negate the Independent mode one simply places "*namōya*" before the rest of the verb as it appears in the conjugation. To answer in the negative follow the same procedures as the above except that one uses "*namōya*" — once for "no" and a second time to negate the verb.

Examples:

Q. kinōhtē-kīwān cī?   A. namōya, namōya ninōhtē-kīwān.

Do you want to go home?   No, I don't want to go home.

This long way of answering in the negative is used to make a point or to answer a written question that requires a complete statement. Although it is cumbersome one will sometimes hear it in the instances above. More often than not however, the answer is a simple "no" – "*mwāc, mōya, namōya*" and other times there are more specific answers that require the additional particle "*ohci*." One may review Chapter 11 for more details on negation.

Independent Mode of Transitive Inanimate -1: VTI-1

Conjugation of VTI-1 follows the same process as that of the VAIs where the verb stem is inserted between the person indicator and the suffixes/endings. Just as with the others, VTI-1 verb stems are found in the singular imperative. The stem, in this case ends in an "*a*" that is dropped, then the remaining word is inserted in the verb pattern.

One can identify a transitive verb by asking two questions:

i) Is the action transferred to or affecting (someone or) something?

ii) Does the verb stem end in an "*a*"?

If the the answer is "Yes" to both questions then it must be a VTI-1. Therefore, one will use the chart below, while following the rule mentioned above, to conjugate the verb.

VTI-1 – Independent mode

1s	ni	_____	ēn	1s	I _____ it
2s	ki	_____	ēn	2s	You _____ it
3s		_____	am	3s	S/he/it _____ it
3's		_____	amiyiwa	3's	His/her/its ____ _____ it
1p	ni	_____	ēnān	1p	We _____ it
21	ki	_____	ēnaw	21	We _____ it
2p	ki	_____	ēnāwāw	2p	You _____ it
3p		_____	amwak	3p	They _____ it
3'p		_____	amiyiwa	3'p	Their ____ _____ it

Example: Independent Mode VTI-1 "wāpahta – see it"

1s	niwāpahtēn	1s	I see it.
2s	kiwāpahtēn	2s	You (sg) see it.
3s	wāpahtam	3s	S/he sees it.
3's	wāpahtamiyiwa	3's	His/her _____ sees it.
1p	niwāpahtēnān	1p	We, not you, see it. (excl)
21	kiwāpahtēnaw	21	We, and you, see it. (incl)
2p	kiwāpahtēnāwāw	2p	You (pl) see it.
3p	wāpahtamwak	3p	They see it.
3'p	wāpahtamiyiwa	3'p	Their _____ see it.

NOTE: Remember: Drop "-*a*" from end of 2s imperative form and insert this stem into the chart.

VTI-1 – Conjunct Mode

1s	ē-	_____	amān	1s	as I ____ it
2s	ē-	_____	aman	2s	as you (sg) _____ it
3s	ē-	_____	ahk	3s	as s/he _____ it
3's	ē-	_____	amiyit	3's	as his/her/its ____ ____ it
1p	ē-	_____	amāhk	1p	as we(excl) _____ it
21	ē-	_____	amahk	21	as we (incl) _____ it
2p	ē-	_____	amēk	2p	as you (pl) _____ it
3p	ē-	_____	ahkik	3p	as they _____ it
3'p	ē-	_____	amiyit	3'p	as their ____ ____ it

Example: VTI-1 miyāhta – smell it

1s	ē-miyāhtamān	1s	as I smell it
2s	ē-miyāhtaman	2s	as you (sg) smell it
3s	ē-miyāhtahk	3s	as s/he smells it
3's	ē-miyāhtamiyit	3's	as his/her/its _____ smells it
1p	ē-miyāhtamāhk	1p	as we(excl) smell it
21	ē-miyāhtamahk	21	as we(incl) smell it
2p	ē-miyāhtamēk	2p	as you (pl) smell it
3p	ē-miyāhtahkik	3p	as they smell it
3'p	ē-miyāhtamiyit	3'p	as their _____ smell it

VTI-1 – Future Conditional Form – if or when

1s	_____amāni	1s	if/when I _____
2s	_____amani	2s	if/when you _____
3s	_____ahki	3s	if/when s/he _____
3's	_____amiyici	3's	if/when his/her _____
1p	_____amāhki	1p	if/when we (excl) _____
21	_____amahko	21	if/when we (incl) _____
2p	_____amēko	2p	if/when you (pl) _____
3p	_____ahkwāwi	3p	if/when they _____
3'p	_____amiyici	3'p	if/when their _____

Example: VTI-1 nisitohta – understand it

1s	nisitohtamāni	1s	if/when I understand it
2s	nisitohtamani	2s	if/when you understand it
3s	nisitohtahki	3s	if/when s/he understands it
3's	nisitohtamiyici	3's	if/when his/her _____ understands it
1p	nisitohtamāhki	21	if/when we (excl) understand it
21	nisitohtamahko	21	if/when we (incl) understand it
2p	nisitohtamēko	2p	if/when you (pl) understand it
3p	nisitohtahkwāwi	3p	if/when they understand it
3'p	nisitohtamiyici	3'p	if/when their _____ understands it

Examples:

1. ēkā nisitohtamēko wīhtamawihkēk ēkwa kīhtwām kika-kanawāpahtēnaw.

   If you(pl) don't understand tell me and we (incl) will look at it again.

2. ispīhk nisitohtamāni anima mistahi nika-miywēyihtēn.

   When I understand that I will be very happy.

Transitive Inanimate-2 Verbs

This set has the same prefixes and suffixes as the VAI conjugation charts that have been been introduced. So it should not be difficult to manage the conjugation of these verbs.

The VTI-2 stems can be identified from the 2s imperative because they always end in an "ā." For this particular set of verbs there is no change to the stem when conjugating.

Some VTI-2 stems are:

osīhtā	make it	kanācihtā	clean it
ayā	have it	kocīhtā	try it
āpacihtā	use it	itohtatā	take it there

VTI-2 – Immediate Imperative

2s	_____
2p	_____k
21	_____tān

Example: "kanācihtā – clean it"

2s	kanācihtā	Clean it.
2p	kanācihtā*k*	Clean it.
21	kanācihtā*tān*	Let's clean it.

VTI-2 – Delayed Imperative

2s	_____ hkan
2p	_____ hkēk
21	_____ hkahk

Example: "kanācihtā – clean it"

2s	kanācihtāhkan	Clean it. (later)
2p	kanācihtāhkēk	Clean it. (later)
21	kanācihtāhkahk	Let's clean it. (later)

NOTE: A reminder: 2s give orders to a single person; 2p gives orders to more than one person; 21 gives or invites one or more persons to do some task or action with you. "Let's read it."

VTI-2 – Independent Mode

1s	ni_____n	1s	I _____ it.
2s	ki_____n	2s	You _____ it.
3s	_____w	3s	S/he/it ____ it.
3's	_____yiwa	3's	His/her/its ____ ____ it.
1p	ni _____nān	1p	We _____ it.
21	ki_____ naw	21	We _____ it.
2p	ki_____nāwāw	2p	You _____ it.
3p	_____wak	3p	They _____ it.
3'p	_____yiwa	3'p	Their ____ _____ it.

Example: "kocīhtā – try/attempt it"

1s	nikocīhtān	1s	I try it.
2s	kikocīhtān	2s	You try it.
3s	kocīhtāw	3s	S/he tries it.
3's	kocīhtāyiwa	3's	His/her/its ____ tries it.
1p	nikocīhtānān	1p	We try it.
21	kikocīhtānaw	21	We try it.
2p	kikocīhtānāwāw	2p	You try it.
3p	kocīhtāwak	3p	They try it.
3'p	kocīhtāyiwa	3'p	Their ____ try it.

VTI-2 – Conjunct Mode

1s	ē-_____yān	1s	as I _____ it.
2s	ē-_____yan	2s	as you ____ it.
3s	ē-_____t	3s	as s/he/it ___ it
3's	ē-_____yit	3's	as his/her/its ____ _____ it.
1p	ē-_____yāhk	1p	as we ____ it.
21	ē-_____ yahk	21	as we ____ it.
2p	ē-_____ yēk	2p	as you ____ it.
3p	ē- _____cik	3p	as they ____ it.
3'p	ē-_____yit	3'p	as their ____ _____it.

Example: "kocihtā – try it"

1s	ē-kocihtāyān	1s	as I try it.
2s	ē-kocihtāyan	2s	as you try it.
3s	ē-kocihtāt	3s	as s/he/it tries it.
3's	ē-kocihtāyit	3's	as his/her/its ____ tries it.
1p	ē-kocihtāyāhk	1p	as we try it.
21	ē-kocihtāyahk	21	as we try it.
2p	ē-kocihtāyēk	2p	as you try it.
3p	ē-kocihtācik	3p	as they try it.
3'p	ē-kocihtāyit	3'p	as their ____ try it.

Future Conditional form for VTI-2

Remember that these follow the VAI charts but you can also refer to Chart 12 in Appendix A.

1s	_____ yāni	1s	if/when I _____ it
2s	_____ yani	2s	if/when you ____ it
3s	_____ ci	3s	if/when s/he ____ it
3's	_____ yici	3's	if/when his/her ____ ___ it
1p	_____ yāhki	1p	if/when we (excl) _____ it
21	_____ yahko	21	if/when we (incl) _____ it
2p	_____ yēko	2p	if/when you (pl) _____ it
3p	_____ twāwi	3p	if/when they _____ it
3'p	_____ yici	3'p	if/when their ____ ____ it

The suffixes here are italicized and the stem is underlined only so one can differentiate the suffixes from the stem.

Example: "osīhtā – use it"

1s	osīhtāyāni	1s	if/when I make it
2s	osīhtāyani	2s	if/when you make it
3s	osīhtāci	3s	if/when s/he makes it
3's	osīhtāyici	3's	if/when his/her _____ makes it
1p	osīhtāyāhki	1p	if/when we (excl) make it
21	osīhtāyahko	21	if/when we (incl) make it
2p	osīhtāyēko	2p	if/when you (pl) make it
3p	osīhtātwāwi	3p	if/when they make it
3'p	osīhtāyici	3'p	if/when their _____ make it

NOTE: A review of these paradigms and those in Chapter 11 will show that VTI-2 are conjugated the same as VAI stems.

Transitive Inanimate – 3 VTI-3

The VTI-3 also follow the charts for VAI. It is not necessary to make any change to the verb stem before inserting it in the chart.

VTI-3 – Immediate Imperative

2s	_____
2p	_____ k
21	_____ tān

Example: "mīci – eat it"

2s	mīci	Eat it.
2p	mīcik	Eat it.
21	mīcitān	Let's eat it.

VTI-3 – Delayed Imperative

2s	_____hkan
2p	_____ihkēk
21	_____ihkahk

Example: "mīci – eat it"

2	mīcihkan	Eat it. (later).
2p	mīcihkēk	Eat it. (later).
21	mīcihkahk	Let's eat it. (later)

NOTE: It has been mentioned before it is not necessary for the word "mwēstas – later" to be used because the suffix itself indicates the idea of "later." It is not a set rule not to use it and one might hear it used anyway.

VTI-3 – Independent Mode

1s	ni_____n	1s	I _____ it.
2s	ki_____n	2s	you _____ it.
3s	_____w	3s	s/he _____ it.
3's	_____yiwa	3's	his/her/its ____ _____ it.
1p	ni _____nān	1p	we _____ it.
21	ki_____naw	21	we _____ it.
2p	ki_____nāwāw	2p	you _____ it.
3p	_____wak	3p	they _____ it.
3'p	_____yiwa	3'p	their ____ _____ it.

Example: "mīci – eat it"

1s	nimīcin	1s	I eat it.
2s	kimīcin	2s	You eat it.
3s	mīciw	3s	S/he eats it.
3's	mīciyiwa	3's	His/her/its ____ eats it.
1p	nimīcinān	1p	We eat it.
21	kimīcinaw	21	We eat it.
2p	kimīcināwāw	2p	You eat it.
3p	mīciwak	3p	They eat it.
3'p	mīciyiwa	3'p	Their ____ eat it.

VTI-3 – Conjunct Mode

1s	ē-_____yān	1s	as I _____ it.
2s	ē-_____yan	2s	as you _____ it.
3s	ē-_____t	3s	as s/he/it _____ it.
3's	ē-_____yit	3's	as his/her/its ____ ____ it.
1p	ē-_____yāhk	1p	as we _____ it.
21	ē-_____yahk	21	as we _____ it.
2p	ē-_____yēk	2p	as you _____ it.
3p	ē-_____cik	3p	as they _____ it.
3'p	ē-_____yit	3'p	as their ____ _____ it.

Example: "mīci – eat it"

1s	ē-mīciyān	1s	as I eat it.
2s	ē-mīciyan	2s	as you eat it.
3s	ē-mīcit	3s	as s/he/it eats it.
3's	ē-mīciyit	3's	as his/her/its ____ eats it.
1p	ē-mīciyāhk	1p	as we eat it.
21	ē-mīciyahk	21	as we eat it.
2p	ē-mīciyēk	2p	as you eat it.
3p	ē-mīcicik	3p	as they eat it.
3'p	ē-mīciyit	3'p	as their ____ eat it.

Future Conditional form of VTI-2 and VTI-3

Remember that these follow the VAI charts but you can also refer to Chart 12 in Appendix A.

Example: "mīci – eat it"

1s	mīciyāni	1s	if/when I eat it
2s	mīciyani	2s	if/when you eat it
3s	mīcici	3s	if/when s/he eat it
3's	mīciyici	3's	if/when his/her ____ eat it

1p	mīciyāhki	1p	if/when we (excl) eat it
21	mīciyahko	21	if/when we (incl) eat it
2p	mīciyēko	2p	if/when you (pl) eat it
3p	mīcitwāwi	3p	if/when they eat it
3'p	mīciyici	3'p	if/when their ____ eat it

Example:

a) mīciyani anima kika-maskawisīn.

    If you eat that you will be strong.

b) mīciyāni ōma niya nama kīkway kiya kika-ayān.

    If I eat this then you will not have any.

Chapter 18: Transitive Animate Verbs-1 (Regular Stems)

The transitive animate verb is used when the object or goal in the sentence is an animate noun. It is uniquely complicated but precise because it addresses, separately with different suffixes, the singular and plural "objects" in each of the modes and forms that have already been introduced for the VTI. There are also three other forms that are addressed in separate chapters: the Inverse form, the Reflexive and the Unspecified Actor form.

In addition to marking the suffixes to indicate the presence of singular and plural objects in a sentence this class of verbs also has some stems which undergo complicated changes. This chapter will present *only* VTA-1 or regular verbs but in the two Imperative modes, the Independent mode, Conjunct mode and the Future Conditional form. All will show the singular and plural conjugation.

The VTA-*2* – "*Vw*" stem is in Chapter 19; VTA-*3* – "*Cw*" stem is in Chapter 20; VTA-*4* – "*t*" stem is in Chapter 21.

NOTE: Although there are these differences they all follow some of the same conjugation charts.

a) Some VTA stems undergo changes.

b) Each of the modes in this and other chapters discussing the VTA will present the singular and plural suffixes.

c) As well, here are some terms that might cause some confusion: *Vw* → refers to a "*Vowel w*" sequence in the spelling of a verb stem; *Cw* → refers to a "*Consonant w*" sequence in the spelling of a verb stem.

Immediate Imperative Mode – VTA-1 Regular Verbs

The verb stem again will be placed in the space indicated by the underscore in the following charts. The stem for any VTA ends in a consonant; this will be the "hook" which will indicate that it is a VTA-1. The stem is from the 2s Imperative or from the 3s, Independent mode, minus the suffix "-*ēw.*"

Singular object (one person/object is affected)

2s _____

2p _____ ihk

21 _____ ātān

NOTE: The slashes between him/her/it indicate "or" rather than all three at the same time. Context will determine whether you use him, or her, or it, in the translation. This will be the case through all the chapters dealing with the VTA.

Example: "VTA-1 "asam – feed him/her/it"

2s	asam	2s	Feed him/her/it.
2p	asamihk	2p	Feed him/her/it.
21	asamātān	21	Let's feed him/her/it.

Plural object (more than one person/object is affected)

2s _____ ik

2p _____ ihkok

21 _____ ātānik

Example: VTA-1 "asam – feed him/her/it"

2s	asamik	2s	Feed them.
2p	asamihkok	2p	Feed them.
21	asamātānik	21	Let's feed them.

NOTE: In a) the slashes between him/her/it indicate "or" rather than all three at the same time. Context will determine whether you use him, or her, or it, in the translation. The charts for the VTA may be found in Appendix A – Verb Chart 5 and Chart 6 for future conditionals.

Delayed Imperative – VTA-1

Singular object (one person/object is affected)

2s _____ āhkan
2p _____ āhkēk
21 _____ āhkahk

Example:

2s	asamāhkan	2s	Feed him/her/it later.
2p	asamāhkēk	2p	Feed him/her/it later.
21	asamāhkahk	21	Let's feed him/her/it later.

Plural object (more than one person/object is affected)

2s _____ āhkanik
2p _____ āhkēkok
21 _____ āhkahkok

Example: VTA-1 "wāpam – see him/her/it"

2s	wāpam<u>āhkan</u>*ik*	2s	See them later.
2p	wāpam<u>āhkēk</u>*ok*	2p	See them later.
21	wāpam<u>āhkahk</u>*ok*	21	Let's see them later.

In the examples above the underlined part of the suffix indicates the singular object (single person is affected). The additional italicized suffix indicates a plural object. (more than one person is affected).

NOTE: Delayed Imperative has often been explained as a command to some one to do something at a later time; in the future.

Independent Mode for VTA-1

Similar to the Transitive Inanimate verbs the Transitive Animate verbs have the structure: Subject, Verb, Object. But in this case, the object will be an animate noun and this object is a person or an animate thing in the singular or plural.

It is most important to remember that with this class of verbs one will be applying suffixes that indicate a singular object and an additional suffix which is attached to this existing suffix to show that there is a plural object involved.

The conjugation pattern below shows the suffixes for a singular object. As was the case with VAI verbs, the suffixes and person indicators remain constant.

Independent mode VTA-1

Singular object (one person/object is affected)

1s	ni	_____ āw	1s	I _____ him/her/it.	
2s	ki	_____ āw	2s	you _____ him/her/it.	
3s		_____ ēw	3s	s/he/it _____ him/her/it.	
3's		_____ ēyiwa	3's	his/her/its _____ _____ him/her/it.	
1p	ni	_____ ānān	1p	we _____ him/her/it. (excl)	
21	ki	_____ ānaw	21	we _____ him/her/it. (incl)	
2p	ki	_____ āwāw	2p	you _____ him/her/it.	
3p		_____ ēwak	3p	they _____ him/her/it.	
3'p		_____ ēyiwa	3'p	their _____ _____ him/her/it.	

Example: VTA-1 "*mow* – eat it" singular (one person/object is affected)

1s	nimowāw		1s	I eat it.
2s	kimowāw		2s	You eat it.
3s	mowēw		3s	He/she/it eats it.
3's	mowēyiwa		3s	His/her/its _____ eats it.
1p	nimowānān		1p	We (excl) eat it.
21	kimowānaw		21	We (incl) eat it.
2p	kimowāwāw		2p	You (pl) eat it.
3p	mowēwak		3p	They eat it.
3'p	mowēyiwa		3'p	Their _____ eats it.

Plural object (more than one object/person is affected)

1s	ni _____ āw*ak*	1s	I _____ them
2s	ki _____ āw*ak*	2s	you ____ them
3s	_____ ēw	3s	s/he/it _____ them
3'	_____ ēyiwa	3's	his/her/its ____ _____ them
1p	ni _____ ānān*ak*	1p	we _____ them (excl)
21	ki _____ ānaw*ak*	21	we _____ them (incl)
2p	ki _____ āwāw*ak*	2p	you _____ them
3p	_____ ēwak	3p	they _____ them
3'p	_____ ēyiwa	3'p	their ____ _____ them

NOTE: The plural suffix is italicized to illustrate that it is added to the singular suffix shown above. An important feature to remember is that the 3rd person forms do not take any further plural object markers. They are obviative and only the context will determine whether the object is singular or plural.

Example: VTA-1 "mow – eat it" – plural (more than one object/person is affected)

1s	nimowāwak		1s	I eat them.
2s	kimowāwak		2s	You eat them.
3s	mowēw		3s	He/she/it eats them.
3's	mowēyiwa		3's	His/her/its _____ eats them.
1p	nimowānānak		1p	We (excl) eat them.
21	kimowānawak		21	We (incl) eat them.
2p	kimowāwāwak		2p	You (pl) eat them.
3p	mowēwak		3p	They eat them.
3'p	mowēyiwa		3'p	Their _____ eats them.

NOTE: "it" and "them" refer to an animate noun which can then be replaced by names of people, animals or objects that are of the animate category. The sentences below represent this.

Examples:

1) nimowāw kinosēw.	I eat the fish or I eat fish.
2) kimowāwāw pahkwēsikan.	You (pl.) eat bannock.
3) nikī-mowāw osāwās anohc.	I ate an orange today.
4) kikī-mowāw*ak* cī osāwās*ak*?	Did you (sg.) eat the oranges?
5) nikī-mowāw*ak* ayōskan*ak*.	I ate the raspberries.

In examples 4) and 5) the objects are plural. Only the transitive animate verbs have this peculiarity where the form of the verb must agree in number with the number of the object. In other words, if the object in the sentence is animate and plural then the verb suffixes must also indicate animate plus pluralization.

NOTE: The stem did not undergo any alterations before being placed in the space between the person prefix and the suffix. The object in the sentence will be an animate noun which may be a person/s or an animate thing/s.

The following are more examples to show this object-verb agreement:

a) niwāpamāw nāpēw (singular object).
    I see the man.

b) niwāpamāwak nāpēwak (plural object).
    I see the men.

c) āsay cī kikī-asamāw kicawāsimis (singular object)?
    Did you feed your child already?

d) āsay cī kikī-asamāwak kicawāsimisak (plural object)?
    Did you feed your children already?

The objects in the sentences b) and d) above show that the plural suffixes on the verbs correspond with the plural suffixes on the nouns. The last letter is always "*k*." These plural suffixes will occur only in the following persons: 1s, 2s 1p, 21, 2p.

Obviative 3s; 3p; 3'; 3'p

But in the third person, singular or plural (3, 3p), and the third person obviative, singular or plural (3', 3'p), the object in a sentence does not follow the regular pluralization of animate nouns. The noun ends in an "-*a*."

For example:

3s   wāpamēw nāpēwa.
      He/she sees the man/men.

3p   wāpamēwak nāpēwa.
      They see the man/men.

3'   otānisa wāpamēyiwa iskwēwa.
      His/her daughter/s see(s) the woman/women.

3'p   otānisiwāwa wāpamēyiwa iskwēwa.
      Their daughter/s see(s) the woman/women.

NOTE: An important observation is that there is a slash (/) between man/men, woman/women, daughter and plural "s." The context of the situation, conversation or the knowledge of the speaker about the people spoken about determines the translation of the Cree sentence. This is especially true for the sentences 3' and 3'p. Suppose there are names for the daughters' parents in the above sentences:

3'   John otānisa wāpamēyiwa iskwēwa.
      John's daughter/s see/s the woman/women.

In this sentence the addressee can identify whether it is "John's (only) daughter…" or "John's daughters…" only if he knows beforehand how many daughters John has. The speaker may also clarify this. For instance, if it is only one daughter, simply by using the daughter's name. The context of the 3'p would be determined likewise.

Conjunct Mode VTA-1

Singular object (one person/object is affected)

1s	ē-_____ak	1s	as I _____ him/her/it.
2s	ē-_____at	2s	as you ____ him/her/it.
3s	ē-_____āt	3s	as he/she _____ him/her.
3's	ē-_____āyit	3's	as his/her _____ ____ him/her/it.
1p	ē-_____āyāhk	1p	as we (excl) _____ him/her/it.
21	ē-_____āyahk	21	as we (incl) _____ him/her/it.

2p	ē-_____āyēk	2p	as you (pl) _____ him/her/it.
3p	ē-_____ācik	3p	as they _____ him/her/it.
3'p	ē-_____āyit	3'p	as their ____ ____ him/her/it.

Example: VTA-1 "wīcih – help him/her/it" (one person/object is affected)

1s	ē-wīcihak	1s	as I help him/her/it.
2s	ē-wīcihat	2s	as you (sg) help him/her/it.
3s	ē-wīcihāt	3s	as he/she helps him/her.
3's	ē-wīcihāyit	3's	as his/her _____ helps him/her/it.
1p	ē-wīcihāyāhk	1p	as we (excl) help him/her/it.
21	ē-wīcihāyahk	21	as we (incl) help him/her/it.
2p	ē-wīcihāyēk	2p	as you (pl) help him/her/it.
3p	ē-wīcihācik	3p	as they help him/her/it.
3'p	ē-wīcihāyit	3'p	as their _____ helps him/her/it.

Plural object (more than one person/object is affected)

1s	ē-_____akik	1s	as I _____ them.
2s	ē-_____acik	2s	as you ____ them.
3s	ē-_____āt	3s	as he/she/it _____ them.
3's	ē-_____āyit	3's	as his/her/its ____ ____ them.
1p	ē-_____āyāhkik	1p	as we (excl) _____ them.
21	ē-_____āyahkok	21	as we (incl) _____ them.
2p	ē-_____āyēkok	2p	as you (pl) _____ them.
3p	ē-_____ācik	3p	as they _____ them.
3'p	ē-_____āyit	3'p	as their ____ ____ them.

Example: VTA-1 "wīcih – help him/her/it" (more than one person/object is affected)

1s	ē-wīcihakik	1s	as I help them.
2s	ē-wīcihacik	2s	as you help them.
3s	ē-wīcihāt	3s	as he/she/it helps them.
3's	ē-wīcihāyit	3's	as his/her/its ____ helps them.
1p	ē-wīcihāyāhkik	1p	as we (excl) help them.
21	ē-wīcihāyahkok	21	as we (incl) help them.
2p	ē-wīcihāyēkok	2p	as you (pl) help them.
3p	ē-wīcihācik	3p	as they help them.
3'p	ē-wīcihāyit	3'p	as their _____ helps them.

One can use the tense markers simply by following the chart below to change form one tense to another. Or one can also add a preverb.

NOTE: A (-) hyphen is required after the "*ē*"; after the tense; and after the preverb. A (+) signifies no hyphen or space between the stem and the suffix.

ē-	Tense -	Preverb -	Verb Stem +	Suffix

Future Conditional – VTA-1

Singular object (one person/object is affected)

1s	_____aki	1s	if/when I _____ him/her/it
2s	_____aci	2s	if/when you (sg) ____ him/her/it
3s	_____āci	3s	if/when s/he ____ him/her/it
3's	_____āyici	3's	if/when his/her ____ ____ him/her/it
1p	_____āyāhki	1p	if/when we (excl) _____ him/her/it

21	_____āyahko	21	if/when we (incl) _____ him/her/it
2p	_____āyēko	2p	if/when you (pl) _____ him/her/it
3p	_____ātwāwi	3p	if/when they _____ him/her/it
3'p	_____āyici	3'p	if their ____ _____ him/her/it

Example: VTA-1 "wāpam – see him/her/it" (one person/object is affected)

1s	wāpamaki	1s	if/when I see him/her
2s	wāpamaci	2s	if/when you (sg) see him/her
3s	wāpamāci	3s	if/when s/he sees him/her
3's	wāpamāyici	3's	if/when his/her ____ sees him/her
1p	wāpamāyāhki	1p	if/when we (excl) see him/her
21	wāpamāyahko	21	if/when we (incl) see him/her
2p	wāpamāyēko	2p	if/when you (pl) see him/her
3p	wāpamātwāwi	3p	if/when they see him/her
3'p	wāpamāyici	3'p	if their ____ sees him/her

Plural object (more than one person/object is affected)

1s	_____akwāwi	1s	if/when I _____ them
2s	_____atwāwi	2s	if/when you (sg) ____ them
3s	_____āci	3s	if/when s/he _____ them
3's	_____āyici	3's	if/when his/her ____ ____ them
1p	_____āyāhkwāwi	1p	if/when we (excl) _____ them
21	_____āyahkwāwi	21	if/when we(incl) _____ them
2p	_____āyēkwāwi	2p	if/when you (pl) _____ them
3p	_____ātwāwi	3p	if/when they _____ them
3'p	_____āyici	3'p	if/when their ____ _____ them

Example: VTA-1 "kakwēcim – ask him/her" (more than one person is affected)

1s	kakwēcimakwāwi	1s	if/when I ask them
2s	kakwēcimatwāwi	2s	if/when you (sg) ask them
3s	kakwēcimāci	3's	if/when s/he asks them
3's	kakwēcimāyici	3's	if/when his/her ____ asks them
1p	kakwēcimāyāhkwāwi	1p	if/when we (excl) ask them
21	kakwēcimāyahkwāwi	21	if/when we(incl) ask them
2p	kakwēcimāyēkwāwi	2p	if/when you (pl) ask them
3p	kakwēcimātwāwi	3p	if/when they ask them
3'p	kakwēcimāyici	3'p	if/when their ____ asks them

NOTE: There are changes to the plural object suffixes for 1s, 2s, 1p, 21p, 2p only. 3s, 3's, 3p, 3'p remain the same in singular and plural. Notice also that the example VTA-1 verb stems end in either an "-m," "-h" or occasionally an "-n" as well, e.g.: "wēpin – throw him/her/it away." The stem "mow – eat it" always remains the same. Another *important* reminder is: *Do not use any of part of the singular suffixes for plural forms. Use only the plural suffixes provided in the chart above.*

Chapter 19: Transitive Animate Verbs-2 (Vw stems)

Except for the fact that the last two letters of the stem are not used in some parts of conjugating the VTA-2 verbs follow the VTA-1 charts. This will become apparent in the chapter discussing the Inverse form.

Some "Vw" stems are:

kapēsīsta<u>w</u> – camp with him/her

kaskikwātama<u>w</u> – sew it for him/her/it

(Vw = Vowel w stem)

atoska<u>w</u> – work for him/her

pētama<u>w</u> – bring it for him/her/it

Immediate Imperative – VTA-2 "Vw" stem

a) Singular object (one person/object is affected)

2s	_____	
2p	_____	ihk
21	_____	ātān

Example: VTA-2 "Vw" "pētamaw – Bring it for him/her/it"

2s	pētamaw	2s	Bring it for him/her/it.
2p	pētam*ā*hk	2p	Bring it for him/her/it.
21	pētamawātān	21	Let's bring it for him/her/it.

NOTE: In 2p above and below the "-*aw*" was dropped from the stem and the "-*i*" in the VTA-1 suffix changed to an "-*ā*" (*in italics*).

b) Plural object (more than one person/object is affected)

2s	_____	ik	2s (Order one person)
2p	_____	ihkok	2p (Order more than one person.)
21	_____	ātānik	21 (Suggestion/invitation to do s.t. with/for s.o.)

Example:

2s	pētamaw*ik*	2s	Bring it for them.
2p	pētam*ā*hkok	2p	Bring it for them.
21	pētamaw*ātānik*	21	Let's bring it for them.

NOTE: The changes which took place in *2p* of the Immediate Imperative, *singular* object, *do not occur* in the Immediate Imperative *plural object*.

Reminder: that VTA-2 follows the VTA-1 charts.

Delayed Imperative – VTA-2 "Vw" stem

a) Singular object (one person/object is affected)

2s	_____	*āhkan*
2p	_____	*āhkēk*
21	_____	*āhkahk*

Example: VTA-2 "Vw" stem "pētamaw – Bring it for him/her/it."

2s	pētamawāhkan	2s	Bring it for him/her/it later.
2p	pētamawāhkēk	2p	Bring it for him/her/it later.
21	pētamawāhkahk	21	Let's bring it for him/her/it later.

b) Plural object (more than one person/object is affected)

2s	_____	āhkanik
2p	_____	āhkēkok
21	_____	āhkahkok

Example:

2s	pētamawāhkan*ik*	2s	Bring it for them. (later)
2p	pētamawāhkēk*ok*	2p	Bring it for them. (later)
21	pētamawāhkahk*ok*	21	Let's bring it for them. (later)

Independent Mode – VTA-2 "Vw"

a) Singular object (one person/object is affected)

1s	ni	_____ āw	1s	I _____	him/her/it.
2s	ki	_____ āw	2s	you ____	him/her/it.
3s		_____ ēw	3s	s/he/it _____	him/her/it.
3's		_____ ēyiwa	3's	his/her/its ____ _____	him/her/it.
1p	ni	_____ ānān	1p	we _____	him/her/it. (excl)
21	ki	_____ ānaw	21	we _____	him/her/it. (incl)
2p	ki	_____ āwāw	2p	you _____	him/her/it.
3p		_____ ēwak	3p	they _____	him/her/it.
3'p		_____ ēyiwa	3'p	their ____ _____	him/her/it.

Example: VTA-2 "nakiskaw – meet him/her/it." (one person/object is affected)

1s	ninakiskawāw	1s	I meet him/her/it.
2s	kinakiskawāw	2s	You meet him/her/it.
3s	nakiskawēw	3s	He/she/it meets him/her/it.
3's	nakiskawēyiwa	3's	His/her/its ____ meets him/her/it.
1p	ninakiskawānān	1p	We (excl) meet him/her/it.
21	kinakiskawānaw	21	We (incl) meet him/her/it.
2p	kinakiskawāwāw	2p	You (pl) meet him/her/it.
3p	nakiskawēwak	3p	They meet him/her/it.
3'p	nakiskawēyiwa	3'p	Their _____ meet him/her/it.

b) Plural object (more than one person/object is affected).

1s	ni	_____ āwak	1s	I _____	them
2s	ki	_____ āwak	2s	you ____	them
3s		_____ ēw	3s	s/he/it _____	them
3'		_____ ēyiwa	3's	his/her/its ____ _____	them
1p	ni	_____ ānānak	1p	we _____	them (excl)
21	ki	_____ ānawak	21	we _____	them (incl)
2p	ki	_____ āwāwak	2p	you _____	them
3p		_____ ēwak	3p	they _____	them
3'p		_____ ēyiwa	3'p	their ____ _____	them

Example: VTA-2 "nakiskaw – meet him/her/it" (plural/more than one person/object).

1s	ninakiskawāw	1s	I meet them.
2s	kinakiskawāwak	2s	You meet them.
3s	nakiskawēw	3s	He/she/it meets them.
3's	nakiskawēyiwa	3's	His/her/its _____meets them.
1p	ninakiskawānānak	1p	We (excl) meet them.
21	kinakiskawānawak	21	We (incl) meet them.
2p	kinakiskawāwāwak	2p	You (pl) meet them.
3p	nakiskawēwak	3p	They meet them.
3'p	nakiskawēyiwa	3'p	Their _____ meet them.

NOTE: There is an additional suffix to mark the plural object only in 1s, 2s, 1p, 21, 2p.

Conjunct Mode VTA-2

a) Singular object (one person/object is affected)

1s	ē-	_____ ak	1s	as I _____	him/her/it.
2s	ē-	_____ at	2s	as you (sg) _____	him/her/it.

3s	ē-_____	āt
3's	ē-_____	āyit
1p	ē-_____	āyāhk
21	ē-_____	āyahk
2p	ē-_____	āyēk
3p	ē-_____	ācik
3'p	ē-_____	āyit

3s	as he/she _____	him/her.
3's	as his/her _____ _____	him/her/it.
1p	as we (excl) _____	him/her/it.
21	as we (incl) _____	him/her/it.
2p	as you (pl) _____	him/her/it.
3p	as they _____	him/her/it.
3'p	as their _____ _____ meet	him/her/it.

Example - VTA-2 "nakiskaw – meet him/her/it" (one person is affected)

1s	ē-nakiskawak	1s	as I meet him/her/it.
2s	ē-nakiskawat	2s	as you (sg) meet him/her/it.
3s	ē-nakiskawāt	3s	as he/she meets him/her.
3's	ē-nakiskawāyit	3's	as his/her _____ meets him/her/it.
1p	ē-nakiskawāyāhk	1p	as we (excl) meet him/her/it.
21	ē-nakiskawāyahk	21	as we (incl) meet him/her/it.
2p	ē-nakiskawāyēk	2p	as you (pl) meet him/her/it.
3p	ē-nakiskawācik	3p	as they meet him/her/it.
3'p	ē-nakiskawāyit	3'p	as their _____ meet him/her/it.

b) Plural object (plural/more than one person/object)

1s	ē- _____	akik
2s	ē- _____	acik
3s	ē- _____	āt
3's	ē- _____	āyit
1p	ē- _____	āyāhkik
21	ē- _____	āyahkok
2p	ē- _____	āyēkok
3p	ē- _____	ācik
3'p	ē- _____	āyit

1s	as I _____	them.
2s	as you _____	them.
3s	as he/she/it _____	them.
3's	as his/her/its _____ _____	them.
1p	as we (excl) _____	them.
21	as we (incl) _____	them.
2p	as you (pl) _____	them.
3p	as they _____	them.
3'p	as their _____ _____	them.

Example: Plural object (plural/more than one person/object)

1s	ē-nakiskawakik	1s	as I meet them.
2s	ē-nakiskawacik	2s	as you meet them.
3s	ē-nakiskawāt	3s	as he/she/it meets them.
3's	ē-nakiskawāyit	3's	as his/her/its _____ meets them.
1p	ē-nakiskawāyāhkik	1p	as we (excl) meet them.
21	ē-nakiskawāyahkok	21	as we (incl) meet them.
2p	ē-nakiskawāyēkok	2p	as you (pl) meet them.
3p	ē-nakiskawācik	3p	as they meet them.
3'p	ē-nakiskawāyit	3'p	as their _____ meet them.

One can use the tense markers simply by following the chart below to change from one tense to another. Or one can also add a preverb.

ē-	Tense -	Preverb -	Verb Stem	Suffix

NOTE: A (-) hyphen is required *after* the "ē-"; *after* the tense; and *after* the preverb. A (+) signifies no hyphen or space between the stem and the suffix.

Future Conditional forms for VTA -2

As always this verb class addresses the singular object with one set of suffixes and another set for plural object.

1s	_____ aki	1s	if/when I _____ him/her
2s	_____ aci	2s	if/when you ____ him/her
3s	_____ āci	3s	if/when s/he ____ him/her
3's	_____ āyici	3's	if/when his/her ____ _____ him/her
1p	_____ āyāhki	1p	if/when we (excl) _____ him/her
21	_____ āyahko	21	if/when we (incl) _____ him/her
2p	_____ āyēko	2p	if/when you (pl) _____ him/her
3p	_____ ātwāwi	3p	if/when they _____ him/her
3'p	_____ āyici	3'p	if their ____ _____ him/her

Example: VTA-2 "*kaskikwātamaw* – Sew it for him/her/it" (more than one person/object)

1s	kaskikwātamawaki	1s	if/when I sew it for him/her
2s	kaskikwātamawaci	2s	if/when you sew it for him/her
3s	kaskikwātamawāci	3s	if/when s/he sews it for him/her
3's	kaskikwātamawāyici	3's	if/when his/her __ sews it for him/her
1p	kaskikwātamawāyāhki	1p	if/when we (excl) sew it for him/her
21	kaskikwātamawāyahko	21	if/when we (incl) sew it for him/her
2p	kaskikwātamawāyēko	2p	if/when you (pl) sew it for him/her
3p	kaskikwātamawātwāwi	3p	if/when they sew it for him/her
3'p	kaskikwātamawāyici	3'p	if their ___ sew it for him/her

b) plural object (plural/more than one person/object)

1s	_____ akwāwi	1s	if/when I _____ them
2s	_____ atwāwi	2s	if/when you (sg) _____ them
3s	_____ āci	3s	if/when s/he _____ them
3's	_____ āyici	3's	if/when his/her ____ _____ them
1p	_____ āyāhkwāwi	1p	if/when we (excl) _____ them
21	_____ āyahkwāwi	21	if/when we(incl) _____ them
2p	_____ āyēkwāwi	2p	if/when you (pl) _____ them
3p	_____ ātwāwi	3p	if/when they _____ them
3'p	_____ āyici	3'p	if/when their ____ _____ them

Example: VTA-2 "kaskikwātamaw – Sew it for him/her/it" (more than one person/object)

1s	kaskikwātamawakwāwi	1s	if/when I sew it for them
2s	kaskikwātamawatwāwi	2s	if/when you (sg) sew it for them
3s	kaskikwātamawāci	3s	if/when s/he sews it for them
3's	kaskikwātamawāyici	3's	if/when his/her _____ sews it for them
1p	kaskikwātamawāyāhkwāwi	1p	if/when we (excl) sew it for them
21	kaskikwātamawāyahkwāwi	21	if/when we(incl) sew it for them
2p	kaskikwātamawāyēkwāwi	2p	if/when you (pl) sew it for them
3p	kaskikwātamawātwāwi	3p	if/when they sew it for them
3'p	kaskikwātamawāyici	3'p	if/when their _____ sew it for them

NOTE: Changes occur only in 1s, 2s, 1p, 21p, 2p.
3s, 3's, 3p, 3'p suffixes remain the same as the singular form in (a) above.

Chapter 20: Transitive Animate Verbs-3 (Cw stems)

Another group of VTA stems may appear odd because they end with two consonants, one of which is a "-w". Complications can arise especially when transcribing spoken Cree because it is not enunciated in some speech forms.

For example this "-w" is not used at all in 2s and 2p of the immediate imperative so it is not written there but it is retained in 21 of the immediate Imperative and in all of the Delayed Imperative and in other verb forms. But for the purpose of identifying this particular VTA stem the "w" is included.

Some VTA "Cw" stems are: (Cw = Consonant w stem)

sāsāpiskisw – Fry it.   cīstahw – Pierce it/him/her.
pakamahw – Hit it/him/her.   pāskisw – Shoot it/him/her.

Immediate Imperative Mode – VTA-3 "Cw stem"

NOTE: Do not include the "-w" in 2s and 2p.

Singular object (one person/object is affected)

2s   _____
2p   _____ ohk
21   _____ ātān

Example: VTA-3 "Cw" stem "kīsisw – "Cook it"

2s   kīsis   2s   Cook it.
2p   kīsisohk   2p   Cook it.
21   kīsiswātān   21   Let's cook it.

Plural object (more than one person/object is affected)

2s   _____ ok
2p   _____ ohkok
21   _____ ātānik

Example: VTA-3 "Cw" stem "kīsisw – "Cook it"

2s   kīsisok   2s   Cook them.
2p   kīsisohkok   2p   Cook them.
21   kīsiswātānik   21   Let's cook them.

NOTE: The "-w" is not used when the suffix begins with an "o-". So the "-w" will be retained on the verb stem in the Delayed Imperative below and in other modes if the suffix does not begin with an "o-".

Delayed Imperative – "Cw" VTA-3 stem

Singular object (one person/object is affected)

2s   _____ āhkan
2p   _____ ākēhk
21   _____ āhkahk

Example: VTA-3 "Cw" stem "kīsisw – "Cook it"

2s   kīsiswāhkan   2s   Cook it later.
2p   kīsiswākēhk   2p   Cook it later.
21   kīsiswāhkahk   21   Let's cook it later.

Plural object (more than one person/object is affected)

2s   _____ āhkanik
2p   _____ ākēhkok
21   _____ āhkahkok

Example: VTA-3 "kīsisw – Cook it"

2s	kīsiswāhkanik	2s	Cook them later.
2p	kīsiswākēhkok	2p	Cook them later.
21	kīsiswāhkahkok	21	Let's cook them later.

Independent Mode for "Cw" VTA-3 stem:

Singular object (one person/object is affected)

1s	ni _____ āw	1s	I _____ him/her/it.
2s	ki _____ āw	2s	you ____ him/her/it.
3s	_____ ēw	3s	s/he/it _____ him/her/it.
3's	_____ ēyiwa	3's	his/her/its ____ _____ him/her/it.
1p	ni _____ ānān	1p	we _____ him/her/it. (excl)
21	ki _____ ānaw	21	we _____ him/her/it. (incl)
2p	ki _____ āwāw	2p	you _____ him/her/it.
3p	_____ ēwak	3p	they _____ him/her/it.
3'p	_____ ēyiwa	3'p	their ____ _____ him/her/it.

Example: VTA-3 "Cw" stem "kīsisw – Cook it"

1s	nikīsiswāw	1s	I cook it.
2s	kikīsiswāw	2s	You cook it.
3s	kīsiswēw	3s	He/she cooks it.
3's	kīsiswēyiwa	3's	His/her ____ cooks it.
1p	nikīsiswānān	1p	We cook it. (excl)
21	kikīsiswānaw	21	We cook it. (incl)
2p	kikīsiswāwāw	2p	You cook it.
3p	kīsiswēwak	3p	They cook it.
3'p	kīsiswēyiwa	3'p	Their ____ cooks it.

Plural object (more than one person/object is affected)

1s	ni _____āwak	1s	I _____them
2s	ki _____āwak	2s	you ____ them
3s	_____ēw	3s	s/he/it _____ them
3's	_____ēyiwa	3's	his/her/its ____ _____ them
1p	ni _____ānānak	1p	we _____ them (excl)
21	ki _____ānawak	21	we _____ them (incl)
2p	ki _____āwāwak	2p	you _____ them
3p	_____ēwak	3p	they _____ them
3'p	_____ēyiwa	3'p	their ____ _____ them

Example: VTA-3 "Cw" stem "kīsisw – Cook it"

1s	nikīsiswāwak	1s	I cook them.
2s	kikīsiswāwak	2s	You cook them.
3s	kīsiswēw	3s	He/she cooks them.
3's	kīsiswēyiwa	3's	His/her ____ cooks them.
1p	nikīsiswānānak	1p	We cook them. (excl)
21	kikīsiswānawak	21	We cook them. (incl)
2p	kikīsiswāwāw	2p	You cook them.
3p	kīsiswēwak	3p	They cook them.
3'p	kīsiswēyiwa	3'p	Their ____ cooks them.

Conjunct Mode – VTA-3 "Cw" stem

Singular object (one person/object is affected)

1s	ē- _____ak	1s	as I _____him/her/it.
2s	ē- _____at	2s	as you (sg) _____ him/her/it.
3s	ē- _____āt	3s	as he/she _____him/her.
3's	ē- _____āyit	3's	as his/her ____ ___ him/her/it.
1p	ē- _____āyāhk	1p	as we (excl) _____him/her/it.
21	ē- _____āyahk	21	as we (incl) _____him/her/it.
2p	ē- _____āyēk	2p	as you (pl) _____him/her/it.
3p	ē- _____ācik	3p	as they _____him/her/it.
3'p	ē- _____āyit	3'p	as their ____ ____ him/her/it.

Example: VTA-3 – "Cw" stem "cīstahw – Pierce him/her/it"

1s	ē-cīstahwak	1s	as I pierce him/her/it.
2s	ē-cīstahwat	2s	as you (sg) pierce him/her/it.
3s	ē-cīstahwāt	3s	as he/she pierces him/her.
3's	ē-cīstahwāyit	3's	as his/her ____ pierces him/her/it.
1p	ē-cīstahwāyāhk	1p	as we (excl) pierce him/her/it.
21	ē-cīstahwāyahk	21	as we (incl) pierce him/her/it.
2p	ē-cīstahwāyēk	2p	as you (pl) pierce him/her/it.
3p	ē-cīstahwācik	3p	as they pierce him/her/it.
3'p	ē-cīstahwāyit	3'p	as their ____ pierces him/her/it.

Plural object (plural/more than one person/object)

1s	ē-_____akik	1s	as I _____them.
2s	ē-_____acik	2s	as you _____ them.
3s	ē-_____āt	3s	as he/she/it ____them.
3's	ē-_____āyit	3's	as his/her/its ____ _____them.
1p	ē-_____āyāhkik	1p	as we (excl) _____them.
21	ē-_____āyahkok	21	as we (incl) _____them.
2p	ē-_____āyēkok	2p	as you (pl) _____them.
3p	ē-_____ācik	3p	as they _____them.
3'p	ē-_____āyit	3'p	as their ____ _____them.

Example: VTA-3 "Cw" stem "cīstahw – Pierce him/her/it"

1s	ē-cīstahwakik	1s	as I pierce them.
2s	ē-cīstahwacik	2s	as you pierce them.
3s	ē-cīstahwāt	3s	as he/she/it pierces them.
3's	ē-cīstahwāyit	3's	as his/her/its ___ pierces them.
1p	ē-cīstahwāyāhkik	1p	as we (excl) pierce them.
21	ē-cīstahwāyahkok	21	as we (incl) pierce them.
2p	ē-cīstahwāyēkok	2p	as you (pl) pierce them.
3p	ē-cīstahwācik	3p	as they pierce them.
3'p	ē-cīstahwāyit	3'p	as their _____ pierces them.

Future Conditional – VTA-3 "Cw" stem

Singular object (one person/object is affected)

1s	_____aki	1s	if/when I _____him/her/it.
2s	_____aci	2s	if/when you (sg) _____him/her/it.
3s	_____āci	3s	if/when he/she _____him/her.
3's	_____āyici	3's	if/when his/her ____ ____ him/her/it.

1p	_____āyāhki	1p	if/when we (excl) _____ him/her/it.
21	_____āyahki	21	if/when we (incl) _____ him/her/it.
2p	_____āyēko	2p	if/when you (pl) _____ him/her/it.
3p	_____ācik	3p	if/when they _____ him/her/it.
3'p	_____āyici	3'p	if/when their ____ _____ him/her/it.

Example: VTA-3 "Cw" stem "pakamahw – Hit him/her/it"

1s	pakamahwaki	1s	if/when I hit him/her/it.
2s	pakamahwaci	2s	if/when you (sg) hit him/her/it.
3s	pakamahwāci	3s	if/when he/she hit him/her.
3's	pakamahwāyici	3's	if/when his/her ___ hit him/her/it.
1p	pakamahwāyāhki	1p	if/when we (excl) hit him/her/it.
21	pakamahwāyahki	21	if/when we (incl) hit him/her/it.
2p	pakamahwāyēko	2p	if/when you (pl) hit him/her/it.
3p	pakamahwātwāwi	3p	if/when they hit him/her/it.
3'p	pakamahwāyici	3'p	if/when their _____ hit him/her/it.

Plural object (plural/more than one person/object)

1s	_____akwāwi	1s	if/when I _____ them.
2s	_____atwāwi	2s	if/when you (sg) _____ them.
3s	_____āci	3s	if/when he/she _____ them.
3's	_____āyici	3's	if/when his/her ____ _____ them.
1p	_____āyāhkwāwi	1p	if/when we (excl) _____ them.
21	_____āyahkwāwi	21	if/when we (incl) _____ them.
2p	_____āyēkwāwi	2p	if/when you (pl) _____ them.
3p	_____ātwāwi	3p	if/when they _____ them.
3'p	_____āyici	3'p	if/when their ____ _____ them.

Example: VTA-3 "Cw" stem "pakamahw – Hit him/her/it"

1s	pakamahwakwāwi	1s	if/when I hit them.
2s	pakamahwatwāwi	2s	if/when you (sg) hit them.
3s	pakamahwāci	3s	if/when he/she hits them.
3's	pakamahwāyici	3's	if/when his/her ____ hits them.
1p	pakamahwāyāhkwāwi	1p	if/when we (excl) hit them.
21	pakamahwāyahkwāwi	21	if/when we (incl) hit them.
2p	pakamahwāyēkwāwi	2p	if/when you (pl) hit them.
3p	pakamahwātwāwi	3p	if/when they hit them.
3'p	pakamahwāyici	3'p	if/when their _____ hits them.

Chapter 21: Transitive Animate Verbs-4 ("t" Stems)

There is yet another set of Transitive Animate verbs: those are the irregular verbs with an aberrant form of the verb stem. The stems end in a "-*t*" which changes to an "-*s*" in the 2s of the imperative mode and in parts of the Inverse form. This consonant "-*s*" is retained for 2s singular and plural but the "-*t*" is used for all of the other modes and verb forms. Here are examples of VTA-4 "-*t*" stems:

nāt – fetch him/her/it
mihtāt – long/grieve for him/her/it
nawaswāt – chase him/her/it
tēpwāt – call him/her/it

pakawāt – dislike him/her/it
nakat – leave him/her/it
piminawat – cook for him/her/it

Examples are in the following modes: the Immediate and Delayed Imperative mode; the Independent and Conjunct modes; the Future Conditional form. All are also in their singular and plural forms.

Immediate Imperative Mode – VTA-4 "t" stem

Singular object (one person/object is affected)

2s	_____
2p	_____ihk
21	_____ātān

Example: VTA-4 "nakat – Leave him/her/it"

2s	nakas	2s	leave him/her/it
2p	nakatihk	2p	leave him/her/it
21	nakatātān	21	let's leave him/her/it

Plural (more than one person/object is affected)

2s	_____ik
2p	_____ihkok
21	_____ātānik

Example: VTA-4 "nakat – Leave him/her/it"

2s	nakasik	2s	leave them
2p	nakatihkok	2p	leave them
21	nakatātānik	21	let's leave them

NOTE: The verb stem is "*nakat*".

The "-*t*" changes to an "-*s*" *only* in the 2s of the Immediate Imperative. It will also change in some persons in the Inverse Mode (discussed in a separate chapter).

Delayed Imperative – VTA-4 "t" stem

Singular object (one person/object is affected)

2s	_____āhkan	2s	_____ later.
2p	_____āhkēk	2p	_____ later.
21	_____āhkahk	21	_____ later.

Example: VTA-4 "t" stem "piminawat – Cook for him/her/it"

2s	piminawatāhkan	2s	Cook/make a meal for him/her later.
2p	piminawatāhkēk	2p	Cook/make a meal for him/her later.
21	piminawatāhkahk	21	Let's make a meal for him/her later.

Plural (more than one person/object is affected)

2s	_____āhkanik
2p	_____ āhkēkok
21	_____ āhkahkok

Example: VTA-4 "t" stem "piminawat – cook for him/her/it"

2s	piminawatāhkanik	2s	Cook for them later.
2p	piminawatāhkēkok	2p	Cook for them later.
21	piminawatāhkahkok	21	Let's cook for them later.

Independent Mode for VTA-4 "t" stem:

Singular object (one person/object is affected)

1s	ni _____ āw	1s	I _____ him/her/it.
2s	ki _____ āw	2s	you ____ him/her/it.
3s	_____ ēw	3s	s/he/it _____ him/her/it.
3's	_____ ēyiwa	3's	his/her/its ____ _____ him/her/it.
1p	ni _____ ānān	1p	we _____ him/her/it. (excl)
21	ki _____ ānaw	21	we _____ him/her/it. (incl)
2p	ki _____ āwāw	2p	you _____ him/her/it.
3p	_____ ēwak	3p	they _____ him/her/it.
3'p	_____ ēyiwa	3'p	their ____ _____ him/her/it.

Example: VTA-4 "t" stem "mihtāt – Long/grieve for him/her/it"

1s	nimihtātāw	1s	I long for him/her/it.
2s	kimihtātāw	2s	You long for him/her/it.
3s	mihtātēw	3s	He/she longs for him/her/it.
3's	mihtātēyiwa	3's	His/her ____ longs for him/her/it.
1p	nimihtātānān	1p	We long for him/her/it. (excl)
21	kimihtātānaw	21	We long for him/her/it. (incl)
2p	kimihtātāwāw	2p	You long for him/her/it.
3p	mihtātēwak	3p	They long for him/her/it.
3'p	mihtātēyiwa	3'p	Their ____ longs for him/her/it.

Plural object (more than one person/object is affected).

1s	ni _____ āw*ak*	1s	I _____ them
2s	ki _____ āw*ak*	2s	you ____ them
3s	_____ ēw	3s	s/he/it _____ them
3's	_____ ēyiwa	3's	his/her/its ____ _____ them
1p	ni _____ ānān*ak*	1p	we _____ them (excl)
21	ki _____ ānaw*ak*	21	we _____ them (incl)
2p	ki _____ āwāw*ak*	2p	you _____ them
3p	_____ ēwak	3p	they _____ them
3'p	_____ ēyiwa	3'p	their ____ _____ them

Example: VTA-4 "t" stem "mihtāt – Long/grieve for him/her/it"

1s	nimihtātāwak	1s	I long for them.
2s	kimihtātāwak	2s	You long for them.
3s	mihtātēw	3s	He/she longs for them.
3's	mihtātēyiwa	3's	His/her ____ longs for them.
1p	nimihtātānānak	1p	1p We long for them. (excl)
21	kimihtātānawak	21	We long for them. (incl)
2p	kimihtātāwāwak	2p	You long for them.
3p	mihtātēwak	3p	They long for them.
3'p	mihtātēyiwa	3'p	Their ____ long for them.

NOTE: The verb stem is "*mihtāt*". The "-*t*" changes to an "-*s*" *only* in the 2s of the Immediate Imperative. The Inverse Mode which will be dealt with in a separate chapter, also has the "-*t*" changing to an "-*s*" in some forms.

Conjunct Mode – VTA-4 "t" stem

Singular object (one person/object is affected)

1s	ē- _____ak	1s	as I _____ him/her/it.
2s	ē- _____at	2s	as you (sg) _____ him/her/it.
3s	ē- _____āt	3s	as he/she _____ him/her.
3's	ē- _____āyit	3's	as his/her ____ _____ him/her/it.
1p	ē- _____āyāhk	1p	as we (excl) _____ him/her/it.
21	ē- _____āyahk	21	as we (incl) _____ him/her/it.
2p	ē- _____āyēk	2p	as you (pl) _____ him/her/it.
3p	ē- _____ācik	3p	as they _____ him/her/it.
3'p	ē- _____āyit	3'p	as their ____ _____ him/her/it.

Example: VTA-4 "t" stem "nawaswāt – Chase him/her/it"

1s	ē- nawaswātak	1s	as I him/her/it.
2s	ē- nawaswātat	2s	as you (sg) chase him/her/it.
3s	ē- nawaswātāt	3s	as he/she chases him/her.
3's	ē- nawaswātāyit	3's	as his/her ____ chases him/her/it.
1p	ē- nawaswātāyāhk	1p	as we (excl) chase him/her/it.
21	ē- nawaswātāyahk	21	as we (incl) chase him/her/it.
2p	ē- nawaswātāyēk	2p	as you (pl) chase him/her/it.
3p	ē- nawaswātācik	3p	as they chase him/her/it.
3'p	ē- nawaswātāyit	3'p	as their ____ chases him/her/it.

Plural object (plural/more than one person/object)

1s	ē-_____akik	1s	as I _____ them.
2s	ē-_____acik	2s	as you _____ them.
3s	ē-_____āt	3s	as he/she/it _____ them.
3's	ē-_____āyit	3's	as his/her/its ____ _____ them.
1p	ē-_____āyāhkik	1p	as we (excl) _____ them.
21	ē-_____āyahkok	21	as we (incl) _____ them.
2p	ē-_____āyēkok	2p	as you (pl) _____ them.
3p	ē-_____ācik	3p	as they _____ them.
3'p	ē-_____āyit	3'p	as their ____ _____ them.

Example: VTA-4 "nawaswāt – Chase him/her/it"

1s	ē- nawaswātakik	1s	as I chase them.
2s	ē- nawaswātacik	2s	as you chase them.
3s	ē- nawaswātāt	3s	as he/she/it chases them.
3's	ē- nawaswātāyit	3's	as his/her/its ____ chases them.
1p	ē- nawaswātāyāhkik	1p	as we (excl) chase them.
21	ē- nawaswātāyahkok	21	as we (incl) chase them.
2p	ē- nawaswātāyēkok	2p	as you (pl) chase them.
3p	ē- nawaswātācik	3p	as they chase them.
3'p	ē- nawaswātāyit	3'p	as their ____ chases them.

Future Conditional – VTA-4 "t" stem

Singular object (one person/object is affected)

1s	_____aki	1s	if/when I _____ him/her
2s	_____aci	2s	if/when you (sg) _____ him/her
3s	_____āci	3s	if/when s/he_____ him/her
3's	_____āyici	3's	if/when his/her ____ _____ him/her

1p	_____āyāhki	1p if/when we (excl) _____him/her
21	_____āyahko	21 if/when we (incl) _____him/her
2p	_____āyēko	2p if/when you (pl) _____him/her
3p	_____ātwāwi	3p if/when they _____him/her
3'p	_____āyici	3'p if their _____ _____him/her

Example: VTA-4 "nāt – Fetch him/her/it"

1s	nātaki	1s if/when I fetch him/her/it
2s	nātaci	2s if/when you (sg) fetch him/her/it
3s	nātāci	3s if/when s/he fetches him/her/it
3's	nātāyici	3's if/when his/her _____ fetches him/her/it
1p	nātāyāhki	1p if/when we (excl) fetch him/her/it
21	nātāyahko	21 if/when we (incl) fetch him/her/it
2p	nātāyēko	2p if/when you (pl) fetch him/her/it
3p	nātātwāwi	3p if/when they fetch him/her/it
3'p	nātāyici	3'p if their _____ fetches him/her

Plural object (more than one person/object is affected)

1s	_____ akwāwi	1s if/when I them
2s	_____ atwāwi	2s if/when you (sg) _____ them
3s	_____ āci	3s if/when s/he _____ them
3's	_____ āyici	3's if/when his/her _____ _____ them
1p	_____ āyāhkwāwi	1p if/when we (excl) _____ them
21	_____ āyahkwāwi	21 if/when we(incl) _____ them
2p	_____ āyēkwāwi	2p if/when you (pl) _____ them
3p	_____ ātwāwi	3p if/when they _____ them
3'p	_____ āyici	3'p if/when their _____ _____ them

Example: VTA-4 "nāt – Fetch him/her/it"

1s	nātakwāwi	1s if/when I fetch them
2s	nātatwāwi	2s if/when you (sg) fetch them
3s	nātāci	3s if/when s/he fetches them
3's	nātāyici	3's if/when his/her _____ fetches them
1p	nātāyāhkwāwi	1p if/when we (excl) fetch them
21	nātāyahkwāwi	21 if/when we(incl) fetch them
2p	nātāyēkwāwi	2p if/when you (pl) fetch them
3p	nātātwāwi	3p if/when they fetch them
3'p	nātāyici	3'p if/when their _____ fetches them

One should observe that VTA-4 "*t*" stems shows that the "-*t*" occurred in all but the 2s in the Immediate Imperative mode where it was replaced by "-*s*".

Whenever one sees a VTA verb stem in the Imperative 2s ending in an "-*s*" then one will use a "-*t*" in all other conjugations. This "-*s*" also occurs in parts of Inverse mode conjugations.

Chapter 22: Numbers and Money

Numbers

pēyak	one	nikotwāsik	six
nīso	two	tēpakohp	seven
nisto	three	ayēnānēw	eight
nēwo	four	kēkā-mitātaht	nine
niyānan	five	mitātaht	ten

The number before an even multiple of ten is expressed as "nearly the next number," whatever that number may be. For example the number nine above is "*kēkā-mitātaht*," which literally means "nearly ten." And so it follows that ten is "*mitātaht*".

Multiples of Ten

mitātaht	ten	nikotwāsomitanaw	sixty
nīsitanaw	twenty	tēpakohpomitanaw	seventy
nistomitanaw	thirty	ayēnānēmitanaw	eighty
nēmitanaw*/nēwomitanaw	forty	kā-mitātahtomitanaw	ninety
niyānanomitanaw	fifty	mitātahtomitanaw	one hundred

*It appears that this may be the preferred term for forty but if anyone uses the other term it will be understood.

The Teen Numbers

The teen numbers are written by adding the suffix "*-sāp*" or "*-osāp*" following a consonant, to the base numbers except nine. Nineteen is unique as it is said *kēkā- mitātahtosāp* but this form is a regional preference because as will be shown in the next section there is another term. Numbers eleven, twelve and the teen numbers are used in conjunction with the multiples of tens to refer to twenty-one up to twenty-eight. Twenty-nine is represented as "nearly thirty," thirty-nine as "nearly forty," and so on. Here are the numbers eleven, twelve and the teen numbers up to nineteen, followed by numbers twenty to twenty-nine.

NOTE: the numbers five and six lose their last syllable when occurring in combinations.

pēyakosāp	eleven	nīsitanaw	twenty
nīsosāp	twelve	nīsitanaw pēyakosāp	twenty-one
nistosāp	thirteen	nīsitanaw nīsosāp	twenty-two
nēwosāp	fourteen	nīsitanaw nistosāp	twenty-three
niyānanosāp	fifteen	nīsitanaw nēwosāp	twenty-four
nikotwāsosāp	sixteen	nīsitanaw niyānanosāp	twenty-five
tēpakohposāp/		nīsitanaw nikotwāsosāp	twenty-six
tēpakohp-tahtosāp	seventeen	nīsitanaw tēpakohposāp	twenty-seven
ayēnānēwosāp	eighteen	nīsitanaw ayēnānēwosāp	twenty-eight
kēkā-mitātahtosāp	nineteen	kēkāc-nistomitanaw	twenty-nine

There are two terms for the number "seventeen" either term is acceptable. Communities may prefer one or they may use them interchangeably, either way they will be understood.

A regional preference is the use of the word "*ayiwāk*" which means in this context "more/plus." Once the multiple of ten is established the next numbers are expressed as that "multiple of ten plus the base number." For example:

nīsitanaw	twenty
nīsitanaw ayiwāk pēyak	twenty-one
nīsitanaw ayiwāk nīso	twenty-two
nīsitanaw ayiwāk nisto	twenty-three
nīsitanaw ayiwāk nēwo	twenty-four

nīsitanaw ayiwāk niyānan	twenty-five
nīsitanaw ayiwāk nikotwāsik	twenty-six
nīsitanaw ayiwāk tēpakohp	twenty-seven
nīsitanaw ayiwāk ayēnānēw	twenty-eight
kēkāc-nistomitanaw	twenty-nine

For the multiples of ten, from thirty to ninety, the suffix "-*mitanaw*" is attached to those base numbers which end with an "-o." "-*omitanaw*" is used for those that end with a consonant.

nistomitanaw	thirty
kēkāc-nēwomitanaw	thirty-nine
nēwomitanaw/nēmitanaw	forty
kēkāc-niyānomitanaw	forty-nine
niyānanomitanaw	fifty
kēkāc-nikotwāsomitanaw	fifty-nine
nikotwāsomitanaw	sixty
kēkāc-tēpakohpomitanaw	sixty-nine
tēpakohpomitanaw	seventy
kēkāc-ayēnānēwomitanaw	seventy-nine
ayēnānēwomitanaw	eighty
kēkāc-kēkā-mitātahtomitanaw	eighty-nine
kēkā-mitātahtomitanaw	ninety
kēkā-mitatahtomitanaw kēkā-mitātaht	ninety-nine

Some regions express the teen numbers by placing *mitātaht* before them, except nineteen is *kēkā-mitātahtosāp*, for example:

mitātaht pēyakosāp	eleven
mitātaht nīsosāp	twelve

They also use this same procedure for the twenty plus numbers but instead of using *mitātaht* they use the teen numbers with the multiple of ten numbers, for example:

nīsitanaw pēyakosāp	twenty-one
nīsitanaw nīsosāp	twenty-two

Another regional difference is *ayinānēw* rather than *ayēnānēw* for the number eight.

Money (sōniyāw)

Money, as it was known in Europe, was not used by the inhabitants of this continent so existing terms were probably applied to the coinage that was introduced to them.

When referring to dollars the word "*tahtwāpisk*" or the suffix "-*āpisk*" is combined with numbers. When referring to quarters the term "*sōniyās*" is used, plus the number of quarters involved. Here is a list of money terms:

pēyak sōniyās	25 cents – one quarter
nīso sōniyās	50 cents – two quarters
nisto sōniyās	75 cents – three quarters
pēyakwāpisk	one dollar
nīswāpisk	two dollars
nistwāpisk	three dollars
nēwāpisk	four dollars
niyānanwāpisk	five dollars
nikotwāswāpisk	six dollars
tēpakohptaht-wāspisk	seven dollars
ayēnānēw-tahtwāpisk	eight dollars
kēkā-mitātahtwāpisk	nine dollars

mitātahtwāpisk	ten dollars
nīsitanawtaht-wāpisk	twenty dollars
nistomitanaw-tahtwāpisk	thirty dollars

Chapter 23: Inverse Mode – Transitive Animate Verbs

A brief review of the Direct form is necessary here to illustrate the change which will occur with word order for the Inverse. Examples of VTA-1 in the Independent and Conjunct modes are given to show the Direct action of this category of verbs. As an attempt to show the differences between the Direct and Inverse detailed explanations and diagrams are presented for both the previous material and the concept of the inverse form.

NOTE: One very important feature of the Inverse is that it *does not* have an Imperative mode. Refer to Chapter 27 which discusses the "you-me" set. There is an imperative for this particular set which may be mistakenly referred to as the Imperative for the Inverse.

Because the Transitive Animate verbs are always in singular and plural forms each of the different verb stems is dealt with separately otherwise all four stems would make for too many conjugation tables in one chapter. So the VTA-1 and VTA-4 are in Chapter 24; VTA-2 is in Chapter 25 and VTA-3 is in Chapter 26.

Word Order

Word order is the most important detail to remember. Earlier explanations gave examples of word order going from left to right. That is the actor (subject) being placed first within the sentence structure, the verb is second and then the goal (object) is placed last. The diagram below reflects this idea with English and Cree sentences.

I	see	him.		niwāpamāw		
S	V	O		S	V	O
======>				======>		

Furthermore, the goal or the object in this form is always the third person singular or plural (it, him, her, them), or obviative. The Actor or subject can be any of the persons in the conjugation charts that have already been introduced. With the SVO order in mind consider the verb conjugation below.

Independent Mode – Direct for VTA-1 – Regular Stems

Singular object (one person/object is affected)

Example: VTA-1 – regular stems "wāpam" – See him/her/it

1s	niwāpamāw nāha atim.		
	I see that dog yonder.	1s → 3s	
2s	kiwāpamāw ana nāpēw.		
	You see that man.	2s → 3s	
3s	wāpamēw anihi iskwēwa.		
	S/he sees that woman.	3s → 3's/3'p	
3's	wāpamēyiwa anihi okimāwa.		
	His/her ____ sees that chief.	3's → 3's/3'p	
1p	niwāpamānān ana maskihkīwiyiniw.		
	We saw that doctor.	1p → 3s	
21	kiwāpamānaw ana maskihkīwiskwēw.		
	We saw that nurse.	21 → 3s	
2p	kiwāpamāwāw ana nahkawiyiniw.		
	You saw that Saulteaux person.	2p → 3s	
3p	wāpamēwak anihi mitāsa.		
	They saw those trousers.	3s → 3's/3'p	
3'p	wāpamēyiwa anihi atimwa		
	Their ____ saw those dogs.	3'p → 3's/3'p	

NOTE: The object in all the examples except for those for 3s, 3's, 3p, 3'p (third persons) is a regular singular noun. Now observe that the object is marked with an unusual ending in 3s, 3's,

3p, 3'p. This "*a*" suffix on an *animate noun* is referred to as the *obviative marker*. It is used to mark the noun as being secondary to some other third person. The object being acted upon is singular or plural. The context dictates whether the object is singular or plural.

NOTE ALSO: once these *animate nouns* undergo obviation they appear to lose their classification of animate. This is indicated by the use of the inanimate demonstrative pronoun "*anihi*" which is usually reserved only for inanimate nouns. Don't worry about this as it occurs only in the obviative and furthermore, the classification remains animate.

Because the objects of the third person forms are either singular or plural, we need not worry about number agreement for 3s, 3's, 3p 3'p like we do for objects in 1s, 2s, 1p, 21, 2p.

NOTE: Remember that in Cree '*niwāpamāw*' and the rest of the conjugated verb, translates to "I see him/her/it." and so on. But then one can add the names of the object or person being seen. The sentences in the conjugation above are used correctly.

Plural object (more than one person/object is affected)

As always with the VTA category there are additional suffixes to indicate that there is a plural object being acted upon. This plural suffix is attached to the singular object suffix. All modes and forms for the VTA follow this idea of verb-noun agreement, singular suffixes for the verb if the object/noun is singular and plural suffixes for the verb if the object/noun is plural. So in the example below the *singular suffixes are italicized* and the **plural and obviative suffixes** for both the nouns and the verbs **are boldfaced**.

Example: VTA-1 – regular stems "wāpam" – See them.

1s	niwāpam*āw***ak** awāsis**ak**.	
	I see the children.	1s → 3p
2s	kiwāpam*āw***ak** aniki nāpē**wak**.	
	You see those men.	2s → 3p
3s	wāpam*ēw* anihi nāpē**wa**.	
	S/he sees those man/men.	3s → 3's/3'p
3's	wāpam*ēyiwa* anihi atimw**a**.	
	His/her ____ sees those dogs.	3's → 3's/3'p
1p	niwāpam*ānān***ak** aniki iyiniw**ak**.	
	We see those people.	1p → 3p
21	kiwāpam*ānaw***ak** aniki maskihkīwiyiniw**ak**.	
	We see those doctors.	21 → 3p
2p	kiwāpam*āwāw***ak** aniki piyēsīs**ak**.	
	You see those birds.	2p → 3p
3p	wāpam*ēw***ak** anihi maskihkīwiyiniw**a**.	
	They see those doctors.	3 → 3's/3'p
3'p	wāpam*ēyiwa* anihi minōs**a**.	
	Their ____ see those cats.	3'p → 3's/3'p

NOTE: 1s, 2s, 1p, 21, 2p, have the additional suffix "*ak*" for the verb noun agreement. 3s, 3's, 3p, 3'p do not. The column of numbers on the right side of page represent the action by 1st, 2nd, 3rd person etc. toward the object 3s, 3's, 3p, 3'p.

Inverse Word Order

The direction of the action in the VTA – Inverse form has always been viewed as going in the opposite direction to that of the Direct, from right to left. The illustrations below show this idea of the direction of action.

VTA – DIRECT: I   see   him.   **ni*wāpam*āw.**
              =======➔   =======➔
               S V O   S V   O

VTA – INVERSE: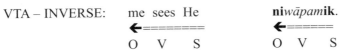

Note that the *first person prefix* for Cree is in first position in **both** the VTA – Direct and the VTA – Inverse. In the Cree example above *"ni"* is identified as the subject **but** although it is still in the first position in the inverse it is now the object of an action by 3s. The important thing to remember is that him/her/it is now the subject and 1s, 2s, 1p, 21, 2p, are now the object in the word order. Consider the diagram below.

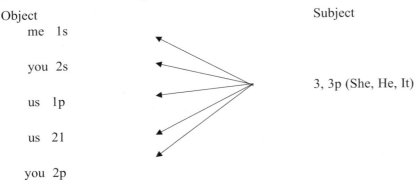

This diagram elaborates on the idea presented in the diagrams above. They both illustrate that the Inverse reverses the assignment of Subject and Object.

NOTE: The 3s, 3's, 3p, 3'p are not included in this diagram for reasons that can be very confusing if explained with linguistic terms. The translation into English cannot accommodate the idea of the obviative. This will become more clear when the Independent Mode of the Inverse is conjugated.

Remember examples of the four different VTA stems are presented as follows:

   Chapter 24 – Inverse 1 – VTA-1 – "reg." stem *and* VTA-4 "t" stem
   Chapter 25 – Inverse 2 – VTA-2 – "Vw" stem
   Chapter 26 – Inverse 3 – VTA-3 – "Cw" stem

Chapter 24:
Inverse 1 – VTA-1 – Regular and VTA-4 – "t" Stems

Of all the modes and forms that have been studied only the Inverse of the VTA stems do not have the Imperative modes. But the examples are in the Independent, Conjunct and Future Conditional paradigms. Each will, of course, be in the singular and plural forms.

The four categories of VTA stems in the previous chapters occur in either of three paradigms for the inverse form. These paradigms, which are in Appendix A, are referred to as:

i) Chart 7 – Inverse 1
> used for VTA-1 **regular** stem and VTA-4 "t" stem

ii) Chart 8 – Inverse 2
> used for VTA-2 "Vw" verb stem

iii) Chart 9 – Inverse 3
> used for VTA-3 "Cw" verb stem

NOTE: Remember: VTA-1 and VTA-4 *"t"* stems use the Inverse 1 chart. VTA-4 *"t"* stems change the *"-t"* to an *"-s"* in the following: Conjunct and Future conditional modes in 1s (singular & plural conjugation).

Examples of verbs which use this chart are:

wāpam – See him/her/it   wīcih – help him/her/it   nakat – Leave him/her/it.
asam – feed him/her/it   pāhpih – laugh at him/her/it   nāt – Fetch/get him/her/it.

Independent Mode – Inverse 1 – VTA-1 regular stems

Singular (3s is acting on 1s through 3'p)

1s	ni___ik	she/he/it _____ me.	1s ← 3s
2s	ki___ik	she/he/it _____ you. (sg.)	2s ← 3s
3s	___ik(ow)	she/he/it is___ by him/her.	3s ← 3's/3'p
3's	___ikoyiwa	his/her/its is ___ ___ by him/her.	3's ← 3's/3'p
1p	ni___ikonān	she/he/it _____ us. (excl)	1p ← 3s
21	ki___ikonaw	she/he/it _____ us. (incl)	21 ← 3s
2p	ki___ikowāw	she/he/it _____ you. (pl.)	2p ← 3s
3p	___ik(ow)ak	they are _____ by him/her.	3p ← 3's/3'p
3'p	___ikoyiwa	his/her/its are ___ ___ by him/her.	3'p ← 3s'/3'p

Example: Inverse 1 VTA-1 "pāhpih – Laugh at him/her/it" regular stem.

1s	nipāhpihik	she/he laughs at me.	1s ← 3s
2s	kipāhpihik	she/he laughs at you. (sg.)	2s ← 3s
3s	pāhpihik(ow)	she/he is laughed at by him/her.	3s ← 3's/3'p
3's	pāhpihikoyiwa	his/her ___ is laughed at by him/her.	3's ←3's/3'p
1p	nipāhpihikonān	she/he laughs at us. (excl)	1p ← 3s
21	kipāhpihikonaw	she/he laughs at us. (incl)	21 ← 3s
2p	kipāhpihikowāw	she/he laughs at you. (pl.)	2p ← 3s
3p	pāhpihik(ow)ak	they are laughed at by him/her.	3p ← 3's/3'p
3'p	pāhpihikoyiwa	their ___ is laughed at by him/her.	3'p ← 3's/3'p

NOTE: *(-ow)* in 3s and 3p may or may not be used as it appears to be either a dialect preference or a personal option. It is in brackets here only to point this out so it is not in brackets elsewhere.

Plural (3p are acting on 1s through 3'p)

1s	ni___ikwak	they _____ me.	1s ← 3p
2s	ki___ikwak	they _____ you.	2s ← 3p
3s	___ikow	s/he/it is _____ by them.	3s ← 3's/3'p

3's		_____ikoyiwa	his/her/its ___ is ____ by them.	3's ← 3's/3'p
1p	ni	_____ikonānak	they ____ us. (excl)	1p ← 3p
21	ki	_____ikonawak	they ____ us. (incl)	21 ← 3p
2p	ki	_____ikowāwak	they ____ you.	2p ← 3p
3p		_____ikowak	they are ____ by them.	3p ← 3's/3'p
3'p		_____ikoyiwa	their ___ are ____ by them.	3'p ← 3's/3'p

Example: Inverse 1 VTA-1 "pāhpih – Laugh at him/her/it"

1s	nipāhpihikwak	they laugh at me.	1s ← 3p
2s	kipāhpihikwak	they laugh at you.	2s ← 3p
3s	pāhpihikow	s/he is laughed at by them.	3s ← 3's/3'p
3's	pāhpihikoyiwa	his/her ___ is laughed at by them.	3's ← 3's/3'p
1p	nipāhpihikonānak	they laugh at us. (excl)	1p ← 3p
21	kipāhpihikonawak	they laugh at us. (incl)	21 ← 3p
2p	kipāhpihikowāwak	they laugh at you.	2p ← 3p
3p	pāhpihikowak	they are laughed at by them.	3p ← 3's/3'p
3'p	pāhpihikoyiwa	their ___ are laughed at by them.	3'p ← 3's/3'p

NOTE: Plural suffixes: "-wak" for 1s, 2s; "-ak" for 1p, 21, 2p. VTA-1 regular stem and VTA-4 *"t"* stem use Inverse 1 chart.

Conjunct Mode – Inverse 1 – VTA-1 regular verbs

Singular (3s is acting on 1s through 3'p)

1s	ē-____it	as s/he it ____ me	1s ← 3s
2s	ē-____isk	as s/he/it ____ you	2s ← 3s
3s	ē-____ikot	as his/her/its ____ by him/her/it	3s ← 3's/3'p
3's	ē-____ikoyit	as his/her/its _____ ____ by him/her/it	3's ← 3's/3'p
1p	ē-____ikoyāhk	as s/he/it ____ us (excl)	1p ← 3s
21	ē-____ikoyahk	as his/her/it ____ us (incl)	21 ← 3s
2p	ē-____ikoyēk	as his/her/it ____ you	2p ← 3s
3p	ē-____ikocik	as they ____ by him/her/it	3p ← 3's/3'p
3'p	ē-____ikoyit	as their ____ are ____ by him/her/it	3'p ← 3's/3'p

Example: Inverse – VTA-1 regular "wīsām" – Invite him/her along

1s	ē- wīsām**it**	as s/he invites me along	1s ← 3s
2s	ē- wīsāmisk	as s/he invites you along	2s ← 3s
3s	ē- wīsāmikot	as s/he is invited along by him/her	3s ← 3's/3'p
3's	ē- wīsāmikoyit	as his/her ___ is invited along by him/her	3's ← 3's/3'p
1p	ē- wīsāmikoyāhk	as s/he invites us (excl) along	1p ← 3s
21	ē- wīsāmikoyahk	as s/he invites us (incl) along	21 ← 3s
2p	ē- wīsāmikoyēk	as s/he invites you along	2p ← 3s
3p	ē- wīsāmikocik	as s/he is invited along by him/her/it	3p ← 3's/3'p
3'p	ē- wīsāmikoyit	as their ___ are invited along by him/her/it	3'p ← 3's/3'p

Plural (3p are acting on 1s through 3'p)

1s	ē-____**icik**	as they ____ me	1s ← 3p
2s	ē-____iskik	as they ____ you	2s ← 3p
3s	ē-____ikot	as he/she/it is ____ by them	3s ← 3's/3'p
3's	ē-____ikoyit	as his/her/its ____is ____ by them	3's ← 3's/3'p
1p	ē-____ikoyāhkik	as they ____ us (excl)	1p ← 3p
21	ē-____ikoyahkok	as they ____ us (incl)	21 ← 3p
2p	ē-____ikoyēkok	as they ____ you	2p ← 3p

| 3p | ē-____ikocik | as they are ____ by them | 3p ← 3's/3'p |
| 3'p | ē-____ikoyit | as their ___ are ____ by them | 3'p ← 3's/3'p |

NOTE: The suffix for 1s: *"-it"* for singular; *"-icik"* for plural. Observe also: the plural suffixes are added to the singular suffixes only in: 1s, 2s, 1p, 21, 2p. They are italicized in all of the paradigms only for ease of locating them.

Example: Inverse – VTA-1 regular *"wīsām"* – Invite him/her along

1s	ē-wīsāmicik	as they invite me	1s ← 3p
2s	ē-wīsāmiskik	as they invite you	2s ← 3p
3s	ē-wīsāmikot	as he/she/it is invited by them	3s ← 3's/3'p
3's	ē-wīsāmikoyit	as his/her/its ___is invited by them	3's ← 3's/3'p
1p	ē-wīsāmikoyāhkik	as they invite us (excl)	1p ← 3p
21	ē-wīsāmikoyahkok	as they invite us (incl)	21 ← 3p
2p	ē-wīsāmikoyēkok	as they invite you	2p ← 3p
3p	ē-wīsāmikocik	as they are invited by them	3p ← 3's/3'p
3'p	ē-wīsāmikoyit	as their ____ are invited by them	3'p ← 3's/3'p

VTA-4 "t" Stems

It was stated that the VTA-4 *"-t"* stems also use the Chart 7, Inverse-1 paradigm. Here is one example conjugated in the Inverse 1. Notice the following changes to the verb stem: the *"-t"* is changed to an *"-s"* only in the following: Conjunct and Future conditional: 1s (singular and plural)

Independent Mode – Inverse 1 – VTA-4 "t" stem

Singular (3p acting on 1s through 3'p)

1s	ni___ik	she/he/it _____ me.	1s ← 3s
2s	ki___ik	she/he/it_____you. (sg.)	2s ← 3s
3s	___ikow	she/he/it is _____ by him/her.	3s ← 3's/3'p
3's	___ ikoyiwa	his/her/its _____is by him/her.	3's ← 3's/3'p
1p	ni__ ikonān	she/he/it _____us. (excl)	1p ← 3s
21	ki__ ikonaw	she/he/it _____us. (incl)	21 ← 3s
2p	ki__ ikowāw	she/he/it _____you. (pl.)	2p ← 3s
3p	__ ikowak	they are_____ by him/her.	3p ← 3's/3'p
3'p	__ ikoyiwa	their ___ are ___ by him/her.	3'p ← 3's/3'p

Example: VTA-4 "t" stem "nakat – Leave him/her/it"

1s	ninakatik	she/he leaves me.	1s ← 3s
2s	kinakatik	she/he leaves to you. (sg.)	2s ← 3s
3s	nakatikow	she/he is left by him/her.	3s ← 3's/3'p
3's	nakatikoyiwa	his/her ___ is left by him/her.	3's ← 3's/3'p
1p	ninakatikonān	she/he leaves us. (excl)	1p ← 3s
21	kinakatikonaw	she/he leaves us. (incl)	21 ← 3s
2p	kinakatikowāw	she/he leaves you. (pl.)	2p ← 3s
3p	nakatikowak	they are left by him/her.	3p ← 3's/3'p
3'p	nakatikoyiwa	their ___ are left by him/her.	3'p ← 3's/3'p

Plural (3p are acting on 1s through 3'p)

1s	ni_____ ikwak	they _____ me.	1s ← 3p
2s	ki_____ ikwak	they _____you.	2s ← 3p
3s	____ ikow	s/he/it is ____by him/her.	3s ← 3's/3'p
3's	_____ ikoyiwa	his/her/its___ is ___ by him/her.	3s ← 3's/3'p
1p	ni_____ ikonānak	they _____us. (excl)	1p ← 3p

21	ki____ ikonawak	they ____ us. (incl)	21 ← 3p
2p	ki____ ikowāwak	they ____ you.	2p ← 3p
3p	____ikwak	they are____ by him/her.	3p ← 3's/3'p
3'p	____ikoyiwa	their ___ are ____ by him/her.	3'p ← 3's/3'p

Example: VTA-4 – *"t"* stem "nakat – Leave him/her/it"

1s	ninakatikwak	they leave me.	1s ← 3p
2s	kinakatikwak	they leave you.	2s ← 3p
3s	nakatikow	s/he is left by them.	3s ← 3's/3'p
3's	nakatikoyiwa	his/her ___ are left by them.	3's ← 3's/3'p
1p	ninakatikonānak	they leave us. (excl)	1p ← 3p
21	kinakatikonawak	they leave us. (incl)	21 ← 3p
2p	kinakatikowāwak	they leave you.	2p ← 3p
3p	nakatikwak	they are left by them.	3p ← 3's/3'p
3'p	nakatikoyiwa	their ___ are left by them.	3'p ← 3's/3'p

Conjunct Mode – Inverse 1 – VTA-4 "t" stem

Singular (3s is acting on 1s through 3'p)

1s	ē-____it	as s/he it ____ me	1s ← 3s
2s	ē-____isk	as s/he/it ____ you	2s ← 3s
3s	ē-____ikot	as his/her/its ____ him/her/it	3s ← 3's/3'p
3's	ē-____ikoyit	as his/her/its ____ ____ him/her/it	3's ← 3's/3'p
1p	ē-____ikoyāhk	as s/he/it ____ us (excl)	1p ← 3s
21	ē-____ikoyahk	as his/her/it ____ us (incl)	21 ← 3s
2p	ē-____ikoyēk	as his/her/it ____ you	2p ← 3s
3p	ē-____ikocik	as they ____ him/her/it	3p ← 3's/3'p
3'p	ē-____ikoyit	as their ____ ____ him/her/it	3'p ← 3's/3'p

Example: VTA-4 – *"t"* stem "nakat – Leave him/her/it"

1s	ē-nakasit*	as s/he/it leaves me	1s ← 3s
2s	ē-nakatisk	as s/he/it leaves you	2s ← 3s
3s	ē-nakatikot	as s/he/it is left by him/her/it	3s ← 3's/3'p
3's	ē-nakatikoyit	as his/her/its ____is left by him/her/it	3's ← 3's/3'p
1p	ē-nakatikoyāhk	as s/he/it leaves us (excl)	1p ← 3s
21	ē-nakatikoyahk	as his/her/it leaves us (incl)	21 ← 3s
2p	ē-nakatikoyēk	as his/her/it leaves you	2p ← 3s
3p	ē-nakatikocik	as they are left by him/her/it	3p ← 3's/3'p
3'p	ē-nakatikoyit	as their ____ is left by him/her/it	3'p ← 3's/3'p

Plural (3p are acting on 1s through 3'p)

1s	ē-____ icik	as they ____ me	1s ← 3p
2s	ē-____ ' iskik	as they ____ you	2s ← 3p
3s	ē-____ikot	as he/she/it is ____ by them	3s ← 3's/3'p
3's	ē-____ikoyit	as his/her/its ___is ____ by them	3's ← 3's/3'p
1p	ē-____ikoyāhkik	as they ____ us (excl)	1p ← 3p
21	ē-____ikoyahkok	as they ____ us (incl)	21 ← 3p
2p	ē-____ikoyēkok	as s/he/it ____ you	2p ← 3s
3p	ē-____ikocik	as they are .____ by him/her/it	3p ← 3's/3'p
3'p	ē-____ikoyit	as their ____ are ____ by him/her/it	3'p ← 3's/3'p

Example: VTA-4 – *"t"* stem "nakat – Leave him/her/it"

1s	ē- nakasicik*	as they leave me	1s ← 3p
2s	ē- nakatiskik	as they leave you	2s ← 3p
3s	ē- nakatikot	as s/he/it is left by them	3s ← 3's/3'p
3's	ē- nakatikoyit	as his/her/its ____ is left by them	3's ← 3's/3'p
1p	ē- nakatikoyāhkik	as they leave us (excl)	1p ← 3p
21	ē- nakatikoyahkok	as they leave us (incl)	21 ← 3p
2p	ē- nakatikoyēkok	as they leave you	2p ← 3p
3p	ē- nakatikocik	as they are left by them.	3p ← 3's/3'p
3'p	ē- nakatikoyit	as their ____ is left by them	3'p ← 3's/3'p

NOTE: The suffix for 1s: *"-it"* for singular; *"-icik"* for plural. This is also noted at the bottom of the page for Verb Chart 7.

Future Conditional Form Inverse 1 – VTA-4 "t" stem

Singular (3s is acting on 1s through 3'p)

1s	____ici *	when/if s/he/it ____ me	1s ← 3s
2s	____iski	when/if s/he/it ____ you	2s ← 3s
3s	____ikoci	when/if his/her/it is ____ by him/her/it	3s ← 3's/3'p
3's	____ikoyici	when/if his/her/its __is ___ by him/her/it	3's ← 3's/3'p
1p	____ikoyāhki	when/if s/he/it ____ us (excl)	1p ← 3s
21	____ikoyahko	when/if s/he/it ____ us (incl)	21 ← 3s
2p	____ikoyēko	when/if s/he/it ____ you	2p ← 3s
3p	____ikotwāwi	when/if they are ____ by him/her/it	3p ← 3's/3'p
3'p	____ikoyici	when/if their __ are ____ by him/her/it	3'p ← 3's/3'p

Example: Inverse 1 – VTA-4 *"t"* stem "nakat – Leave him/her/it"

1s	nakasici*	when/if s/he leaves me	1s ← 3s
2s	nakatiski	when/if s/he leaves you	2s ← 3s
3s	nakatikoci	when/if s/he is left by him/her	3s ← 3's/3'p
3's	nakatikoyici	when/if his/her __ is left by him/her	3's ← 3's/3'p
1p	nakatikoyāhki	when/if s/he leaves us (excl)	1p ← 3s
21	nakatikoyahki	when/if s/he leaves us (incl)	21 ← 3s
2p	nakatikoyēko	when/if s/he leaves you	2p ← 3s
3p	nakatikotwāwi	when/if they are left by him/her	3p ← 3's/3'p
3'p	nakatikoyici	when/if their ____ is left by him/her	3'p ← 3's/3'p

Plural (3p are acting on 1s through 3'p)

1s	____itwāwi *	when/if they ____ me	1s ← 3p
2s	____iskwāwi	when/if they ____ you	2s ← 3p
3s	____ikoci	when/if he/she/it is____ by them	3s ← 3's/3'p
3's	____ikoyici	when/if his/her/its ____is .____ by them	3's ← 3's/3'p
1p	____ikoyāhkwāwi	when/if they ____ us (excl)	1p ← 3p
21	____ikoyahkwāwi	when/if they ____ us (incl)	21 ← 3p
2p	____ikoyēkwāwi	when/if they ____ you	2p ← 3p
3p	____ikotwāwi	when/if they ____ by them	3p ← 3's/3'p
3'p	____ikoyici	when/if their ____ are ____ by them	3'p ← 3's/3'p

Example: Inverse 1 – VTA-4 *"t"* stem "nakat – Leave him/her/it"

1s	nakasitwāwi*	when/if they leave me	1s ← 3p
2s	nakatiskwāwi	when/if they leave you	2s ← 3p
3s	nakatikoci	when/if s/he/it is left by them	3s ← 3's/3'p

3's	nakatikoyici	when/if his/her/its ____ is left by them	3's ← 3's/3'p
1p	nakatikoyāhkwāwi	when/if they leave us (excl)	1p ← 3p
21	nakatikoyahkwāwi	when/if they leave us (incl)	21 ← 3p
2p	nakatikoyēkwāwi	when/if they leave you	2p ← 3p
3p	nakatikotwāwi	when/if they are left by them	3p ← 3's/3'p
3'p	nakatikoyici	when/if their ____ are left by them	3'p ← 3's/3'p

NOTE: The suffix for 1s: *"-ici"* for singular; *"-itwāwi"* for plural. Observe that in all of the above conjugations: the *"t"* in *nakat* is changed to *"nakas"* for the "1s" in the Conjunct and Future Conditional singular and plural forms.

Chapter 25: Inverse 2 – VTA-2 – "Vw" Stems

There is a change to the *"Vw"* stem in some modes. Any change will be brought to your attention whenever it is required.

NOTE: Remember Inverse of VTA do not have Imperatives.

Independent Mode – Inverse 2 – VTA- "Vw" stem

Some verbs with *"Vw"* stems are:

nitoht**aw** – Listen to him/her/it   nakisk**aw** – meet him/her/it

misk**aw** – Find him/her/it   atamisk**aw** – shake his/her hand

NOTE: The verb stem loses the "-*aw*" for both the singular and plural of the Independent mode.

Singular (3s is acting on 1s through 3'p)

1s	ni___āk	she/he/it _____ me.	1s ← 3s
2s	ki___āk	she/he/it_____you.	2s ← 3s
3s	___ākow	she/he/it is _____ by him/her	3s ← 3's/3'p
3's	___ākoyiwa	his/her/its ___is ____ by him/her	3's ← 3's/3'p
1p	ni___ākonān	she/he/it _____us. (excl)	1p ← 3s
21	ki___ākonaw	she/he/it _____us. (incl)	21 ← 3s
2p	ki___ākonāw	she/he/it _____you.	2p ← 3s
3p	___ākwak	they are_____ by him/her.	3p ← 3's/3'p
3'p	___ākoyiwa	their ___ are ____ by him/her	3'p ← 3's/3'p

Example: VTA-2 – "Vw" stem "nitohtaw – Listen to him/her/it"

1s	ninitohtāk	she/he listens to me.	1s ← 3s
2s	kinitohtāk	she/he listens to you.	2s ← 3s
3s	nitohtākow	she/he is listened to by him/her	3s ← 3's/3'p
3's	nitohtākoyiwa	his/her ___ is listened to by him/her	3's ← 3's/3'p
1p	ninitohtākonān	she/he listens to us. (excl)	1p ← 3s
21	kinitohtākonaw	she/he listens to us. (incl)	21 ← 3s
2p	kinitohtākowāw	she/he listens to you.	2p ← 3s
3p	nitohtākwak	they are listened to by him/her	3p ← 3's/3'p
3'p	nitohtākoyiwa	their ___ are listened to by him/her	3'p ← 3's/3'p

Plural (3p are acting on 1s through 3'p)

1s	ni_____ākwak	they _____ me.	1s ← 3p
2s	ki_____ākwak	they _____you.	2s ← 3p
3s	_____ākow	s/he is _____ by them.	3s ← 3's/3'p
3's	_____ākoyiwa	his/her ___ is ___ by them	3's ← 3's/3'p
1p	ni_____ākonānak	they _____us. (excl)	1p ← 3p
21	ki_____ākonawak	they _____us. (incl)	21 ← 3p
2p	ki_____ākowāwak	they _____you.	2p ← 3p
3p	_____ākwak	they are_____ by them.	3p ← 3's/3'p
3'p	_____ākoyiwa	their ___ are _____ by them	3'p ← 3's/3'p

Example: VTA-2 – *"Vw"* stem "nitohtaw – Listen to him/her/it"

1s	ninitohtākwak	they listen to me.	1s ← 3p
2s	kinitohtākwak	they listen to you.	2s ← 3p
3s	nitohtākow	s/he is listened to by them	3s ← 3's/3'p
3's	nitohtākoyiwa	his/her ___ is listened to by them	3's ← 3's/3'p
1p	ninitohtākonānak	they listen to us. (excl)	1p ← 3p
21	kinitohtākonawak	they listen to us. (incl)	21 ← 3p
2p	kinitohtākowāwak	they listen to you.	2p ← 3p

| 3p | nitohtākwak | they are listened to by them | 3p ← 3's/3'p |
| 3'p | nitohtākoyiwa | their ___ are listened to by them | 3'p ← 3's/3'p |

Conjunct Mode – Inverse 2 – VTA-2 "Vw" stem

NOTE: This time the verb stem *does not* change in 1s for both singular and plural for the Conjunct mode.

Singular (3s is acting on 1s through 3'p)

1s	ē-____ it	as s/he it ____ me	1s ← 3s
2s	ē-____ āsk	as s/he/it ____ you	2s ← 3s
3s	ē-____ ākot	as his/her/its ____ him/her/it	3s ← 3's/3'p
3's	ē-____ ākoyit	as his/her/its ____ ___ him/her/it	3's ← 3's/3'p
1p	ē-____ ākoyāhk	as s/he/it ____ us (excl)	1p ← 3s
21	ē-____ ākoyahk	as his/her/it ____ us (incl)	21 ← 3s
2p	ē-____ ākoyēk	as his/her/it ____ you	2p ← 3s
3p	ē-____ ākocik	as they ____ him/her/it	3p ← 3's/3'p
3'p	ē-____ ākoyit	as their ____ are ____ him/her/it	3'p ← 3's/3'p

Example: Inverse 2 – VTA-2 -*"Vw"* stem "nitohtaw – Listen to him/her/it"

1s	ē-nitohtawit	as s/he/it listens to me	1s ← 3s
2s	ē-nitohtāsk	as s/he/it listens to you	2s ← 3s
3s	ē-nitohtākot	as s/he/it is listened to by him/her/it	3s ← 3's/3'p
3's	ē-nitohtākoyit	as his/her/its ___ is listened to by him/her/it	3's ← 3's/3'p
1p	ē-nitohtākoyāhk	as s/he/it listens to us (excl)	1p ← 3s
21	ē-nitohtākoyahk	as his/her/it listens to us (incl)	21 ← 3s
2p	ē-nitohtākoyēk	as his/her/it listens to you	2p ← 3s
3p	ē-nitohtākocik	as they are listened to by him/her/it	3p ← 3's/3'p
3'p	ē-nitohtākoyit	as their ____ are listened to by him/her/it	3'p ← 3's/3'p

Plural (3p are acting on 1s through 3'p)

1s	ē-____ icik	as they ____ me	1s ← 3p
2s	ē-____āskik	as they ____ you	2s ← 3p
3s	ē-____ākot	as he/she/it is ____ by them	3s ← 3's/3'p
3's	ē-____ākoyit	as his/her/its ___ is ___ by them	3's ← 3's/3'p
1p	ē-____ākoyāhkik	as they ____ us (excl)	1p ← 3p
21	ē-____ākoyahkok	as they ____ us (incl)	21 ← 3p
2p	ē-____ākoyēkok	as they ____ you	2p ← 3p
3p	ē-____ākocik	as they ____ by them	3p ← 3's/3'p
3'p	ē-____ākoyit	as their ____ are ____ by them	3'p ← 3's/3'p

Example: Inverse VTA-2 –*"Vw"* stem "nitohtaw – Listen to him/her/it"

1s	ē-nitohtawicik	as they listen to me	1s ← 3p
2s	ē- nitohtāskik	as they listen to you	2s ← 3p
3s	ē- nitohtākot	as s/he/it is listened to by them	3s ← 3's/3'p
3's	ē- nitohtākoyit	as his/her/its ___ is listened to by them	3's ← 3's/3'p
1p	ē- nitohtākoyāhkik	as they listen to us (excl)	1p ← 3p
21	ē-nitohtākoyahkok	as they listen to us (incl)	21 ← 3p
2p	ē- nitohtākoyēkok	as they listen to you	2p ← 3p
3p	ē- nitohtākocik	as they are listened to by them	3p ← 3p
3'p	ē- nitohtākoyit	as their ___ are listened to by them	3'p ← 3p

NOTE: The suffix for 1s: "*-it*" for singular; "*-icik*" for plural. This is noted at the bottom of the page for Verb Chart 8.

Future Conditional Form Inverse 2 – VTA-2 "Vw" stem

Notice that the stem is not changed for the "1s" in the Conjunct and Future Conditional singular and plural forms.

Singular (3s is acting on 1s through 3'p)

1s	____ici *	when/if s/he/it ____ me	1s ← 3s
2s	____āski	when/if s/he/it ____ you	2s ← 3s
3s	____ākoci	when/if his/her/it is ___ by him/her/it	3s ← 3's/3'p
3's	____ākoyici	when/if his/her/its __ is __ by him/her/it	3's ← 3's/3'p
1p	____ākoyāhki	when/if s/he/it ____ us (excl)	1p ← 3s
21	____ākoyahko	when/if his/her/it ____ us (incl)	21 ← 3s
2p	____ākoyēko	when/if his/her/it ____ you	2p ← 3s
3p	____ākotwāwi	when/if they are ___ by him/her/it	3p ← 3's/3'p
3'p	____ākoyici	when/if their ___ are ___ by him/her/it	3'p ← 3's/3'p

Example: Inverse 2 – VTA - 2 – "Vw" stem "nitohtaw – Listen to him/her/it"

1s	nitohtawici*	when/if s/he listens to me	1s ← 3s
2s	nitohtāski	when/if s/he listens to you	2s ← 3s
3s	nitihtākoci	when/if s/he is listened to by him/her	3s ← 3's/3'p
3's	nitohtākoyici	when/if his/her __ is listened to by him/her	3's ← 3's/3'p
1p	nitohtākoyāhk	when/if s/he listens to us (excl)	1p ← 3s
21	nitohtākoyahki	when/if s/he listens to us (incl)	21 ← 3s
2p	nitohtākoyēko	when/if s/he listens to you	2p ← 3s
3p	nitohtākotwāwi	when/if they are listened to by him/her	3p ← 3's/3'p
3'p	nitohtākoyici	when/if their ____ are listened to by him/her	3'p ← 3's/3'p

Plural (3p are acting on 1s through 3'p)

1s	____itwāwi *	when/if they ____ me	1s ← 3p
2s	____āskwāwi	when/if they ____ you	2s ← 3p
3s	____ākoci	when/if he/she/it is ___ by them	3s ← 3's/3'p
3's	___ākoyici	when/if his/her/its ___ is ____ by them	3's ← 3's/3'p
1p	___ākoyāhkwāwi	when/if they ____ us (excl)	1p ← 3p
21	___ākoyahkwāwi	when/if they ____ us (incl)	21 ← 3p
2p	___ākoyēkwāwi	when/if they ____ you	2p ← 3p
3p	___ākotwāwi	when/if they ____ by them	3p ← 3's/3'p
3'p	___ākoyici	when/if their ____ are ____ by them	3'p ← 3's/3'p

Example: Inverse 2 – VTA-2 – *"Vw"* stem "nitohtaw – Listen to him/her/it"

1s	nitohtawitwāwi*	when/if they listen to me	1s ← 3p
2s	nitohtāskwāwi	when/if they listen to you	2s ← 3p
3s	nitohtākoci	when/if s/he/it is listened to by them	3s ← 3's/3'p
3's	nitohtākoyici	when/if his/her/its __ is listened to by them	3's ← 3's/3'p
1p	nitohtākoyāhkwāwi	when/if they listen to us (excl)	1p ← 3p
21	nitohtākoyahkwāwi	when/if they listen to us (incl)	21 ← 3p
2p	nitohtākoyēkwāwi	when/if they listen to you	2p ← 3p
3p	nitohtākotwāwi	when/if they are listened to by them	3p ← 3's/3'p
3'p	nitohtākoyici	when/if their ____ are listened to by them	3'p ← 3's/3'p

NOTE: The suffix for 1s: *"-it"* for singular; *"-icik"* for plural.

Chapter 26: Inverse VTA-3 – "Cw" Stems

Before looking at the paradigms remember that there are no imperatives for inverse of the Transitive Animate verbs.

The VTA-3 – *"Cw"* stems all end in a "Consonant plus a *"w"*. This may look complicated but it does not have to be, if one follows the rules. Here are some verbs which fit this category. Notice the *"Cw"* endings on the stems.

pakamahw – strike/hit him/her/it	wīsakatahw – hurt him/her/it
pistisw – cut him/her/it accidently	nātisahw – send for him/her/it
pasastēhw – whip him/her/it	papāmitisahw – follow him/her/it around

NOTE: "Cw" = (Consonant w stem)

Independent Inverse 3 – VTA-3 "Cw" stem "pakamahw – Strike him/her/it"

Singular (3s is acting on 1s through 3'p)

1s	ni____ok	s/he/it ____ me	1s ← 3s
2s	ki____ok	s/he/it ____ you	2s ← 3s
3s	____okow	his/her/it is ____ by him/her/it	3s ← 3's/3'p
3's	____okoyiwa	his/her/its ___ is ____ by him/her/it	3's ← 3's/3'p
1p	ni____okonān	s/he/it ____ us (excl)	1p ← 3s
21	ki____okonaw	his/her/it ____ us (incl)	21 ← 3s
2p	ki____okowāw	his/her/it ____ you	2p ← 3s
3p	____okowak	they are ____ by him/her/it	3p ← 3's/3'p
3'p	____okoyiwa	their ____ are ____ by him/her/it	3'p ← 3's/3'p

Example: Inverse 3 – VTA-3 "Cw" stem "pakamahw – Strike him/her/it"

1s	nipakamahok	s/he/it strikes me	1s ← 3s
2s	kipakamahok	s/he/it strikes you	2s ← 3s
3s	pakamahokow	s/he/it is struck by him/her/it	3s ← 3's/3'p
3's	pakamahokoyiwa	his/her/its ___ is struck by him/her/it	3's ← 3's/3'p
1p	nipakamahokonān	s/he/it strikes us (excl)	1p ← 3s
21	kipakamahokonaw	s/he/it strikes us (incl)	21 ← 3s
2p	kipakamahokowāw	s/he/it strikes you	2p ← 3s
3p	pakamahokowak	they are struck by him/her/it	3p ← 3's/3'p
3'p	pakamahokoyiwa	their ___ are struck by him/her/it	3'p ← 3's/3'p

Plural (3p are acting on 1s through 3'p)

1s	ni____okwak	they ____ me	1s ← 3p
2s	ki____okwak	they ____ you	2s ← 3p
3s	____okow	s/he/it is ____ by them	3s ← 3's/3'p
3's	____okoyiwa	his/her/its ____ is ____ by them	3's ← 3's/3'p
1p	ni____okonānak	they ____ us (excl)	1p ← 3p
21	ki____okonawak	they ____ us (incl)	21 ← 3p
2p	ki____okowāwak	they ____ you	2p ← 3p
3p	____okwak	they are ____ by them	3p ← 3's/3'p
3'p	____okoyiwa	their ____ ____ by them	3'p ← 3's/3'p

Example: Inverse 3 – VTA-3 "Cw" stem "pakamahw – Strike him/her/it"

1s	nipakamahokwak	they strike me	1s ← 3p
2s	kipakamahokwak	they strike you	2s ← 3p
3s	pakamahokow	s/he is struck by them	3s ← 3's/3'p
3's	pakamahokoyiwa	his/her/its ____ is struck by them	3's ← 3's/3'p
1p	nipakamahokonānak	they strike us (excl)	1p ← 3p

21	kipakamahokonawak	they strike us (incl)	21 ← 3p
2p	kipakamahokowāwak	they strike you	2p ← 3p
3p	pakamahokwak	they are struck by them	3p ← 3's/3'p
3'p	pakamahokoyiwa	their _____ are struck by them	3'p ← 3's/3'p

NOTE: If one looks closely at the above conjugation it shows that the *"w"* is being dropped from the spelling. Study the rest of the paradigms below and you will find that the *"w"* is not needed at all.

The suffix for 1s: *"-ok"* for singular and *"-okwak"* for plural. The plural suffix *"wak"* was attached to the Inverse singular suffix.

Conjunct Inverse 3 – VTA-3 "Cw" stem

Singular (3s is acting on 1s through 3'p)

1s	ē-_____ot	as s/he it _____ me	1s ← 3s
2s	ē-_____osk	as s/he/it _____ you	2s ← 3s
3s	ē-_____okot	as s/he/it is _____ by him/her/it	3s ← 3's/3'p
3's	ē-_____okoyit	as his/her/its _____ _____ by him/her/it	3's ← 3's/3'p
1p	ē-_____okoyāhk	as s/he/it _____ us (excl)	1p ← 3s
21	ē-_____okoyahk	as his/her/it _____ us (incl)	21 ← 3s
2p	ē-_____okoyēk	as his/her/it _____ you	2p ← 3s
3p	ē-_____okocik	as they _____ at by him/her/it	3p ← 3's/3'p
3'p	ē-_____okoyit	as their _____ _____ at by him/her/it	3'p ← 3's/3'p

Example: Inverse 3 – VTA-3 *"Cw"* stem "pakamahw – Strike him/her"

1s	ē-pakamahot	as s/he/it strikes me	1s ← 3s
2s	ē-pakamahosk	as s/he/it strikes you	2s ← 3s
3s	ē-pakamahokot	as s/he/it is struck by him/her/it	3s ← 3's/3'p
3's	ē-pakamahokoyit	as his/her/its ___ is struck by him/her/it	3's ← 3's/3'p
1p	ē-pakamahokoyāhk	as s/he/it strikes us (excl)	1p ← 3s
21	ē-pakamahokoyahk	as s/he/it strikes us (incl)	21 ← 3s
2p	ē-pakamahokoyēk	as s/he/it strikes you	2p ← 3s
3p	ē-pakamahokocik	as they are struck by him/her/it	3p ← 3's/3'p
3'p	ē-pakamahokoyit	as their _____ are struck by him/her/it	3'p ← 3's/3'p

Plural (3p are acting on 1s through 3'p)

1s	ē-_____ocik	as they _____ me	1s ← 3p
2s	ē-_____oskik	as they _____ you	2s ← 3p
3s	ē-_____okot	as he/she/it is _____ by them	3s ← 3's/3'p
3's	ē-_____okoyit	as his/her/its _____ _____ by them	3's ← 3's/3'p
1p	ē-_____okoyāhkik	as they _____ us (excl)	1p ← 3p
21	ē-_____okoyahkok	as they _____ us (incl)	21 ← 3p
2p	ē-_____okoyēkok	as they _____ you	2p ← 3p
3p	ē-_____okocik	as they _____ by them	3p ← 3's/3'p
3'p	ē-_____okoyit	as their _____ are _____ by them	3'p ← 3's/3'p

Example: Inverse 3 – VTA-3 *"Cw"* stem "pakamahw – Strike him/her"

1s	ē-pakamahocik	as they strike me	1s ← 3p
2s	ē-pakamahoskik	as they strike you	2s ← 3p
3s	ē-pakamahokot	as he/she/it is struck by them	3s ← 3's/3'p
3's	ē-pakamahokoyit	as his/her/its _____ struck by them	3's ← 3's/3'p
1p	ē-pakamahokoyāhkik	as they strike us (excl)	1p ← 3p
21	ē-pakamahokoyahkok	as they strike us (incl)	21 ← 3p

21	____okoyahkwāwi	when/if they ____ us (incl)	21 ← 3p
2p	____okoyēkwāwi	when/if they ____ you	2p ← 3p
3p	____okotwāwi	when/if they ____ by them	3p ← 3's/3'p
3'p	____okoyici	when/if their ____ are ____ by them	3'p ← 3's/3'p

Example: Inverse 3 – VTA-3 *"Cw"* stem "pakamahw – Strike him/her"

1s	pakamahotwāwi	when/if they strike me	1s ← 3p
2s	pakamahoskwāwi	when/if they strike you	2s ← 3p
3s	pakamahokoci	when/if he/she/it is struck by them	3s ← 3's/3'p
3's	pakamahokoyici	when/if his/her/its ____ is struck by them	3's ← 3's/3'p
1p	pakamahokoyāhkwāwi	when/if they strike us (excl)	1p ← 3p
21	pakamahokoyahkwāwi	when/if they strike us (incl)	21 ← 3p
2p	pakamahokoyēkwāwi	when/if they strike you	2p ← 3p
3p	pakamahokotwāwi	when/if they are struck by them	3p ← 3's/3'p
3'p	pakamahokoyici	when/if their ____ are struck by them	3'p ← 3's/3'p

NOTE: The suffix for 1s: *"-oci"* for singular; *"-otwawi"* for plural.

Chapter 27: The You–Me Set

So far we have looked at grammatical structures where actions were towards another person or thing. In other words the action was towards a third person, *him/her/it*. This was referred to as being a *Direct* action. Next the discussion was on the structure where those third persons or things were the ones who were doing the action. In other words the third person was acting on those that were acting in the direct form. This was called the *Inverse*. The *Reflexive* form of a verb, where the action is directed towards oneself, has also been discussed before. Another new chapter discusses a form where the actor is not identified. That is labelled as the Unspecified Actor form. So now this chapter will give an additional form that was not presented in the last edition.

As the title suggests this next form called the *"you- me set"* represents the interaction of second person, *"you,"* singular or plural, with: *1s - "me"; 1p - "us."* There are many paradigms with their unique prefixes and suffixes presented here which will indicate the direction of the action that is taking place. They occur in the Imperatives, the Independent mode—direct and inverse; in the Conjunct mode—direct and inverse and in the Future Conditional—direct and inverse.

A reminder here is that there are four kinds of VTA stems: VTA-1; VTA-2; VTA-3; VTA-4. We will begin with the VTA-1 regular stems.

NOTE: The arrows and figures on the right show the direction of the action by those persons that are represented by the numbers.

VTA-1 Regular Stems

a) Immediate Imperative – Inverse 1 – VTA-1 Regular Stems

2s	____in	____ me.	1s ← 2s
2s/2p	____inān	____ us.	1p ← 2s/2p
2p	____ik	____ me.	1s ← 2p

Example: VTA-1 – "wīcih – Help him/her/it"

2s	wīcihin	Help me.	1s ← 2s
2s/2p	wīcihinān	Help us.	1p ← 2s/2p
2p	wīcihik	Help me.	1s ← 2p

b) Delayed Imperative – Inverse 1 – VTA-1 Regular Stems

2s	____ihkan	____me. (later)	1s ← 2s
2s/2p	____ihkāhk	____us. (later)	1p ← 2s/2p
2p	____ihkēk	____me. (later)	1s ← 2p

Example – VTA -1 "wīcih – Help him/her/it"

2s	wīcihihkan	Help me.	1s ← 2s
2s/2p	wīcihihkāhk	Help us.	1p ← 2s/2p
2p	wīcihihkēk	Help me.	1s ← 2p

a) Independent Mode – Direct

1s	ki____itin	I ____ you	1s → 2s
1p	ki____itinān	We ____ you	1p → 2s/2p
1s	ki____itināwāw	I ____ you	1s → 2p

Example: VTA-1 – "wīcih – Help him/her/it"

1s	kiwīcihitin	I help you	1s → 2s
1p	kiwīcihitinān	We help you	1p → 2s/2p
1s	kiwīcihitināwāw	I help you	1s → 2p

b) Independent Mode – Inverse

2s	ki_____in	You _____ me	1s ← 2s
2s/2p	ki_____inān	You _____ us	1p ← 2s/2p
2p	ki _____ināwāw	You _____ me	1s ← 2p

Example: VTA-1 – "wīcih – Help him/her/it"

2s	kiwīcihin	You help me.	1s ← 2s
2s/2p	kiwīcihinān	You help us.	1p ← 2s/2p
2p	kiwīcihināwāw	You help me.	1s ← 2s

a) Conjunct Mode Direct

1s	ē-_____itān	as I _____ you	1s → 2s
1p	ē-_____itāhk	as we ____ help you	1p → 2s/2p
1s	ē-_____ititakohk	as I _____ you	1s → 2p

Example: VTA-1 – "wīcih – Help him/her/it"

1s	ē-wīcihitān	as I help you	1s → 2s
1p	ē-wīcihitāhk	as we help you	1p → 2s/2p
1s	ē-wīcihititakohk	as I help you	1s → 2p

b) Conjunct Mode Inverse

2s	ē-_____yan	as you _____ me	1s ← 2s
2s/2p	ē-_____iyāhk	as you _____ us	1p ← 2s/2p
2p	ē-_____iyēk	as you _____ me	1s ← 2p

Example: VTA-1 – "wīcih – Help him/her/it"

2s	ē-wīcihiyan	as you help me	1s ← 2s
2s/2p	ē-wīcihiyāhk	as you help us	1p ← 2s/2p
2p	ē-wīcihiyēk	as you help me	1s ← 2p

a) Future Conditional – Direct

1s	_____itāni	if/when I _____ you	1s → 2s
1p	_____itāhki	if/when we _____ you	1p → 2s/2p
1s	_____itako	if/when I _____ you	1s → 2p

Example: VTA-1 – "wīcih – Help him/her/it"

1s	wīcihitāni	if/when I help you	1s → 2s
1p	wīcihitāhki	if/when we help you	1p → 2s/2p
1s	wīcihitako	if/when I help you	1s → 2p

b) Future Conditional – Inverse

2s	_____iyani	if/when you _____ me	1s ← 2s
2s/2p	_____iyāhki	if/when you_____ us	1p ← 2s/2p
2p	_____iyēko	if/when you _____ me	1s ← 2p

Example: VTA-1 –"wīcih – Help him/her/it"

2s	wīcihiyani	if/when you help me	1s ← 2s
2s/2p	wīcihiyāhki	if/when you help us	1p ← 2s/2p
2p	wīcihiyēko	if/when you help me	1s ← 2p

VTA-4 "t" Stems

Examples of the "t" stems are:

pakwāt – dislike/hate him/her/it   nāt – fetch him/her/it kāt – hide him/her/it   sakahpit – tie him/her/it

pōtāt – blow him/her/it   mowihkāt – cry for him/her/it

    VTA-4 *"t"* stems change the *"-t"* to an *"-s"* in the Immediate and Delayed Imperative: 2s, 1p, 2p, and in the Conjunct inverse.

a) Immediate Imperative – Inverse 1

2s	_____in	____ me.	1s ← 2s
2s/2p	_____inān	____ us.	1p ← 2s/2p
2p	_____ik	____ me.	1s ← 2p

Example: VTA-4 "t" stem – "nakat – Leave him/her/it"

2s	nakasin	Leave me.	1s ← 2s
2s/2p	nakasinān	Leave us.	1p ← 2s/2p
2p	nakasik	Leave me.	1s ← 2p

b) Delayed Imperative

2s	____ihkan	____me. (later)	1s ← 2s
2s/2p	____ihkāhk	____us. (later)	1p ← 2s/2p
2p	____ihkēk	____me. (later)	1s ← 2p

Example: Inverse 1 – VTA-4 "t" stem – "nakat – Leave him/her/it"

2s	nakasihkan	Leave me. (later)	1s ← 2s
2s/2p	nakas*ihkāhk*	Leave us. (later)	1p ← 2s
2p	nakasihkēk	Leave me. (later)	1s ← 2p

a) Independent Mode – Direct

1s	ki____itin	I _____ you	1s → 2s
1p	ki____itinān	We _____ you	1p → 2s/2p
1s	ki____itināwāw	I _____ you	1s → 2p

Example: VTA-1 – "nakat – Leave help him/her/it"

1s	kinakatitin	I leave you.	1s → 2s
1p	kinakatitinān	We leave you.	1p → 2s/2p
1s	kinakatitināwāw	I leave you.	1s → 2p

b) Independent Mode – Inverse

2s	ki____in	You _____ me.	1s ← 2s
2s/2p	ki____inān	You _____ us.	1p ← 2s/2p
2p	ki____ināwāw	You _____ me.	1s ← 2p

Example: VTA-1 "nakat – Leave him/her/it"

2s	kinakasin	You leave me.	1s ← 2s
2s/2p	kinakasinān	You leave us.	1p ← 2s/2p
2p	kinakasināwāw	You leave me.	1s ← 2s

a) Conjunct Mode Direct

1s	ē-____itān	as I _____ you	1s → 2s
1p	ē-____itāhk	as we _____ you	1p → 2s/2p
1s	ē-____ititakok	as I _____ you	1s → 2p

Example:

1s	ē-nakatitān	as I leave you	1s → 2s
1p	ē-nakatitāhk	as we leave you	1p → 2s/2p
1s	ē-nakatitakok	as I leave you	1s → 2p

b) Conjunct Mode Inverse

2s	ē-____yan	as you _____ me	1s ← 2s
2s/2p	ē-____iyāhk	as you _____ us	1p ← 2s/2p
2s	ē-____iyēk	as you _____ me	1s ← 2p

Example:

2s	ē-nakasiyan	as you leave me	1s ← 2s
2s/2p	ē-nakasiyāhk	as you leave us	1p ← 2s/2p
2p	ē-nakasiyēk	as you leave me	1s ← 2p

a) Future Conditional – Direct

1s	____itani	if/when I _____ you	1s → 2s
1p	____itāhki	if/when we ____ you	1p → 2s/2p
1s	____itako	if/when I _____ you	1s → 2p

Example: VTA-4 "t" stem – "nakat – Leave him/her/it"

1s	nakatitāni	if/when I leave you	1s → 2s
1p	nakatitāhki	if/when we leave you	1p → 2s/2p
1s	nakatitako	if/when I leave you	1s → 2p

b) Future Conditional – Inverse

2s	____iyani	if/when you _____ me	1s ← 2s
2s/2p	____iyāhki	if/when you_____ us	1p ← 2s/2p
2p	____iyēko	if/when you ____ me	1s ← 2p

Example: VTA-4 "t" stem – "nakat – Leave him/her/it"

2s	nakasiyani	if/when you leave me	1s ← 2s
2s/2p	nakasiyāhki	if/when you leave us	1p ← 2s/2p
2p	nakasiyēko	if/when you leave me	1s ← 2p

VTA-2 "Vw" Stems ("Vw" = Vowel w)

VTA-2 – "Vw" stems do not undergo any changes in the two Imperative forms and whenever there are changes that will be noted.

Some verbs with *"Vw"* stems:

| nitohtaw – Listen to him/her/it. | nakiskaw – meet him/her/it |
| miskaw – find him/her/it | atamiskaw – shake his/her hand |

a) Immediate Imperative – VTA-2 "Vw" Stems (Vw = Vowel w stem)

2s	_____in	____ me.	1s ← 2s
2s/2p	_____inān	____ us.	1p ← 2s/2p
2p	_____ik	____ me.	1s ← 2p

Example: VTA-2 – "Vw" "nitohtaw – Listen to him/her/it"

2s	nitohtawin	Listen to me.	1s ← 2s
2s/2p	nitohtawinān	Listen to us.	1p ← 2s/2p
2p	nitohtawik	Listen to me.	1s ← 2p

b) Delayed Imperative – VTA-2 "Vw" Stem

2s	_____ihkan	____me. (later)	1s ← 2s
2s/2p	_____ihkāhk	____us. (later)	1p ← 2s/2p
2p	_____ihkēk	____me. (later)	1s ← 2p

Example: VTA-2 – "Vw" "nitohtaw – Listen to him/her/it"

| 2s | nitohtawihkan | Listen to me. (later) | 1s ← 2s |

| 2s/2p | nitohtawihkāhk | Listen to us. (later) | 1p ← 2s/2p |
| 2p | nitohtawihkēk | Listen to me. (later) | 1s ← 2p |

a) Independent Mode – Direct

1s	ki_____ātin	I _____ you	1s → 2s
1p	ki_____ātinān	We _____ you	1p → 2s/2p
1s	ki_____ātināwāw	I _____ you	1s → 2p

Example: VTA-2 – "Vw" "nitohtaw – Listen to him/her/it"

1s	kinitohtātin	I listen to you	1s → 2s
1p	kinitohtātinān	We listen to you	1p → 2s/2p
1s	kinitohtātināwāw	I listen to you	1s → 2p

NOTE: The *"-aw"* was dropped from the stem in the Independent – Direct.

b) Independent Mode – Inverse

2s	ki_____in	You _____ me.	1s ← 2s
2s/2p	ki_____inān	You _____ us.	1p ← 2s/2p
2p	ki_____ināwāw	You _____ me.	1s ← 2p

Example: VTA-2 – "nitohtaw – Listen to him/her/it"

2s	kinitohtawin	You listen to me.	1s ← 2s
2s/2p	kinitohtawinān	You listen to us.	1p ← 2s/2p
2p	kinitohtawināwāw	You listen to me.	1s ← 2s

a) Conjunct Mode – Direct

1s	ē- _____ātān	as I _____ you	1s → 2s
1p	ē- _____ātāhk	as we _____ you	1p → 2s/2p
1s	ē-_____ātakohk	as I _____ you	1s → 2p

Example: VTA-2 – "nitohtaw – Listen to him/her/it"

1s	ē- nitohtātān	as I listen to you	1s → 2s
1p	ē- nitohtātāhk	as we listen to you	1p → 2s/2p
1s	ē- nitohtātakok	as I listen to you	1s → 2p

NOTE: The *"-aw"* was dropped from the verb stem in the Conjunct – Direct.

b) Conjunct Mode Inverse

2s	ē-_____yan	as you _____ me.	1s ← 2s
2s/2p	ē-_____iyāhk	as you_____ us.	1p ← 2s/2p
2p	ē-_____iyēk	as you _____ me.	1s ← 2p

Example: VTA-2 – "nitohtaw – Listen to him/her/it"

2s	ē- nitohtawiyan	as you listen to me	1s ← 2s
2s/2p	ē- nitohtawiyāhk	as you listen to us	1p ← 2s/2p
2p	ē- nitohtawiyēk	as you listen to me	1s ← 2p

a) Future Conditional – Direct

1s	_____ātāni	if/when I _____ you	1s → 2s
1p	_____ātāhko	if/when we _____ you	1p → 2s/2p
1s	_____ātako	if/when I _____ you	1s → 2p

Example: VTA-2 – "nitohtaw – Listen to him/her/it"

1s	nitohtātāni	if/when I listen to you	1s → 2s
1p	nitohtātāhko	if/when we listen to you	1p → 2s/2p
1s	nitohtātahko	if/when I listen to you	1s → 2p

NOTE: The *"-aw"* was dropped from the stem in the Future Conditional – Direct.

b) Future Conditional – Inverse

2s	_____ iyani	if/when you _____ me	1s ← 2s
2s/2p	_____ iyāhki	if/when you _____ us	1p ← 2s/2p
2p	_____ iyēko	if/when you _____ me	1s ← 2p

Example: VTA-2 – "nitohtaw – Listen to him/her/it"

2s	nitohtawiyani	if/when you listen to me	1s ← 2s
2s/2p	nitohtawiyāhki	if/when you listen to us	1p ← 2s/2p
2p	nitohtawiyēko	if/when you listen to me	1s ← 2p

NOTE: The *"-aw"* was dropped from the stem in the Independent Direct, the Conjunct Direct and the Future Conditional – Direct.

VTA-3 "Cw" Stems (Cw = Consonant w stem)

Some examples of VTA-3 "Cw" stems are:

pasastēhw – whip/strap him/her/it   pakamahw – strike/hit him/her/it
pāskisw – shoot him/her/it   pimitisahw – follow him/her/it

NOTE: The *"w"* is dropped from the stem in the two Imperative modes.

a) Immediate Imperative Inverse 3 – VTA-3 "Cw" Stems

2s	_____on	_____ me.	1s ← 2s
2s/2p	_____onān	_____ us.	1p ← 2s/2p
2p	_____ok	_____ me.	1s ← 2p

Example: Inverse 3 – VTA-3 –"Cw" stem pakamahw – strike him/her/it

2s	pakamahon	Strike me.	1s ← 2s
2s/2p	pakamahonān	Strike us.	1p ← 2s/2p
2p	pakamahok	Strike me.	1s ← 2p

b) Delayed Imperative Inverse 3 – VTA-3 "Cw" Stems

2s	_____ohkan	_____me. (later)	1s ← 2s
2s/2p	_____ohkāhk	_____us. (later)	1p ← 2s/2p
2p	_____ohkēk	_____me. (later)	1s ← 2p

Example: Inverse 3 – VTA-3 – "Cw" stem pakamahw – Strike him/her/it

2s	pakamahohkan	Strike me. (later)	1s ← 2s
2s/2p	pakamahohkāhk	Strike us. (later)	1p ← 2s/2p
2p	pakamahohkēk	Strike me. (later)	1s ← 2p

a) Independent Mode – Direct

1s	ki_____otin	I _____ you	1s → 2s
1p	ki_____otinān	We _____ you	1p → 2s/2p
1s	ki_____otināwāw	I _____ you	1s → 2p

Example: VTA-3 – "Cw" pakamahw – Hit him/her/it

1s	kipakamahotin	I strike you.	1s → 2s
1p	ki pakamahotinān	We strike you.	1p → 2s/2p
1s	kipakamahotināwāw	I strike you.	1s → 2p

b) Independent Mode – Inverse

2s	ki_____on	You _____ me.	1s ← 2s
2s/2p	ki_____onān	You _____ us.	1p ← 2s/2p
1p	ki_____onāwāw	You _____ me.	1s ← 2p

Example: VTA-3 – "Cw" pakamahw – hit him/her/it

2s	kipakamahon	You strike me.	1s ← 2s
2s/2p	kipakamahonān	You strike us.	1p ← 2s/2p
2p	kipakamahonāwāw	You strike me.	1s ← 2p

a) Conjunct Mode – Direct

1s	ē-_____otān	as I _____ you	1s → 2s
1p	ē-_____otāhk	as we _____ you	1p → 2s/2p
1s	ē-_____otakok	as I _____ you	1s → 2p

Example: VTA-3 – "Cw" pakamahw – hit him/her/it

1s	ē- pakamahotān	as I strike you	1s → 2s
1p	ē- pakamahotāhk	as we strike you	1p → 2s/2p
1s	ē- pakamahotakok	as I strike you	1s → 2p

b) Conjunct Mode – Inverse

2s	ē-_____ oyan	as you _____ me.	1s ← 2s
2s/2p	ē-_____ oyāhk	as you_____ us.	1p ← 2s/2p
2p	ē-_____oyēk	as you _____ me.	1s ← 2p

Example: VTA-3 – "Cw" pakamahw – Hit him/her/it

2s	ē- pakamahoyan	as you strike me	1s ← 2s
2s/2p	ē- pakamahoyāhk	as you strike us	1p ← 2s/2p
2p	ē- pakamahoyēk	as you strike me	1s ← 2p

a) Future Conditional – Direct

1s	_____ otāni	if/when I _____ you	1s → 2s
1p	_____ otāhki	if/when we _____ you	1p → 2s/2p
1s	_____ otako	if/when I _____ you	1s → 2p

Example: VTA-3 – "Cw" pakamahw – Hit him/her/it

1s	pakamahotāni	if/when I strike you	1s → 2s
1p	pakamahotāhk	if/when we strike you	1p → 2s/2p
1s	pakamahotako	if/when I strike you	1s → 2p

b) Future Conditional – Inverse

2s	_____ oyani	if/when you _____ me	1s ← 2s
2s/2p	_____ oyāhki	if/when you _____ us	1p ← 2s/2p
2p	_____ oyēko	if/when you _____ me	1s ← 2p

Example: VTA-3 – "Cw" pakamahw – Hit him/her/it

2s	pakamahoyani	if/when you strike me	1s ← 2s
2s/2p	pakamahoyāhki	if/when you strike us	1p ← 2s/2p
2p	pakamahoyēko	if/when you strike me	1s ← 2p

Chapter 28: Unspecified Actor

This form of Cree verbs is also known as the Indefinite actor form but it seems that it is more appropriate to say that a specific subject is not identified. This unspecified actor form is used extensively in Cree for a number of reasons so one will hear it in everyday conversations. It may be used when referring to topics and incidents where the action takes precedence over one specific actor. The action may be viewed as a collective one that does not allow the action to be attributed to one specific actor.

It can also be useful when one wants to keep a promise not to divulge the source of the information being discussed but it offers an opportunity for others to ask questions.

The verb stems of both Transitive and Intransitive verbs can be found in this particular form. Since those forms that occur with the Animate Intransitive verb stems are not as involved as the VTA stems they are presented first.

Animate Intransitive verbs – VAI – Unspecified Actor

In other situations, one uses this form to refer to group activities, incidents or occasions such as a banquet, dance, wake or other activity.

These verbs are not conjugated but they do occur in the future and past tense. A peculiar characteristic is that they appear to be Intransitive Inanimate verbs but the stem is a VAI. Some verbs will appear in two forms for the Independent mode which may be a personal or perhaps a regional preference but they are both understood.

The charts with the prefixes are not included here but there are charts in the appendices that should be consulted if necessary.

In the following examples the suffixes, *-nāniwiw* and *-nāniwan* which indicate that there is an unspecified actor or subject are italicized. They are in the independent and the conjunct modes.

NOTE: In the examples below both forms for the independent mode are correct.

	Mode	Verb	Translation
1.	Independent	- mīciso*nāniwiw*	There is eating going on.
	Independent	- mīciso*nāniwan*	There is eating going on.
	Conjunct	- ē-mīciso*hk*	as there is eating going on.
	Future conditional - mīciso*hki*		if/when there is eating
2.	Independent	- mētaw*āniwiw*	There is a sports day going on.
	Independent	- mētaw*āniwan*	There is a sports day going on.
	Conjunct	- ē-mētawē*hk*	as there is a sports day going on.
	Future conditional - mētawē*hki*		if/when there is a sports day
3.	Independent	- māto*nāniwiw*	There was crying going on.
	Independent	- māto*nāniwan*	There was crying going on.
	Conjunct	- ē-māto*hk*	as there was crying going on.
	Future conditional - māto*hki*		if/when there is crying
4.	Independent	- nīmā*niwiw*	There is lunch taken along.
	Independent	- nīmā*niwan*	There is lunch taken along.
	Conjunct	- ē-nīmā*hk*	as there is lunch taken along.
	Future conditional - nīmā*hki*		if/when there is lunch taken along
5.	Independent	- nīpēpi*nāniwiw*	There is a wake being held.
	Independent	- nīpēpi*nāniwan*	There is a wake being held.
	Conjunct	- ē-nīpēpi*hk*	as there is a wake being held.
	Future conditional - nīpēpi*hki*		if/when there is a wake

6.	Independent	- itwā*niwiw*	It is said.
	Independent	- itwā*niwan*	It is said.
	Conjunct	- ē-itwē*hk*	as it is said
	Future conditional - itwē*hki*		if/when it is said
7.	Independent	- nōtinito*nāniwiw*	There is fighting/war going on.
	Independent	- nōtinito*nāniwan*	There is fighting/war going on.
	Conjunct	- ē-nōtinito*hk*	as there is fighting/war going on.
	Future conditional - nōtinito*hki*		if/when there is fighting/war going on.

NOTE: The verb stems do not change when used in the Conjunct. In the examples above notice "ē" to "ā" rule is applied only for the Independent mode for the examples, "*itwē*" and "*mētawē*". The suffixes for these are "*-āniwiw*" and "*-āniwan*".

Observe the following examples which show the many uses of this particular form:

1) ē-mēkwā-mētawēhk ēsa anima ēkota kā-takohtēyāhk.

   Apparently there was a sports day going on there when we arrived.

2) kī-mētawāniwiw ayis māna ōtēnāhk kā-nipihk ēkosi māna nikī-itohtānān nīstanān.

   There used to be playing (sports day) in town so we used to go too.

3) ē-mēkwā-mīcisohk ēcik ānima kā-nito-pīhtokwēyān ēkota.

   There was eating going on when I entered there (that I didn't know about).

4) nitawi-nahapitān, āsay ōma ēkwa wī-mīcisonāniwan.

   Let's go sit down as the eating is going to start.

5) āsay ē-māc-ātoskēhk awa pēyak iskwēw kā-pē-nitomikoyāhk.

   Work was already in progress when this woman came to call us.

6) nikī-sipwēyāmonān anima Germany ēsa nētē ē-nōtinitohk ē-itwēhk.

   We fled when it was said that there was fighting in Germany.

7) kī-tapasīnāniwiw anima ēkospīhk ka-mēscihikawinaw ē-itēyihtamihk.

   There was fleeing that time as it was thought that we would all be killed.

8) matwē-mōcikihtāniwan wīkiwāhk.

   There is a lively party going on at their house.

Transitive Animate Verbs – Unspecified Actor

The unspecified actor form for the VTA can be conjugated in the Independent, Conjunct, and Future Conditional paradigms. For a look at these verb forms examples of all four VTA verb stems are fully conjugated below.

Examples of VTA-1, 2, 3, and 4, in the past tense, follow:

Independent Mode of Unspecified Actor Form:

VTA-1 regular stem – itācim – talk about him/her/it

1s	nikī - itācimikawin	1s	I was talked about
2s	kikī - itācimikawin	2s	You were talked about
3s	kī - itācimāw	3s	S/he/it was talked about
3's	kī - itācimimāwa	3's	His/her/its _____ was talked about
1p	nikī - itācimikawinān	1p	We were talked about (excl)
21	kikī - itācimikawinaw	21	We were talked about (incl)
2p	kikī - itācimikawināwāw	2p	You were talked about
3p	kī - itācimāwak	3p	They were talked about
3'p	kī - itācimimāwa	3'p	Their _____ were talked about

Conjunct Mode of Unspecified Actor Form:

VTA-1 regular stem – itācim – talk about him/her/it

1s	ē-kī - itācimikawiyān	1s	as I was talked about
2s	ē-kī - itācimikawiyan	2s	as you were talked about
3s	ē-kī - itācimiht	3s	as s/he/it was talked about
3's	ē-kī - itācimimiht	3's	as his/her/its ____ was talked about
1p	ē-kī - itācimikawiyāhk	1p	as we were talked about (excl)
21	ē-kī - itācimikawiyahk	21	as we were talked about (incl)
2p	ē-kī - itācimikawiyēk	2p	as you were talked about
3p	ē-kī - itācimihcik	3p	as they were talked about
3'p	ē-kī - itācimimiht	3'p	as their ____ were talked about

Future Conditional of Unspecified Actor Form:

VTA-1 regular stem – itācim – talk about him/her/it

1s	itācimikawiyāni	1s	if/when I am talked about
2s	itācimikawiyani	2s	if/when you are talked about
3s	itācimihci	3s	if/when s/he/it is talked about
3's	itācimimihci	3's	if/when his/her/its ____ is talked about
1p	itācimikawiyāhki	1p	if/when we are talked about (excl)
21	itācimikawiyahki	21	if/when we are talked about (incl)
2p	itācimikawiyēko	2p	if/when you are talked about
3p	itācimihtwāwi	3p	if/when they are talked about
3'p	itācimimihci	3'p	if/when their ____ are talked about

Independent Mode of Unspecified Actor Form:

VTA-2 Vw stem – pēhtaw – hear him/her/it

1s	nikī-pēhtākawin	1s	I was heard
2s	kikī-pēhtākawin	2s	You were heard
3s	kī-pēhtawāw	3s	S/he/it was heard
3's	kī-pēhtāwimāwa	3's	His/her/its ____
1p	nikī-pēhtākawinān	1p	We were heard (excl)
21	kikī-pēhtākawinaw	21	We were heard (incl)
2p	kikī-pēhtākawināwāw	2p	You were heard
3p	kī-pēhtawāwak	3p	They were heard
3'p	kī-pēhtāwimāwa	3'p	Their ____ were heard

Conjunct Mode of Unspecified Actor Form:

VTA-2 Vw stem – pēhtaw – hear him/her/it

1s	ē-kī-pēhtākawiyān	1s	as I was heard
2s	ē-kī-pēhtākawiyan	2s	as you were heard
3s	ē-kī-pēhtāht	3s	as s/he/it was heard
3's	ē-kī-pēhtāmiht	3's	as his/her/its ____ was heard
1p	ē-kī-pēhtākawiyāhk	1p	as we were heard (excl)
21	ē-kī-pēhtākawiyahk	21	as we were heard (incl)
2p	ē-kī-pēhtākawiyēk	2p	as you were heard
3p	ē-kī-pēhtāhcik	3p	as they were heard
3'p	ē-kī-pēhtāmiht	3'p	as their ____ were heard

Future Conditional of Unspecified Actor Form:

VTA-2 Vw stem – pēhtaw – hear him/her/it

1s	pēhtākawiyāni		1s	if/when I am heard
2s	pēhtākawiyani		2s	if/when you are heard
3s	pēhtāhci		3s	if/when s/he/it is heard
3's	pēhtāmihci		3's	if/when his/her/its ____ is heard
1p	pēhtākawiyāhki		1p	if/when we are heard (excl)
21	pēhtākawiyahki		21	if/when we are heard (incl)
2p	pēhtākawiyēko		2p	if/when you are heard
3p	pēhtāhtwāwi		3p	if/when they are heard
3'p	pēhtāmihci		3'p	if/when their ____ are heard

Independent Mode Unspecified Actor Form:

VTA-3 Cw stem – pasastēhw – whip him/her/it

1s	nikī-pasastēhokawin		1s	I was whipped
2s	kikī-pasastēhokawin		2s	You were whipped
3s	kī-pasastēhwāw		3s	S/he was whipped
3's	kī-pasastēhomāwa		3's	His/her/its ____ was whipped
1p	nikī-pasastēhokawinān		1p	We were whipped (excl)
21	kikī-pasastēhokawinaw		21	We were whipped (incl)
2p	kikī-pasastēhokawināwāw		2p	You were whipped
3p	kī-pasastēhwāwak		3p	They were whipped
3'p	kī-pasastēhomāwa		3'p	Their ____ were whipped

Conjunct Mode of Unspecified Actor Form:

VTA-3 Cw stem – pasastēhw – whip him/her/it

1s	ē-kī-pasastēhokawiyān		1s	as I was whipped
2s	ē-kī-pasastēhokawiyan		2s	as you were whipped
3s	ē-kī-pasastēhoht		3s	as s/he/it was whipped
3's	ē-kī-pasastēhomiht		3's	as his/her/its ____ was whipped
1p	ē-kī-pasastēhokawiyāhk		1p	as we were whipped (excl)
21	ē-kī-pasastēhokawiyahk		21	as we were whipped (incl)
2p	ē-kī-pasastēhokawiyēk		2p	as you were whipped
3p	ē-kī-pasastēhohcik		3p	as they were whipped
3'p	ē-kī-pasastēhomiht		3'p	as their ____ were whipped

Future Conditional of Unspecified Actor Form:

VTA-3 "Cw stem – pasastēhw – whip him/her/it"

1s	pasastēhokawiyāni		1s	if/when I am whipped
2s	pasastēhokawiyani		2s	if/when you are whipped
3s	pasastēhohci		3s	if/when s/he/it is whipped
3's	pasastēhomihci		3's	if/when his/her/its ____ is whipped
1p	pasastēhokawiyāhki		1p	if/when we are whipped (excl)
21	pasastēhokawiyahki		21	if/when we are whipped (incl)
2p	pasastēhokawiyēko		2p	if/when you are whipped
3p	pasastēhohtwāwi		3p	if/when they are whipped
3'p	pasastēhomihci		3'p	if/when their ____ are whipped

Independent Mode Unspecified Actor Form:

VTA-4 t stem – nawasēwāt – chase him/her/it"

1s	nikī-nawaswātikawin	1s	I was chased
2s	kikī-nawaswātikawin	2s	you were chased
3s	kī-nawaswātāw	3s	s/he/it was chased
3's	kī-nawaswātimāwa	3's	his/her/its _____ was chased
1p	nikī-nawaswātikawinān	1p	we were chased (excl)
21	kikī-nawaswātikawinaw	21	we were chased (incl)
2p	kikī-nawaswātikawināwāw	2p	you were chased
3p	kī-nawaswātāwak	3p	they were chased
3'p	kī-nawaswātimāwa	3'p	their _____ were chased

Conjunct Mode of Unspecified Actor Form:

VTA-4 t stem" – nawaswāt – chase him/her/it

1s	ē-kī-nawaswātikawiyān	1s	as I was chased
2s	ē-kī-nawaswātikawiyan	2s	as you were chased
3s	ē-kī-nawaswātiht	3s	as s/he/it was chased
3's	ē-kī-nawaswātimiht	3's	as his/her/its _____ was chased
1p	ē-kī-nawaswātikawiyāhk	1p	as we were chased (excl)
21	ē-kī-nawaswātikawiyahk	2	as we were chased (incl)
2p	ē-kī-nawaswātikawiyēk	2p	as you were chased
3p	ē-kī-nawaswātihcik	3p	as they were chased
3'p	ē-kī-nawaswātimiht	3'p	as their _____ were chased

Future Conditional of Unspecified Actor Form:

VTA-4 t stem – nawaswāt – chase him/her/it

1s	nawaswātikawiyāni	1s	if/when I am chased
2s	nawaswātikawiyani	2s	if/when you are chased
3s	nawaswātihci	3s	if/when s/he/it is chased
3's	nawaswātimihci	3's	if/when his/her/its _____ is chased
1p	nawaswātikawiyāhki	1p	if/when we are chased (excl)
21	nawaswātikawiyahki	21	if/when we are chased (incl)
2p	nawaswātikawiyēko	2p	if/when you are chased
3p	nawaswātihtwāwi	3p	if/when they are chased
3'p	nawaswātimihci	3'p	if/when their _____ are chased

Transitive Inanimate Verbs – Unspecified Actor

There is no independent mode for the Transitive Inanimate verb unspecified actor because once the suffix *"-ikatēw"* is attached to the VTI stem, the verb cannot be conjugated like other Transitive Inanimate verbs. However it can follow VII-2 paradigms where there are four Independent forms.

Here is how the verb stem and the suffix was put together.

VTI-1	suffix		unspecified actor – VII-2
wēpina +	-ikātēw	→	wēpinikātēw
(throw it away) +	(it is affected so)	→	It is thrown away.

For instance the VTI-1 *"wēpina – throw it away"* changes when this suffix is attached to it.

It will be conjugated here as a VII-2:

VTI – "*wēpina* – throw it away"

Independent Mode

wēpinikātēw	It is thrown away.
wēpinikātēwa	They are thrown away
wēpinikātēyiw	His/her/its ____ is thrown away
wēpinikātēyiwa	His/her/its ____ are thrown away

Conjunct Mode

ē-wēpinikātēk	as it is thrown away
ē-wēpinikātēki	as they are thrown away
ē-wēpinikātēyik	as his/her/its ____ is thrown away
ē-wēpinikātēyiki	as his/her/its ____ are thrown away

Future Conditional

wēpinikātēki	if/when it is thrown away
wēpinikātēkwāwi	if/when they are thrown away
wēpinikātēyiki	if/when his/her/its ____ is thrown away
wēpinikātēyikwāwi	if/when his/her/its ____ are thrown away

NOTE: For VTI-1stems the "-a" is dropped before adding the suffix "-*ikātēw*".

There are two changes that occur when the suffix "-*ikātēw*" is to be attached to VTI-1 stems: i) the "-*a*" is dropped from the stem. ii) the "*t*" on the stem is changed to a "*c*".

VTI-1	suffix	unspecified actor – VII-2
nitohta +	-ikātēw →	nitohcikātēw
(listen to it) +	(it is affected so) →	It is listened to

VTI – "*nitohta* – listen to it" "it" = an inanimate object.

Independent Mode

nitohcikātēw	It is listened to
nitohcikātēwa	They are listened to
nitohcikātēyiw	His/her/its ____ is listened to
nitohcikātēyiwa	His/her/its ____ are listened to

Conjunct Mode

ē-nitohcikātēk	as it is listened to
ē-nitohcikātēki	as they are listened to
ē-nitohcikātēyik	as his/her/its ____ is listened to
ē-nitohcikātēyiki	as his/her/its ____ are listened to

Future Conditional

nitohcikātēki	If/when it is listened to
nitohcikātēkwawi	If/when they are listened to
nitocikātēyiki	If/when his/her/its ____ is listened to
nitohcikātēyikwāwi	If/when his/her/its ____ are listened to

NOTE: With this stem the "-a" was dropped from the stem. The "-*t-*" is replaced by a "-*c-*" then the suffix "-*ikatēw*" is attached. For the Future conditional "-*ikātēw*" is attached to the stem similar to what was done for the Independent mode.

There is a common alternate form for the conjunct which cannot be conjugated. Here are some examples:

ē-wēpinamihk	as it is thrown away
ē-nohtamihk	as it is listened to
ē-nisitohtamihk	as it is understood

Chapter 29: Reflexive Forms

Animate Intransitive verbs

The reflexive forms of verb stems are derived by the addition of three distinct suffixes: *"-iso"*, *"-oso"*, and *"-āso"* to existing transitive verb stems. One such VTA-1 stem is *"wīcisimōm – dance with him/her"* which changes to *"wīcisimōmiso"* when one wants to say "Dance by/with yourself." Note the addition of *"-iso"* to the existing verb stem. With this change the verb stem is now an Animate Intransitive verb derived from a VTA and they follow the Animate Intransitive verb paradigms in Chart 1 in Appendix A.

Let's view the two imperative forms for the Reflexive form of verbs. The verb inflections are italicized so one can begin to see the suffixes needed to write or say the proper form of a verb.

The paradigm for Immediate Imperative is:

2 _____
2p _____ k
21 _____ tān

Immediate Imperative – VAI – *"asamiso – feed yourself"*

2	wīcisimōm*iso*	2 Dance by/with yourself.
2p	wīcisimōmiso*k*	2p Dance by/with yourselves(individually).
21	wīcisimōmiso*tān*	21 Let's dance by/with ourselves (individually).

For the Delayed Imperative the paradigm is:

2 _____ hkan
2p _____ hkēk
21 _____ hkahk

Delayed Imperative – VAI – *"wīcisimōmiso – dance with yourself"*

2	wīcisimōmiso*hkan*	2 Danceby/with yourself. (later).
2p	wīcisimōmiso*hkēk*	2p Dance by/with yourselves (individually) (later).
21	wīcisimōmiso*hkahk*	21 Let's dance by/with ourselves (individually) (later).

As was mentioned above there are three different verb stems that will reflect the idea of doing something for or to yourself. Each will be presented in the two Imperatives, Independent, Conjunct and in the Future Conditional form. The three special suffixes that will help to spot the reflexive form are: *"-iso"*; *"-āso"* and *"-oso"*. Except for the Future conditional form and the imperatives, the examples are conjugated in the past tense.

NOTE: Refer to chart 1 in Appendix A to review the VAI paradigms.

First there are those verb stems that end in *-iso*:

kisīpēkiniso	bathe/wash yourself
pāhpihiso	laugh at yourself
asamiso	feed yourself
wīcihiso	help yourself

One of these examples VAI – *"asamiso – feed yourself"* is conjugated here; in the two imperatives, the independent, conjunct, and future conditional form.

Immediate Imperative VAI – "asamiso – feed yourself"

2	asamiso	2 Feed yourself.
2p	asamisok	2p Feed yourselves.
21	asamisotān	21 Let's feed ourselves.

Delayed Imperative VAI – "asamiso – feed yourself"

2	asamisohkan	2 Feed yourself. (later)
2p	asamisohkēk	2p Feed yourselves. (individually later)
21	asamisohkahk	21 Let's feed ourselves. (individually later)

Independent mode VAI – "*asamiso* – feed yourself" (past tense)

1s	nikī-asamison	1s	I fed myself
2s	kikī-asamison	2s	you fed yourself
3s	kī-asamisow	3s	s/he/it fed himself/herself
3's	kī-asamisoyiwa	3's	his/her/its ____ fed himself/herself
1p	nikī-asamisonān	1p	we fed ourselves (excl)
21	kikī-asamisonaw	21	we fed ourselves (incl)
2p	kikī-asamisonāwāw	2p	you fed yourselves
3p	kī-asamisowak	3p	they fed themselves
3'p	kī-asamisoyiwa	3'p	their ____ fed themselves

Conjunct VAI – "*asamiso* – feed yourself" (past tense)

1s	ē-kī-asamisoyān	1s	as I fed myself
2s	ē-kī-asamisoyan	2s	as you fed yourself
3s	ē-kī-asamisot	3s	as s/he/it fed himself/herself
3's	ē-kī-asamisoyit	3's	as his/her/its ____ fed himself/herself
1p	ē-kī-asamisoyāhk	1p	as we fed ourselves (excl)
21	ē-kī-asamisoyahk	21	as we fed ourselves (incl)
2p	ē-kī-asamisoyēk	2p	as you fed yourselves
3p	ē-kī-asamisocik	3p	as they fed themselves
3'p	ē-kī-asamisoyit	3'p	as their ____ fed themselves

Future Conditional VAI – "*asamiso* – feed yourself"

1s	asamisoyāni	1s	if/when I feed myself
2s	asamisoyani	2s	if/when you feed yourself
3s	asamisoci	3s	if/when s/he feeds him/herself
3's	asamisoyici	3's	if/when his/her ____ feeds him/herself
1p	asamisoyāhki	1p	if/when we feed ourselves (excl)
21	asamisoyahko	21	if/when we feed ourselves (incl)
2p	asamisoyēko	2p	if/when you feed yourselves
3p	asamisotwawi	3p	if/when they feed themselves
3'p	asamisoyici	3'p	if/when their ____ feed themselves

Below are examples of the second set which end in "*–āso*":

atāwēstamāso	buy it for yourself	kīsisamāso	cook it for yourself
pētamāso	bring it for yourself	sāsisamāso	fry it for yourself
kiskinwahamāso	teach/educate yourself	itōtamāso	do it for yourself
kisīpēkinamāso	wash it for yourself		

Immediate Imperative VAI – "*kīsisamāso* – cook it for yourself"

2	kīsisamāso	2	cook it for yourself.
2p	kīsisamāsok	2p	cook it for yourselves
21	kīsisamāsotān	21	Let's cook it for ourselves

Delayed Imperative VAI – "*kīsisamāso* – cook it for yourself"

2	kīsisamāsohkan	2	Cook it for yourself. (later)
2p	kīsisamāsohkēk	2p	Cook it for yourselves. (individually later)
21	kīsisamāsohkahk	21	Let's cook it for ourselves. (individually later)

Independent Mode VAI – "*kīsisamāso* – cook it for yourself" (past tense)

1s	nikī- kīsisamāson	1s	I cooked it for myself.
2s	kikī-kīsisamāson	2s	you cooked it for yourself
3s	kī-kīsisamāsow	3s	s/he cooked it for himself/herself
3's	kī-kīsisamāsoyiwa	3's	his/her ____ cooked it for himself/herself

1p	nikī-kīsisamāsonān	1p	we cooked it for ourselves (excl)
21	kiki-kīsisamāsonaw	21	we cooked it for ourselves (incl)
2p	kiki-kīsisamāsonāwāw	2p	you cooked it for yourselves
3p	kī-kīsisamāsowak	3p	they cooked it for themselves
3'p	kī-kīsisamāsoyiwa	3'p	their ____ cooked it for themselves

Conjunct VAI – "kīsisamāso – cook it for yourself" (past tense)

1s	ē-kī-kīsisamāsoyān	1s	as I cooked it for myself
2s	ē- kī-kīsisamāsoyan	2s	as you cooked it for yourself
3s	ē- kī-kīsisamāsot	3s	as s/he cooked it for herself/himself
3's	ē- kī-kīsisamāsoyit	3's	as his/her ____ cooked it for herself/himself
1p	ē- kī-kīsisamāsoyāhk	1p	as we cooked it for ourselves (excl)
21	ē- kī-kīsisamāsoyahk	21	as we cooked it for ourselves (incl)
2p	ē- kī-kīsisamāsoyēk	2p	as you cooked it for yourselves
3p	ē- kī-kīsisamāsocik	3p	as they cooked it for themselves
3'p	ē- kī-kīsisamāsoyit	3'p	as their ____ cooked it for themselves

Future Conditional VAI – "kīsisamāso – cook it for yourself"

1s	kīsisamāsoyāni	1s	if/when I cook it for myself
2s	kīsisamāsoyani	2s	if/when you cook it for yourself
3s	kīsisamāsoci	3s	if/when s/he cooks it for yourself
3's	kīsisamāsoyici	3's	if/when his/her ____ cooks it for yourself
1p	kīsisamāsoyāhki	1p	if/when we cook it for ourselves (excl)
21	kīsisamāsoyahko	21	if/when we cook it for ourselves (incl)
2p	kīsisamāsoyēko	2p	if/when you cook it for yourself
3p	kīsisamāsotwawi	3p	if/when they cook it for themselves
3'p	kīsisamāsoyici	3'p	if/when their ____ cook it for themselves

Some VAI stems ending with "-oso" are:

pakamahoso hit yourself sīkahoso comb your hair wīsakahoso hurt yourself

Immediate Imperative VAI – "sīkahoso – comb your hair"

2	sīkahoso	2	comb your hair for yourself.
2p	sīkahosok	2p	comb your hair for yourselves.
21	sīkahosotān	21	Let's comb our hair for ourselves.

Delayed Imperative VAI – "sīkahoso – comb your hair"

2	sīkahosohkan	2	comb your hair for yourself. (later)
2p	sīkahosohkēk	2p	comb your hair foryourselves. (individually later)
21	sīkahosohkahk	21	Let's comb our hair for ourselves. (individually later)

Independent Mode VAI – "sīkahoso – comb your hair" (past tense)

1s	nikī-sīkahoson	1s	I combed my hair for myself
2s	kiki-sīkahoson	2s	you combed your hair for yourself
3s	kī-sīkahosow	3s	s/he/it combed his/her hair for himself/herself
3's	kī-sīkahosoyiwa	3's	his/her/its ____ combed his/her hair for himself/herself
1p	nikī-sīkahosonān	1p	we combed our hair for ourselves (excl)
21	kiki-sīkahosonaw	21	we combed our hair for ourselves (incl)
2p	kiki-sīkahosonāwāw	2p	you combed your hair for yourselves
3p	kī-sīkahosowak	3p	they combed their hair for themselves
3'p	kī-sīkahosoyiwa	3'p	their ____ combed their hair for themselves

Conjunct VAI – "sīkahoso – comb your hair" (past tense)

1s	ē-kī-sīkahosoyān	1s	as I combed my hair for myself
2s	ē-kī-sīkahosoyan	2s	as you combed your hair for yourself

3s	ē-kī-sīkahosot	3s	as s/he/it combed his/her hair for himself/herself
3's	ē-kī-sīkahosoyit	3's	as his/her/its _____ combed his/her hair for him/herself
1p	ē-kī-sīkahosoyāhk	1p	as we combed our hair for ourselves (excl)
21	ē-kī-sīkahosoyahk	21	as we combed our hair for ourselves (incl)
2p	ē-kī-sīkahosoyēk	2p	as you combed your hair for yourselves
3p	ē-kī-sīkahosocik	3p	as they combed their hair for themselves
3'p	ē-kī-sīkahosoyit	3'p	as their _____ combed their hair for themselves

Future Conditional VAI – "sīkahoso – comb your hair"

1s	sīkahosoyāni	1s	if/when I comb my hair for myself
2s	sīkahosoyani	2s	if/when you comb your hair for yourself
3s	sīkahosoci	3s	if/when s/he/it comb his/her hair for himself/herself
3's	sīkahosoyici	3's	if/when his/her _____ comb his/her hair for him/herself
1p	sīkahosoyāhki	1p	if/when we comb our hair for ourselves (excl)
21	sīkahosoyahko	21	if/when we comb our hair for ourselves (incl)
2p	sīkahosoyēko	2p	if/when you comb your hair for yourselves
3p	sīkahosotwawi	3p	if/when they comb their hair for themselves
3'p	sīkahosoyici	3'p	if/when their _____ comb their hair for themselves

NOTE: The three suffixes that will let you know that a verb is in the reflexive form are: "*iso*", "*oso*", and "*-āso*". If or when you hear these last suffixes especially in the Imperative form someone is telling someone to do something for himself or for herself; in the Independent mode someone, from 1s to 3'p, is expressing the fact they did something for themselves.

This reflexive form of verbs is common in both Cree and English. Examples are not hard to find; just consider the many scenarios that are played out in most homes every day of the week. Examples may be as simple as giving last minute instructions to children as one is leaving for work. For instance, "Make yourself a sandwich." Or when children are asking one another to get something and the replies that would invariably include, "Do it yourself!" or "Get it yourself!"

Chapter 30: Auxiliary Verb

"To Be" or not "To Be"

So far the English verb "to be" has been in the translations in many of the sample Cree sentences but its presence has not been explained or questioned. Consequently some non-speakers attempt to use the Cree verb *"ayā"* in much the same way as the verb "to be" is utilized in the English language. This chapter will show, through various examples, that the English verb "to be" is only matched by the Cree verb *"ayā"* in one instance, while different Cree constructions are needed for other uses of English "to be."

A review of the verb "to be" is necessary for clarity so it is conjugated in both Cree and English here.

person	Cree	person	English	person	Cree	person	English
1s	nitayān	1s	I **am**	1p	nitayānān	1p	We **are**
–	–	–	–	21	kitayānaw	21	We **are**
2s	kitayān	2s	You **are**	2p	kitayānāw	2p	You **are**
3s	ayāw	3s	S/he/it **is**	3p	ayāwak	3p	They **are**
3's	ayāyiwa	3's	His/her/its __ **is**	3'p	ayāyiwa	3'p	Their __ **is**/ **are**

It is important to know that these verbs are used differently in Cree and English expressions. English uses the verb "to be" in a number of different constructions which can indicate a location, express the state of being, or as an auxiliary verb.

• It is locative in nature when indicating the place at which someone or something is located or where an incident happened (as in the (1) examples below).

• It is referred to as a *"copular" or "equational" verb* when indicating a state of being in which case it is followed by either an adjective (as in the (2) examples)

• or a noun (in the (3) examples).

And it is an *"auxiliary" or "helping" verb* when it is used in conjunction with another verb (as in the (4) examples). As an English auxiliary it can be used with another verb to form the progressive construction.

Along with corresponding Cree constructions the following sentences show how the verb "to be" is used in English. It is important to note that the Cree verb *"ayā"* is used only in the locative sense. When a copular verb is needed in English, the Cree equivalent is not *"ayā"*, but rather the notion of "to be" is merely understood when Cree constructions use demonstrative pronouns or it is inherent in other Cree verbs. Furthermore, *"ayā"* is never used as an auxiliary verb in Cree.

1. Locative "to be" – *"ayā"*:

a) "Here I *am*!" he said as he came into sight there on the path.

"ōta ōma ē-*ayā*yān," itwēw ē-pē-sākēwēt anita mēskanāsihk.

b) Mary *was* here a minute ago.

anohcihkē piko ana ōta kī-ay-*ayā*w mēriy.

c) We *were* there but we did not see anyone.

ēkotē anima nikī-*ayā*nān māka mōy āwiyak nikī-wāpamānān.

d) They were there also.

wīstawāw aniki ēkota kī-*ayā*wak.

e) All who *were* there?

awīniki kahkiyaw ēkota ē-kī-*ayā*cik?

One will notice that in the Cree examples above *"ayā"* is used to talk about being at a location. However, the above usage of "to be" is only one way the English language uses this verb. In the following examples, "to be" is only visible in the English translation, while it is inherent in the Cree verbs.

2. Copular verb "to be" where it helps to describe a 'quality' or 'state' expressed by an English adjective.

"quality or state" – adjective	Verb "to be" is inherent.
a) Kevin *is* tall.	kinosiw Kevin.
b) Our relatives *are* patient.	niwāhkōmākaninānak sīpēyihtamwak.
c) Those gooseberries *are* green.	askihtakonākosiwak aniki sāpōminak.
d) All the people *were* angry.	kahkiyaw ayisiyiniwak kī-kisiwāsiwak.
e) That one *is* foolish	kakēpātisiw ana.
f) The dish *is* clean.	kanātan anima wiyākan.
g) The curtain *is* torn.	yāyikipitēw anima ākoyēkahikan.

Note that none of the inflections of *'ayā'* - "be" are visible in the construction of the Cree sentences above whereas the English sentences have the verb plus an adjective. In effect the Cree verbs are adjectival (e.g. "be angry," "be patient," "be torn," etc.).

3. Copular verb "to be" where *it equates* one entity (person, thing, etc.) with another, as expressed by an English noun.

a) That one *is* a fool.	okakēpātis wiya ēwako.
b) That one *is* a nurse.	maskihkīwiskwēwiw wiya ēwako. (or)
	maskihkīwiskwēw ana.
c) I *am* a singer.	onikamow ōma niya.

In the examples above one should note there are three forms in Cree, none of which use the verb *"ayā"*. In Cree "non-verbal predicates" such as *ēwako, ana* and *ōma* function as the English verb "be" and verbs and nouns which also include the action of the entity. Recall that *ēwako, ana* and *ōma* have been previously labelled as demonstrative pronouns.

Notice also that the Cree verb *"kakēpātisi"* in 2e) has been changed to a noun and is used with these non-verbal predicates.

Of course, the personal pronouns *"niya"* and *"wiya"* specify exactly who is being referred to.

4. Auxiliary verb "to be" is used when expressing a progressive or ongoing activity.

a) Our son John will *be* arriv*ing* this evening.

nikosisinān awa John otākosiki ē-wī-takosihk.

b) They *were* swimm*ing* all afternoon.

kapē aniki ē-kī-pakāsimocik kā-āpihtā-kīsikāyik.

c) We (incl) *are* review*ing* that proposal again today.

kihtwām kiwī-kanawāpahtēnānaw anima kakwēcihkēmowi-masinahikan anohc.

d) I *am* eat*ing* right now but I can be there shortly.

mēkwāc ōma ē-mīcisoyān māka wīpac ēkotē nika-kī-takosinin.

e) We *are* meeting my husband at the cafe.

mīcisowikamikohk awa niwīkimākan ē-wī-nakiskawāyāhk.

Although the progressive or "-ing" form of the verb is usually represented by the conjunct form of Cree verbs note that this is not a set rule. Example c) is in the Independent form and is acceptable.

To recap the English sentences:

- In 1 the verb "to be" is used to indicate location.

- In 2 the "copula" verb precedes the adjectives in the English sentences. In Cree the demonstrative pronouns are used like verbs.

- In e the verb is used to introduce a description of someone or something in the form of a noun.

- In 4 the "auxiliary" verb helps other verbs, but other forms of Cree verbs serve this function. Now a review of the Cree examples follows:

- In 1, there is no change for the verb "to be" in either language. The verb *"ayā"* is used to specify that one is at a location.

- In 2, the verb "to be" is an inherent part of Cree verbs and therefore not visible.

- In 3, either a noun or a non-verbal predicate in the form of a demonstrative pronoun or noun changed into a verb is used in place of *"ayā"*. The noun and the verb have a descriptive element which refers to the condition of the entity.

- In 4, except for c), the verbs are in the conjunct and the verb *"ayā"* is still not used.

NOTE: An interesting and useful observation, in some of the above sentences, is the use of the demonstrative pronouns. The demonstrative pronouns can be used to point out an object to explain, point out its location or define it; all without a verb. They are usually translated with the verb "to be." So English requires the verb but Cree does not.

Inanimate Intransitive Verbs and "to be"

The VII-1 and the VII-2 which refer to states or conditions such as weather, color of inanimate nouns, and seasons are another consideration when discussing the verb "to be." Although these have been discussed in other chapters, it is relevant and important to note that the English translations of the VII-1 terms contain the verb "to be." Here are some examples with the third person (neutral) *"is"* boldfaced.

kisināw	It **is** cold.		nīpin.	It **is** summer.
miyo-kīsikāw.	It **is** a nice day.		mihkwāw.	It **is** red.
nīso-kīsikāw	It **is** the second day/Tuesday.			

These examples and those in the next section should be considered when looking at the translation of verbs. As an example of the translation of Intransitive verbs consider the VAI *"mīciso – eat,"* presented here in both the Independent and the Conjunct mode.

Independent VAI "mīciso – eat"

1s	nimīcison.	I eat.
2s	kimīcison	You eat.
3s	mīcisow	S/he eats.
3s'	mīcisoyiwa	His/her ____ eats.
1p	nimīcisonān	We eat (excl).
21	kimīcisonaw	We eat (incl).
2p	kimīcisonāwāw	You eat.
3p	mīcisowak	They eat.
3'p	mīcisoyiwa	Their ____ eat.

The verb "to be" is not present in the Independent mode of Cree or in the English translation. But observe the translation of this same verb conjugated in the Conjunct mode. The verb "to be" is in the translation.

Conjunct VAI "mīciso – eat"

1s	ē-mīcisoyān	as I **am** eating.
2s	ē-mīcisoyan	as you **are** eating.
3s	ē-mīcisot	as s/he **is** eating.
3's	ē-mīcisoyit	as his/her ____ **is** eating.
1p	ē-mīcisoyāhk	as we (excl) **are** eating.
21	ē-mīcisoyahk	as we (incl) **are** eating.

2p	ē-mīcisoyēk	as you (pl) **are** eating.
3p	ē-mīcisocik	as they **are** eating.
3'p	ē-mīcisoyit	as their _____ **are** eating.

Although *"ayā"* is not visible in the spelling of Cree, "be" is required in the English translation. So even if it is not visible the previous examples show that *"ayā"* has its use in the Cree language but should not be equated with all the uses of "be" in the English language.

Chapter 31: Possession

Animate and Inanimate Nouns

It is important to know what is meant by dependent and independent when discussing animate or inanimate nouns. In this chapter each category is dealt with separately. In addition to the information on dependent and independent nouns a section is devoted to kinship terms in their possessed forms.

Nouns like verbs can be conjugated so it should not be too complicated an idea to understand who owns what or indeed, how many. But the word "declension" will be used, instead of conjugation, to describe this process.

Independent Nouns

An Independent noun, inanimate or animate, is one which makes sense on its own, without prefixes or suffixes. Nouns such as *awāsis* – a child, *masinahikan* – a book, and *okimāhkān* – a chief are examples.

To show possession of *Independent nouns* prefixes *"ni-"*, *"ki-"*, *"o-"* are attached to the beginning of nouns. These are used for two reasons: a) to show that they belong to someone; b) to specify who owns them.

Declension of Independent Nouns

Recall in the verb conjugation paradigms that: *"ni-"* is only for 1s or I; 1p or we; *"ki-"*, is for 2s or you (sg); 21 or we; and 2p or you (pl). This same idea is applied to specify who the owner is when talking about possession but now:

1s	ni ____		=	my ____ .
1p	ni ____		=	our (excl) ____ .
2s	ki ____	n	=	your ____
21	ki ____	naw	=	our (incl) ____ .
2p	ki ____	niwāw	=	your ____ .

To show that 3s, 3's, 3p, 3'p owns an inanimate noun a special prefix *"o-"* is attached to the inanimate nouns in the examples.

3s	o ____	n	=	his/her/its ____ .
3's	o ____	yiw	=	his/her/its ____ ____ .
3p	o ____	niwāw	=	their ____ .
3'p	o ____	yiw	=	their ____ ____ .

To put all of this in a format that we have been using for the conjugation here is a paradigm for the declension of possession of a singular object:

1s	ni ____		1s	My ____	
2s	ki ____		2s	Your ____	
3s	o ____		3s	His/her/its ____	
3's	o ____	iyiw	3's	His/her/its ____ ____	
1p	ni ____	inān	1p	Our ____ (excl)	
21	ki ____	naw	21	Our ____ (incl)	
2p	ki ____	iwāw	2p	Your ____	
3p	o ____	wāw	3p	Their ____	
3'p	o ____	yiw	3'p	Their ____ ____	

The plural suffix *"-a"* is needed for inanimate plural nouns.

1s	ni ____ a	1s	My ____
2s	ki ____ a	2s	Your ____
3s	o ____ a	3s	His/her/its ____

3's o _____ iyiw<u>a</u>   3's His/her/its _____ _____
1p ni _____ inān<u>a</u>   1p Our _____ (excl)
21 ki _____ inaw<u>a</u>   21 Our _____ (incl)
2p ki _____ iwāw<u>a</u>   2p Your _____
3p o _____ wāw<u>a</u>   3p Their _____
3'p o _____ yiw<u>a</u>   3'p Their _____ _____

Independent Inanimate Nouns

i) Example: Inanimate Noun (singular) "maskisin" – a shoe:

1s nimaskisin   my shoe
2s kimaskisin   your shoe
3s omaskisin   his/her/its shoe
3's omaskisiniyiw   his/her/its _____ 's shoe
1p nimaskisininān   our shoe (excl)
21 kimaskisininaw   our shoe (incl)
2p kimaskisiniwāw   your shoe
3p omaskisiniwāw   their shoe
3'p omaskisiniyiw   their _____ 's shoe

NOTE: On the plural side "shoe" should be pluralized because "we," "you (pl)," and "they" cannot collectively own one shoe. But for this example of how possession works for only one object we just pretend these persons own a shoe collectively.

Now this next example shows the declension when everyone owns more than one shoe!

ii) Example: Inanimate Noun (plural) "maskisin" – a shoe

1s nimaskisin<u>a</u>   my shoes
2s kimaskisin<u>a</u>   your shoes
3s omaskisin<u>a</u>   his/her/its shoes
3's omaskisiniyiw<u>a</u>   his/her/its _____ 's shoes
1p nimaskisininān<u>a</u>   our shoes (excl)
21 kimaskisininaw<u>a</u>   our shoes (incl)
2p kimaskisiniwāw<u>a</u>   your shoes
3p omaskisinisniwāw<u>a</u>   their shoes
3'p omaskisiniyiw<u>a</u>   their _____ 's shoes

Remember an *"-a"* is added onto inanimate nouns to pluralize them. In the example above the *"-a"* is attached to the noun *only* in 1s, 2s. For 1p, 21, 2p, 3p the plural suffix is attached to the very end of the suffix and *not on the noun*. This suffix is underlined for emphasis only.

Independent Animate Nouns

Animate nouns owned by 3s, 3's, 3p and 3'p will always have only an *"-a"* suffix whether or not the noun is singular or plural. The examples below have this *"-a"* for the third persons. An explanation will follow the declension of the plural noun.

i) Example: Animate Noun (singular) "asikan – a sock/stocking"

1s nitasikan   my sock
2s kitasikan   your sock
3s otasikana   his/her/its sock
3's otasikaniyiwa   his/her/its _____ 's sock
1p nitasikaninān   our sock (excl)
21 kitasikaninaw   our sock (incl)
2p kitasikaniwāw   your sock
3p otasikaniwāwa   their sock
3'p otasikaniyiwa   their _____ 's sock

NOTE: As with the vowel initial verb stems nouns that begin with a vowel will require the connective *"-t-"* when placed in the declension paradigm.

ii) Example: Animate Noun (plural) "asikan – a sock/stocking"

1s	nitasikanak	my socks
2s	kitasikanak	your socks
3s	otasikana	his/her/its socks
3's	otasikaniyiwa	his/her/its _____ 's socks
1p	nitasikaninānak	our socks (excl)
21	kitasikaninawak	our socks (incl)
2p	kitasikaniwāwak	your socks
3p	otasikaniwāwa	their socks
3'p	otāsikaniyiwa	their _____ 's socks

Recall: Whether animate nouns are Independent or Dependent the plural suffix is *"-ak"*. *Exceptions* are for the 3s, 3's, 3p', 3'p; they use only the suffix *"-a"*. This suffix denotes the obviative form of nouns but it does not specify whether the noun is singular or plural. That is determined through context.

Other Possessive Suffixes

In addition to the prefixes introduced, in the declensions thus far, there is a special suffix *"-im"* applied to some nouns. Here is one example:

i) Example: Animate Noun (singular) " pahkwēsikan – bannock"

1s	nipahkwēsikanim	my bannock
2s	kipahkwēsikanim	your bannock
3s	opahkwēsikanima	his/her/its bannock
3's	opahkwēsikanimiyiwa	his/her/its _____ 's bannock
1p	nipahkwēsikaniminān	our bannock (excl)
21	kipahkwēsikaniminaw	our bannock (incl)
2p	kipahkwēsikanimiwāw	your bannock
3p	opahkwēsikanimiwāwa	their bannock
3'p	opahkwēsikanimiyiwa	their_____ 's bannock

NOTE: Here is what happened to the noun: the possessive prefixes were attached to the noun; the special suffix *"-im"* was attached to the *end* of the *noun* for 1s through to 3'p; then from 3s, 1p, 21, 2p, 3p, 3'p the regular declension suffix was then attached onto the *"-im"* suffix.

ii) Example: Animate Noun (plural) "pahkwēsikan – bannock"

1s	nipahkwēsikanimak	my bannock
2s	kipahkwēsikanimak	your bannock
3s	opahkwēsikanima	his/her/its bannock
3's	opahkwēsikanimiyiwa	his/her/its_____ 's bannock
1p	nipahkwēsikaniminānak	our bannock (excl)
21	kipahkwēsikaniminawak	our bannock (incl)
2p	kipahkwēsikanimiwāwak	your bannock
3p	opahkwēsikanimiwāwa	their bannock
3'p	opahkwēsikanimiyiwa	their _____ 's bannock

NOTE: Here is what happened to the noun:the possessive prefixes were attached to the noun; the special suffix *"-im"* was attached to the *end* of the *noun* for 1s through to 3'p; from 3s, 1p, 21, 2p, 3p'p the regular declension suffix was then attached onto the *"-im"* suffix; then the animate noun plural suffix was attached. The Independent Inanimate noun *"wiyās – meat"* would have this suffix.

Another special suffix is found in nouns that have a "*-kw*" stem. Such words include:

amiskw – a beaver   wāposw – a rabbit
mistikw – a stick   askihkw – a pail
mahkahkw – a tub or barrel.

i) Example: Animate Noun (singular) "wāpos – a rabbit"

1s	niwāposom	my rabbit
2s	kiwāposom	your rabbit
3s	owāposoma	his/her/its rabbit
3's	owāposomiyiwa	his/her/its _____'s rabbit
1p	niwāposominān	our rabbit (excl)
21	kiwāposominaw	our rabbit (incl)
2p	kiwāposomiwāw	your rabbit
3p	owāposomiwāwa	their rabbit
3'p	owāposomiyiwa	their _____'s rabbit

NOTE: Here is what happened to the noun: the possessive prefixes were attached to the noun; the special suffix "*-om*" was attached to the *end* of the *noun* for 1s through to 3'p; from 3s, 1p, 21, 2p, 3p, 3'p the regular declension suffix was then attached onto the "*-om*" suffix.

ii) Example: Animate Noun (plural) "wāpos – rabbit"

1s	niwāposomak	my rabbits
2s	kiwāposomak	your rabbits
3s	owāposoma	his/her/its rabbits
3's	owāposomiyiwa	his/her/its _____'s rabbits
1p	niwāposominānak	our rabbits (excl)
21	kiwāposominawak	our rabbits (incl)
2p	kiwāposomiwāwak	your rabbits
3p	owāposomiwāwa	their rabbits
3'p	owāposomiyiwa	their _____'s rabbits

NOTE: Here is what happened to the noun: the possessive prefixes were attached to the noun; the special suffix "*-om*" was attached to the *end* of the *noun* for 1s through to 3'p; from 3s, 1p, 21, 2p, 3p'p the regular declension suffix was then attached onto the "*-om*" suffix' then the animate noun plural suffix "*ak*" was attached.

Animate nouns with initial "*o-*" and "*Vw*" stems undergo certain changes when referring to them as possessed nouns/objects. One such noun is the word for chief/leader – *okimāw* used in the following example.

i) Example: Animate Noun (singular) "okimāw – a chief/leader"

1s	nitōkimām	my chief
2s	kitōkimām	your chief
3s	otōkimāma	his/her chief
3's	otōkimāmiyiwa	his/her _____'s chief
1p	nitōkimāminān	our chief
21	kitōkimāminaw	our chief
2p	kitōkimāmiwāw	your chief
3p	otōkimāmiwāwa	their chief
3'p	otōkimāmiyiwa	their _____'s chief

NOTE: This is what happened to the noun: connective "*-t-*" rule was applied; the initial "*o-*" changes to "*ō-*"; "*-w*" was dropped and the "*m*" was added.

Although these next examples do not have an initial *"o"* stem they do follow the "Vw" paradigm above.

iskwēw – a woman   →   nitiskwēm – my woman

nāpēw – a man   →   nināpēm – my husband (my man).

But the "-w" is replaced with an *"-m"*.

ii) Example: Animate Noun (plural) "okimāw – a chief/leader"

1s	nitōkimāmak	my chiefs
2s	kitōkimāmak	your chiefs
3s	otōkimāma	his/her chiefs
3's	otōkimāmiyiwa	his/her _____ 's chiefs
1p	nitōkimāminānak	our chiefs
21	kitōkimāminawak	our chiefs
2p	kitōkimāmiwāwak	your chiefs
3p	otōkimāmiwāwa	their chiefs
3'p	otōkimāmiyiwa	their _____ 's chiefs

The plural suffix *"-ak"* is added to the singular possessed form of the nouns.

Dependent Nouns

Dependent nouns are exactly that; they are dependent on prefixes to make sense. These prefixes cannot be detached from the words because if they were the words would not have meaning. Both Inanimate and Animate nouns can occur as Dependent nouns. A more detailed explanation follows below.

Declension of Dependent Nouns

The same declension processes used in the previous section can be applied to dependent inanimate nouns.

Some dependent nouns can be identified by the initial consonant *"m-"* as in the words *mīpit* and *maniway*. When dependent nouns beginning with this initial consonant are declined this consonant is replaced by *"n-"*, *"k-"*, or *"w-"*. Observe the declension paradigm below.

NOTE: In the paradigms used previously it was noted that: *"ni-"* is for 1s, and 1p. *"ki-"*, is for 2s, 21 and 2p. This same idea applies to determine the owner when speaking of possession *except* that the *"i"* is *not* used so now:

1s	n _____	1p	n _____inān (excl)
		21	k _____inaw (incl)
2s	k _____	2p	k _____iwāw
3s	w _____	3p	w _____iwāw
3's	w _____iyiw	3'p	w _____iyiw

Nouns such as *"mīpit* – a tooth," *"mahkwan* – a heel" are dependent inanimate nouns and will therefore require the *special* prefix "w-" on the 3s, 3's, 3p' 3'p. There are some nouns which will have an *"o-"* possessive prefix for 3s, 3's, 3p' 3'p. Most dependent inanimate nouns are either body parts or clothing. Here is an example of how the noun *"mīpit* – a tooth" is declined. Remember the *"m"* is not used and *"w"* is required for 3s, 3's, 3p, 3'p.

i) Example: Dependent Inanimate noun (singular) "mīpit – a tooth"

1s	nīpit	my tooth
2s	kīpit	your tooth
3s	wīpit	his/her/its tooth
3's	wīpitiyiw	his/her/its _____ tooth
1p	nīpitinān	our tooth
21	kīpitinaw	our tooth
2p	kīpitiwāw	your tooth

| 3p | wīpitiwāw | their tooth |
| 3'p | wīpitiyiw | their _____'s tooth |

NOTE: On the plural side "tooth" should be pluralized because "we," "you (pl)," and "they" cannot collectively own one tooth. But for this example of how possession works for only one object just pretend these persons own a "tooth" collectively perhaps a dinosaur tooth.

ii) Example: Dependent Inanimate Noun (plural) "mīpita – teeth"

1s	nīpita	my teeth
2s	kīpita	your teeth
3s	wīpita	his/her/its teeth
3's	wīpitiyiwa	his/her/its _____ teeth
1p	nīpitināna (excl)	our teeth
21	kīpitinawa (incl)	our teeth
2p	kīpitiwāwa	your teeth
3p	wīpitiwāwa	their teeth
3'p	wīpitiyiwa	their _____'s teeth

The changes which occurred are: the prefixes *"n-"*, *"k-"* are retained; but a *"w-"* is used for the 3s, 3's, 3p, 3'p; the stem *"-ipit"* was inserted in the paradigm; no suffixes are added to the noun for 1s, 2s, 3s; the suffix for 3's, 3'p is *"-iyiw"* for Inanimate possessive obviative; the 1p, 21, 2p, 3p suffixes remain as *"-inān"*, *"-inaw"*, *"-iwāw"* and *"-iwāw"*.

Plural suffix: "-a" is attached to the noun in 1s, 2s, 3s; "-a" is attached to the suffixes in 1p, 21, 2p, 3p, 3's, 3'p.

i) Example: Dependent Inanimate Noun (singular) "mīkiwāhp – a home→ nīki"

This is definitely a different word which maybe from the word *mīkiwāhp* as opposed to *wāskahikan* – a house but is a dependent noun.

1s	nīki	my home
2s	kīki	your home
3s	wīki	his/her home
3's	wīkiyiw	his/her _____'s home
1p	nīkinān	our home
21	kīkinaw	our home
2p	nīkiwāw	your home
3p	wīkiwāw	their home
3'p	wīkiyiw	their _____'s home

The changes which occurred are: the prefixes *"n-"*, *"k-"* are retained; but a *"w-"* is used for the 3s, 3's, 3p, 3'p; the stem *"-īk-"* was inserted in the paradigm; the suffixes are different for 1s, 2s, 3s, – it is only an *"-i"*; the suffix for 3's, 3'p is *"-iyiw"* for Inanimate possessive obviative; the 1p, 21, 2p 3p suffixes remain as *"-inān"*, *"-inaw"*, *"-iwāw"*; and *"-iwāw"*.

NOTE: This word does not have a plural form.

i) "mahkwan" – a heel is another Dependent Inanimate noun that follows this paradigm.

1s	nahkwan	my heel
2s	kahkwan	your heel
3s	wahkwan	his/her heel
3's	wahkwaniyiw	his _____'s heel
1p	nahkwaninān	our heel
21	kahkwaninaw	our heel
2p	kahkwaniwāw	your heel
3p	wahkwaniwāw	their heel
3'p	wahkwaniyiw	their _____'s heel

ii) Example: Dependent Inanimate Noun (plural) "mahkwana – a heel"

1s	nahkwana	my heels
2s	kahkwana	your heels
3s	wahkwana	his/her heels
3's	wahkwaniyiwa	his _____'s heels
1p	nahkwanināna	our heels (excl)
21	kahkwaninawa	our heels (incl)
2p	kahkwaniwāwa	your heels
3p	wahkwaniwāwa	their heels
3'p	wahkwaniyiwa	their _____'s heels

The changes which occurred are: a *"w-"* is used for the 3s, 3's, 3p, 3'p to show 3rd person possession; the stem *"-ahkwan"* was inserted in the paradigm; no suffixes added to noun for 1s, 2s, 3s; the suffix for 3's, 3'p is *"-iyiw"* for Inanimate possessive obviative; the 1p, 21, 2p 3p suffixes remain as *"-inān", "-inaw", "-iwāw"*; and *"-iwāw"*.

Plural suffix: "-a" is attached to the noun in 1s, 2s, 3s; "-a" is attached to the suffixes in 1p, 21, 2p, 3p, 3's, 3'p.

i) Example: Dependent Inanimate Noun (singular) "mispiton – an arm"

1s	nispiton	my arm
2s	kispiton	your arm
3s	ospiton	his/her/its arm
3's	ospitoniyiw	his/her/its _____ arm
1p	nispitoninān	our arm (excl)
21	kispitonāninaw	our arm (incl)
2p	kispitoniwāw	your arm
3p	ospitoniwāw	their arm
3'p	ospitoniyiw	their _____'s arm

ii) Example: Dependent Inanimate Noun (plural) "mispitona – arms"

1s	nispitona	my arms
2s	kispitona	your arms
3s	ospitona	his/her/its arms
3's	ospitoniyiwa	his/her/its _____ arms
1p	nispitonināna	our arms (excl)
21	kispitoninawa	our arms (incl)
2p	kispitoniwāwa	your arms
3p	ospitoniwāwa	their arms
3'p	ospitoniyiwa	their _____'s arms

The changes which occurred are: the prefixes are *"ni-", "ki-"*; but an **"o-"** is used for the 3s, 3's, 3p, 3'p; the stem *"-spiton"* was inserted in the paradigm; no suffixes are added to the noun for 1s, 2s, 3s; the suffix for 3's, 3'p is *"-iyiw"* for Inanimate possessive obviative; the 1p, 21, 2p 3p suffixes remain as *"inān", "-inaw", "-iwāw"*; and *"-iwāw"*.

Plural suffix: "-a" is attached to the noun in 1s, 2s, 3s; "-a" is attached to the suffixes in 1p, 21, 2p, 3p, 3's, 3'p.

5a) This Dependent *Animate* noun begins with *"mi-"* and it also follows the same paradigm as those that begin with *"mī-"*. In addition the 3s, 3's, 3p, 3'p use the possessive prefix **"o-"**. It will have singular and plural paradigms.

Example: Dependent Animate Noun (Singular) "mitās – a pair of pants"

1s	nitās	my pants
2s	kitās	your pants

3s	otāsa	his/her/its pants
3's	otāsiyiwa	his/her/its _____ pants
1p	nitāsinān	our pants (excl)
21	kitāsinaw	our pants (incl)
2p	kitāsiwāw	your pants
3p	otāsiwāwa	their pants
3'p	otāsiyiwa	their _____'s pants

ii) Example: Dependent Animate Noun (plural) "mitās – more than one pair of pants"

1s	nitāsak	my pants
2s	kitāsak	your pants
3s	otāsa	his/her/its pants
3's	otāsiyiwa	his/her/its _____ pants
1p	nitāsinānak	our pants (excl)
21	kitāsinawak	our pants (incl)
2p	kitāsiwāwak	your pants
3p	otāsiwāwa	their pants
3'p	otāsiyiwa	their _____'s pants

There are also these forms that have an entirely different form to indicate possession: For instance: i) dog – *atim*→ my dog – *nitēm.* However they can be declined with the possessive paradigm too.

i) Example: Dependent Animate Noun (singular) "atim" – a dog → nitēm

1s	nitēm	my dog
2s	kitēm	your dog
3s	otēma	his/her dog
3's	otēmiyiwa	his/her _____'s dog
1p	nitēminān	our dog (excl)
21	kitēminaw	our dog (incl)
2p	kitēmiwāw	your dog
3p	otēmiwāwa	their dog
3'p	otēmiyiwa	their _____'s dog

ii) Example: Dependent Animate Noun (plural) "atim" – a dog → nitēm

1s	nitēmak	my dogs
2s	kitēmak	your dogs
3s	otēma	his/her dogs
3's	otēmiyiwa	his/her _____'s dogs
1p	nitēminānak	our dogs (excl)
21	kitēminawak	our dogs (incl)
2p	kitēmiwāwak	your dogs
3p	otēmiwāwa	their dogs
3'p	otēmiyiwa	their _____'s dogs

The changes which occurred are: the prefixes *"ni-", "ki-"* are retained; but an *"o-"* is used for the 3s, 3's, 3p, 3'p; the stem *"-tēm"* was inserted in the paradigm; there is no suffix 1s, 2s in the singular; the suffix for 3s is an *"-a"*; for 3's and 3'p it is *"-yiwa"*; the suffix for 3p *"-iwāwa"*; the 1p, 21, 2p, 3p suffixes remain as *"-inān", "-inaw", "-iwāw"*; and *"-iwāw"*.

Kinship Terms – Dependent Nouns

Perhaps the most common dependent nouns are those that refer to relatives, the kinship terms. These terms are quite precise so that one can differentiate whether relatives are from the mother's or father's side of the family: that is *maternal* and *paternal* genealogy.

The possessive prefixes mentioned above, are the same prefixes used in the verb conjugation charts that have already been introduced with the verbs. But there is an additional prefix *"o-"* to show possession by 3s, 3's, 3p, 3'p.

Here are examples of kinship terms in the format that is used in the declension of nouns. Some terms may differ from region to region or from one dialect to another.

NOTE: ni- = my

	ni- = our (excl)
	ki- = our (incl)
ki- = your (sg)	ki- = your (pl)
o- = his/her	o- = their
o- = his/her ____'s	o- = his/her/their ____'s

1s	ni ____ n	1s	My ____
2s	ki ____ n	2s	Your ____
3s	o ____ n	3s	His/her/its ____
3's	o ____ iyiw	3's	His/her/its ____ ____
1p	ni ____ inān	1p	Our ____ (excl)
21	ki ____ naw	21	Our ____ (incl)
2p	ki ____ iwāw	2p	Your ____
3p	o ____ wāw	3p	Their ____
3'p	o ____ yiw	3'p	Their ____ ____

The plural suffix *"-a"* is needed for inanimate plural nouns and *"ak"* for animat nouns.

1s	ni ____ na	1s	My ____
2s	ki ____ na	2s	Your . ____
3s	o ____ na	3s	His/her/its ____
3's	o ____ iyiwa	3's	His/her/its ____ ____
1p	ni ____ ināna	1p	Our ____ (excl)
21	ki ____ inawa	21	Our ____ (incl)
2p	ki ____ iwāwa	2p	Your ____
3p	o ____ wāwa	3p	Their ____
3'p	o ____ yiwa	3'p	Their ____ ____

okāwīmāw – a mother

1s nikāwiy
   my mother
2s kikāwiy
   your mother
3s okāwiya
   his/her mother
3's okāwīyiwa
   his ____'s mother
1p nikāwīnān
   our mother
21 kikāwīnaw
   our mother
2p kikāwīwāw
   your mother
3p okāwīwāwa
   their mother
3'p okāwīyiwa
   their ____'s mother

otānisimāw – a daughter

1s nitānis
   my daughter
2s kitānis
   your daughter
3s otānisa
   his/her daughter
3's otānisiyiwa
   his/her ____'s daughter
1p nitānisinān
   our daughter (excl)
21 kitānisinaw
   our daughter (incl)
2p kitānisiwāw
   your daughter
3p tānisiwāwa
   their daughter
3'p otānisiyiwa
   their ____'s daughter

son – okosisimāw

1s nikosis
my son

2s kikosis
your son

3s okosisa
his/her son

3's okosisiyiwa
his/her _____'s son

1p nikosisinān
our son

21 kikosisinaw
our son

2p kikosisiwāw
your son

3p okosisiwāwa
their son

3'p okosisiyiwa
their _____'s son

father – ōhtāwīmāw

1s nōhtāwiy
my father

2s kōhtāwiy
your father

3s ōhtāwiya
his/her father

3's ōhtāwīyiwa
his/her _____'s father

1p nōhtāwīnān
our father

21 kōhtāwīnaw
our father

2p kōhtāwīwāw
your father

3p ōhtāwīwāwa
their father

3'p ōhtāwīyiwa
their _____'s father

younger sister/brother – osīmimāw

1s nisīmis
my younger sibling

2 kisīmis
your younger sibling

3s osīmisa
his/her younger sibling

3's osīmisiyiwa
his _____'s younger sibling

my man (husband)

1s nināpēm
my husband

2s kināpēm
your husband

3s onāpēma
her husband

3's onāpēmiyiwa
his/her _____'s husband

1p nināpēminānak
our husbands (excl)

21 kināpēminawak
our husbands (incl)

2p kināpēmiwāwak
your husbands

3p onāpēmiwāwa
their husbands

3'p onāpēmiyiwa
their _____'s husbands

spouse – wīkimākan

1s niwīkimākan
my spouse

2s kiwīkimākan
your spouse

3s owīkimākana
his/her spouse

3's owīkimākaniyiwa
his/her _____'s spouse

1p niwīkimākaninānak
our spouses (excl)

21 kiwīkimākaninawak
our spouses (incl)

2p kiwīkimākaniwāwak
your spouses

3p owīkimākaniwāwa
their spouses

3'p owīkimākaniyiwa
their _____'s spouses

older brother – ostēsimāw

1s nistēs
my older brother

2s kistēs
your older brother

3s ostēsa
his/her older brother

3's ostēsiyiwa
his/her _____'s older brother

1p nisīmisinān
     our younger sibling
21 kisīmisinaw
     our younger sibling
2p kisīmisiwāw
     your younger sibling
3p osīmisiwāwa
     their younger sibling
3'p osīmisiyiwa
     their ___ 's younger sibling

older sister – omisimāw
1s nimis
     my older sister
2s kimis
     your older sister
3s omisa
     his/her older sister
3's omisiyiwa
     his/her ___ 's older sister
1p nimisinān
     our older sister
21 kimisinaw
     our older sister
2p kimisiwāw
     your older sister
3p omisiwāwa
     their older sister
3'p omisiyiwa
     their ___ 's older sister

grandmother – ōhkomimāw
1s nōhkom
     my grandmother
2s kōhkom
     your grandmother
3s ōhkoma
     his/her grandmother
3's ōhkomiyiwa
     his/her ___ 's grandmother
1p nōhkominān
     our grandmother
21 kōhkominaw
     our grandmother
2p kōhkomiwāw
     your grandmother
3p ōhkomiwāwa
     their grandmother
3'p ōhkomiyiwa
     their ___ 's grandmother

1p nistēsinān
     our older brother (excl)
21 kistēsinaw
     our older brother (incl)
2p kistēsiwāw
     your older brother
3p ostēsiwāwa
     their older brother
3'p ostēsiyiwa
     their ___ 's older brother

sister or brother
1s nītisān
     my sibling
2s kītisān
     your sibling
3s wītisāna
     his/her sibling
3's wītisāniyiwa
     his/her ___ 's sibling
1p nītisāninān
     our sibling (excl)
21 kītisāninaw
     our sibling (incl)
2p kītisāniwāw
     your sibling
3p wītisāniwāwa
     their sibling
3'p wītisāniyiwa
     their ___ 's sibling

grandfather – omosōmimāw
1s nimosōm
     my grandfather
2s kimosōm
     grandfather
3s omosōma
     grandfather
3's omosōmiyiwa
     his/her ___ grandfather
1p nimosōminān
     our grandfather (excl)
21 kimosōminaw
     our grandfather (incl)
2p kimosōmiwāw
     your grandfather
3p omosōmiwāwa
     their grandfather
3'p omosōmiyiwa
     their ___ 's grandfather

The terms in the following list can also be written in the same format as those above but it is left to the reader to practice writing them in the same format:

my aunt (mother's sister)	nikāwīs
my uncle (mother's brother)	nisis (also father-in-law)
my aunt (father's sister)	nisikos (also mother-in-law)
my uncle (father's brother)	nohcāwis
my cousin	*niciwām, niciwāmis
my cousin	nistēs, nisīmis (father's brother's sons)
my cousin	nimis, nistēs (father's brother's daughters)
my cousin	*nīstāw, nīscās (also brother-in-law) if you are male
my cousin	*nītim, nīcimos (mother's brother's sons) if you are female
my cousin	*nicāhkos (also sister-in-law)
my grandchild	nōsisim (both male or female)

The meaning and usage of a couple of the forms above have changed over the years. This is epecially true in northern communities:

nikāwīs – my maternal aunt is now applied to "my godmother"

nohcāwis – my paternal uncle is applied to "my godfather."

There is a unique Cree term used in Cree society to refer to or to address the parents of a daughter- or son-in-law. There is no commonly used term for this in English but "co-in-law" may suffice for the term "*nitihtāwāw* – my co-in-law." Both sets of parents use this word when speaking of or talking to their "co-in-law." In conversation others can refer to "*kitihtāwāw* – your co-in-law."

Chapter 32: Conjunct Mode and Relative Clauses

The first brief discussion in this chapter will be on the Conjunct mode which is sometimes referred to as the Subjunctive mode. Next the relative clause which is also a subordinate clause will be presented.

Conjunct Forms in Cree

Changing the name from Subjunctive to Conjunct mode does not necessarily take away the confusion that this form has presented. It is rather confusing for a number of reasons:

a) The translation of the conjugated form has caused others to take that as the only way to translate the verbs. e.g.: as I am eating.

b) The translated verbs end in "ing." Combined with the information above the verb form results in this awkward format. e.g.: as I am eating.

c) Translations quite often do not use "as."

d) This form is often but not always a subordinate clause.

e) Explanations about when to use this mode are not clear.

In this book the translation of the conjugated verbs were and still are translated with "as ____" in all the persons in the paradigms *only as an example* and *as a hint* that it can introduce a subordinate clause. Actually "as" can be replaced by other terms depending on the context. It is most important that translations use the proper term to reflect the context of what is being said.

Examples may help to see how this mode is used. They will also show that in some contexts the conjunct form of a verb is a principal clause (P) rather than a subordinate clause (S).

1a) ē-wī-āpacihtāyan cī mōhkomān?
     Are you going to use a knife? (P)

1b) ē-wī-āpacihtāyan cī ōma mōhkomān?
     Are you going to use this knife? (P)

1c) mōhkomān ōma ē-wī-āpacihtāyān.
     (It is that –) I am going to use this knife.
     It's a knife that I am going to use. (S)

1d) ēwako ōma mōhkomān <u>kā</u>-wī-āpacihtāyān.
     This is the knife *that* I am going to use. (S)

2a) niwī-ati-kīwānān ēkwa ē-pē-māyinākwahk ōma. (S)
     We are going home now; it is looking like it is going to storm.
     We are on our way home now as it looks like it's going to storm.

2b) ē-pē-māyinākwahk ōma ēkosi niwi-ati-kīwānān ēkwa. (P)
     It is looking like it is going to storm so we are on our way home.
     (*As it is/since* it is looking like it is going to storm we are on our way home.)

2c) niwī-ati-kīwānān ēkwa *ayisk* ē-pē-māyinākwahk. (S)
     We are on our way home *because* it looks like it is going to storm.
     (We are on our way home *because it is* looking like it is going to storm.)

3a) *ē-māyimahcihot* awa. (P)
     This one is feeling ill.
     (This is information referring to somebody's state of health at that moment.)

3b) ē-māyimahcihot awa ēkosi āhkosiwikamikohk niwī-itohtahāw. (P)
     This one is feeling ill so I am going to take him/her to the hospital

3c) *ē-māyimahcihot* ōma awa *ēkosi* āhkosiwikamikohk niwī-itohtahāw. (P)
     (*This is the situation*) s/he (*this one*) is feeling ill so I am taking him/her to the hospital.

3d)   ē-māyimahcihot ōma ēkosi āhkosiwikamikohk niwī-itohtahāw. (P)
        (*This is the situation*) s/he is feeling ill so I am taking him/her to the hospital.

3e)   āhkosiwikamikohk awa niwī-itohtahāw ayisk ē-māyimahcihot. (S)
        I am taking him/her (this one) to the hospital *because* s/he is not feeling well.

4)   ē-kī-nitawi-kiyokēcik aniki ēkotē. (P)
        They (those ones) went visiting over there.

5a)   tānitē ana Bill ē-itohtēt? (P)
        Where is (it) Bill going?

5b)   tānitē ana kā-kī-itohtēt Bill? (S)
        Where was it that Bill went?

5c)   tānitē anima Bill ē-itohtēt? (P)
        Where is Bill going?
        Where is it that Bill is going(to)?

5d)   tānitē anima Bill kā-itohtēt? (S)
        Where is that that Bill is going (to)?

6)   kīkwāy ē-osīhtāyan? (P)
        What are you *doing*?

In these examples above not all of the verbs in the Conjunct mode are subordinate clauses.

1a) In the first instance, the scenario might be that the person is asking someone whether s/he was going to use a knife for the task at hand. The meaning seems to be that of surprise that he would use a knife at all.

– "cī" is used.

– the verb is in the conjunct.

It is a principal clause.

1b) If one were to change this sentence from a question to a statement it becomes obvious that this a principal clause.

– ē-wī-āpacihtāyān ōma mōhkomān. I am going to use this knife.

1c) In the this sentence however, the demonstrative pronoun "ōma" refers to a statement exclaiming "(It is) that I AM going to be using a knife." A subordinate clause.

– ōma – this

– verb is in the conjunct.

1d) In this sentence we have a relative clause which makes it a subordinate clause.

– ēwako – the one

– ōma – this

– "kā – introduces a relative clause.

2a) Subordinate clause.

– ēkwa – now, and

– ōma – this

– verb is in conjunct.

2b) The literal translation (in brackets) is below what would be a proper English sentence.

– ōma – this

– verb is in conjunct.

– ēkosi – so

2c) The subordinate clause is introduced by " because."

– ayisk is used.

– verb is in conjunct.

3a) This is a statement giving information about the condition of a person. It is a principal clause.
– awa – him/her/it
– verb is in conjunct

3b) A principal clause.
– ēkosi – so
– verb is in conjunct

3c) A principal clause.
– ōma – it
– awa – this one
– ēkosi – so
– verb is in conjunct.

3d) A principal clause
– ōma – him/her/it
– verb is in conjunct.

3e) A subordinate clause.
– ayisk – because
– verb is in conjunct.

4) A principal clause.
– aniki – those
– conjunct

5a) A principal clause.
– ana – it/him/her
– conjunct

5b) A subordinate clause.
– ana – it/him/her
– "kā-" is used in verb.

5c) A principal clause.
– anima – that
– conjunct

5d) A subordinate clause.
– anima – that
– "kā-" introduces a relative clause.

6) A subordinate clause.
– conjunct

The meaning of the demonstrative pronouns, *ōma, awa, ana, anima*, changes depending on the context or different situations.

Most often when the verb is in the conjunct mode it is a subordinate clause except when they occur with the interrogative pronouns. And those that begin with the preverb "*kā-*" are always subordinate.

Tense

Some of the questions are asked using Interrogative and demonstrative pronouns that act as predicates. These are followed by verbs that begin with the "*kā-*". Now in the following example note that the verb in the Independent mode is in the past tense and the conjunct form of the second verb is not. This is not unusual because the time line is already determined by the first tense particle so it would be redundant to use the past tense again.

i)   *nīki*-pakāsimonān ispīhk kā-itohtēyāhk sākahikanihk.
      We swam when we went to the lake.

ii)   māci-mētawēwak māna awāsisak mayaw kā-waniskācik.
      The children usually begin playing as soon as they get up.

But if it is the only verb, the following prefixes will indicate the time:

kā-	→	indicates the present
kē-	→	indicates the future
kā-kī-	→	indicates the past tense.

i)   tānihi kē-atāwēyan.
      Which ones will you buy?

ii)   anihi kā-mihkwāki.
      Those that are red.

iii) ēwako cī ana kā-kī-nikamot.
      Is that the one who sang?

"mēkwāc" or "mēkwā"

Terms *"mēkwāc"* and *"ispīhk"* quite often occur with verbs in the conjunct mode. When *mēkwāc* occurs before the verb it is pronounced with the *"-c"* but if it is used between *"ē-"* and the rest of the verb then the *"-c"* is dropped. If it is placed before the verb it is a particle but if it is placed between the prefix *"ē-"* and the verb stem then it is a preverb.

The meaning is still the same either way and there are no changes to anything else at all. Here is an example:

i)   nikī-wāpamāwak aniki mēkwāc ē-atoskēcik.
      I saw them (those ones) while they were working.

ii)   nikī-wāpamāwak aniki ē-mēkwā-atoskēcik.
      I saw them (those ones) while they were working.

Relative Clauses

One other verb form which needs to be addressed is the relative clause. Relative clauses of course modify nouns in sentences. English terms such as "that," "which," "who," "when" and "where" usually indicate that a relative clause is being used.

An easily recognizable particle *"kā-"*, which replaces the *"ē-"* in front of verb stems that are in the Conjunct mode, is used to introduce relative clauses in Cree. It sounds simple and it is but it can cause a bit of confusion during translation from Cree to English.

Writing a proper grammatical English sentence, when translating Cree, will often obscure a relative clause. And in doing so the English translation does not capture the thought process of the Cree and the way they express that thought. If a Cree sentence were to be translated literally one would have a rather awkwardly constructed English sentence but then it would be more accurate.

The translation of a verb that has the particle *"kā-"* in its construction may be determined by the context of the sentence. Terms such as: "that …," "as …," "which …," or "who" should be used appropriately in the translation. Consider the examples below:

1.   tānispīhk anima kisīmis *kā*-kī-wāpamat?
      When was it *that* you saw your younger sibling?

2.   ē-nitawēyihtaman cī anihi maskisina *kā*-mihkwāki?
      Do you want those shoes *that* are red?
      Literally: You want those shoes *which/that* are red?

3.   ēwakoni cī anihi maskisina *kā*-mihkwāki kā-nitawēyihtaman?
      Are those shoes *that* are red the ones that you want?

4. kikī-wāpamāwak cī aniki iskwēsisak *kā*-nikamocik?
    Did you (sg.) see those girls *that/who* were singing?

5. ēwako cī ana *kā*-kī-nikamot.
    Is that the one *who* sang?

6. tāniwēhkāk aniki awāsisak *kā*-nihtā-nikamocik.
    Where are those children who sing well.
    Literally: Where are they those children *that/who* can sing well.

7. kī-pimohtatāw cī anima maskimot *kā*-osāwāyik.
    Did he carry that bag *which* is orange? (literal translation)
    Did he carry that orange bag?

8. kīkwāy anima kā-kī-atāwēyan.
    What is that *that* you (sg.) bought?

Tense and Relative Clauses

Although the tense markers and word order have already been discussed in Chapter 6 and numerous examples have been given throughout the book the relative clause was not addressed. So here is an observation that explains how to apply the tense markers and where they are placed.

Some of the relative clause examples above, and below as well, are in the past tense. The past tense indicator "*kī-*" or Future Intentional tense "*wī-*" can be paired with "*kā-*" resulting in "*kā-kī-*" and "*kā-wī-*" in sentences to show past or future intentional tense. The chart below shows the order that one would follow for the relative clause paradigm.

kā-	Tense -	Preverb -	Verb Stem +	Suffix

Chapter 33: Conclusion

This volume has presented only a brief glimpse of the Cree language. The focus on its grammatical structure fulfills an immediate need. Although an attempt to use practical examples has been made, the rich and vivid colloquial and idiomatic nature of Cree cannot be captured in written text. One might attempt to simulate conditions but the Cree-speaking community would be the best teacher.

However, it is hoped that this book introduces enough practical information for the reader to understand and to be aware of the complexity of this language. Educators may want to use this text as a reference when questions arise.

References

Ahenakew, Freda. 1987. *Cree Language Structures: A Cree Approach*. Winnipeg: Pemmican Publications, Inc.

Ahenakew, Freda and H.C. Wolfart. 1997. *kwayask ē-kī-pē-kiskinowāpahtihicik/Their Example Showed Me the Way*. Told by Emma Minde. Edited and Translated by Freda Ahenakew and H.C. Wolfart. Edmonton: The University of Alberta Press.

Edwards, Mary. 1961. *Cree: An Intensive Language Course*. Northern Canada Evangelical Mission (first edition, 1954).

Hengeveld, Kees. 1992. Functional Grammar Series 15. *Non-verbal Predication Theory, Typology, Diachrony*. Berlin/New York: Mouton de Gruyter.

Hives, the Rev. H.E. 1952. *Cree Grammar, Being a Simplified Approach to the Study of the Language of the Cree Indians of Canada*. Toronto: Missionary Society of the Church of England in Canada.

Ratt, S., T. Klokeid and M. Cote. 1986. "The Morphological Structure of Conditional Sentences in Cree and Saulteaux" (paper presented at the 18th Algonquian Conference, Winnipeg).

Stevens, the Rev. F.G. 1955. *English-Cree Primer and Vocabulary*. Toronto: Board of Home Mission, the United Church of Canada.

Wolvengrey, Arok. 2001. *nēhiyawēwin: itwēwina/Cree: Words*. Volume 1: Cree–English, Volume 2: English–Cree. Regina: Canadian Plains Research Center, University of Regina.

Appendix A: Verb Charts
Sample Verb Charts

Immediate Imperative Mode			
person	preverb-	verb stem +	suffix
2s			
2p			
21			

Delayed Imperative Mode			
person	preverb-	verb stem +	suffix
2s			
2p			
21			

Independent Mode						
person	person indicator	connective	tense-	preverb-	verb stem +	suffix
1s	ni					
2s	ki					
3s						
3's						
1p	ni					
21	ki					
2p	ki					
3p						
3'p						

Verb Chart 1
Animate Intransitive Verbs

Immediate Imperative Mode			
person	preverb-	verb stem +	suffix
2s			Ø
2P			k
21			tān

Delayed Imperative Mode			
person	preverb-	verb stem +	suffix
2s			hkan
2p			hkēk
21			hkahk

Independent Mode						
person	person indicator	connective	tense-	preverb-	verb stem +	suffix
1s	ni					n
2s	ki					n
3s						w *or n
3's						yiwa
1p	ni					nān
21	ki					naw
2p	ki					nāwāw
3p						wak
3'p						yiwa

Conjunct Mode					
person	ē-	tense-	preverb-	verb stem +	suffix
1s	ē-				yān
2s	ē-				yan
3s	ē-				t
3's	ē-				yit
1p	ē-				yāhk
21	ē-				yahk
2p	ē-				yēk
3p	ē-				cik
3'p	ē-				yit

* n is used only for the VAI n-stem – The instructor will advise which verbs require this suffix.

Verb Chart 2
Transitive Inanimate-1 Verbs

Immediate Imperative Mode			
person	preverb-	verb stem +	suffix
2s			a
2p			amok
21			ētān

Delayed Imperative Mode			
person	preverb-	verb stem +	suffix
2s			amohkan
2p			amohkēk
21			amohkahk

Independent Mode						
person	person indicator	connective	tense-	preverb-	verb stem+	suffix
1s	ni					ēn
2s	ki					ēn
3s						am
3's						amiyiwa
1p	ni					ēnān
21	ki					ēnaw
2p	ki					ēnāwāw
3p						amwak
3'p						amiyiwa

Conjunct Mode					
person	ē-	tense-	preverb-	verb stem +	suffix
1s	ē-				amān
2s	ē-				aman
3s	ē-				ahk
3's	ē-				amiyit
1p	ē-				amāhk
21	ē-				amahk
2p	ē-				amēk
3p	ē-				ahkik
3'p	ē-				amiyit

Verb Chart 3
Transitive Inanimate-2 Verbs

Immediate Imperative Mode			
person	preverb-	verb stem +	suffix
2s			∅
2p			k
21			tān

Delayed Imperative Mode			
person	preverb-	verb stem +	suffix
2s			hkan
2p			hkēk
21			hkahk

Independent Mode						
person	person indicator	connective	tense-	preverb-	verb stem+	suffix
1s	ni					n
2s	ki					n
3s						w
3's						yiwa
1p	ni					nān
21	ki					naw
2p	ki					nāwāw
3p						wak
3'p						yiwa

Conjunct Mode					
person	ē-	tense-	preverb-	verb stem +	suffix
1s	ē-				yān
2s	ē-				yan
3s	ē-				t
3's	ē-				yit
1p	ē-				yāhk
21	ē-				yahk
2p	ē-				yēk
3p	ē-				cik
3'p	ē-				yit

Verb Chart 4
Transitive Inanimate-3 Verbs Conjunct Mode

Immediate Imperative Mode			
person	preverb-	verb stem +	suffix
2s			Ø
2p			k
21			tān

Delayed Imperative Mode			
person	preverb-	verb stem +	suffix
2s			hkan
2p			hkēk
21			hkahk

Independent Mode						
person	person indicator	connective	tense-	preverb-	verb stem+	suffix
1s	ni					n
2s	ki					n
3s						w
3's						yiwa
1p	ni					nān
21	ki					naw
2p	ki					nāwāw
3p						wak
3'p						yiwa

Conjunct Mode					
person	ē-	tense-	preverb-	verb stem +	suffix
1s	ē-				yān
2s	ē-				yan
3s	ē-				t
3's	ē-				yit
1p	ē-				yāhk
21	ē-				yahk
2p	ē-				yēk
3p	ē-				cik
3'p	ē-				yit

Verb Chart 5
Transitive Animate Verbs

Immediate Imperative Mode				
person	preverb-	verb stem +	singular suffix +	plural suffix
2s			Ø	ik
2p			ihk	ok
21			ātān	ik

Delayed Imperative Mode				
person	preverb-	verb stem +	suffix +	plural suffix
2s			āhkan	ik
2p			āhkēhk	ok
21			āhkahk	ok

Independent Mode							
person	person indicator	connective	tense-	preverb	verb stem+	singular suffix +	plural suffix
1s	ni					āw	ak
2s	ki					āw	ak
3s						ēw	Ø
3's						ēyiwa	Ø
1p	ni					ānān	ak
21	ki					ānaw	ak
2p	ki					āwāw	ak
3p						ēwak	Ø
3'p						ēyiwa	Ø

Conjunct Mode						
person	ē-	tense-	preverb-	verb stem +	singular suffix +	plural suffix
1s	ē-				ak	ik
2s	ē-				at*	cik
3s	ē-				āt	Ø
3's	ē-				āyit	Ø
1p	ē-				āyāhk	ik
21	ē-				āyahk	ok
2p	ē-				āyēk	ok
3p	ē-				ācik	Ø
3'p	ē-				āyit	Ø

* delete this "t" before adding the plural suffix for plural object.

Verb Chart 6
Future Conditional Forms

Transitive Animate Verbs – 1, 2, 3, 4 – Future Conditional				
person	preverb-	verb stem +	singular suffix	plural suffix
1s			aki*	akwāwi
2s			aci	atwāwi
3s			āci	āci
3's			āyici	āyici
1p			āyāhki	āyāhkwāwi
21			āyahko	āyahkwāwi
2p			āyēko	āyēkwāwi
3p			ātwāwi	ātwāwi
3'p			āyici	āyici

Transitive Inanimate Verbs - 1 Future Conditional			
person	preverb-	verb stem +	singular suffix
1s			amāni
2s			amani
3s			ahki
3's			amiyici
1p			amāhko
21			amahko
2p			amēko
3p			amātwāwi
3'p			amiyici

Transitive Inanimate Verbs - 2 & 3 Future Conditional			
person	preverb-	Verb stem +	singular suffix
1s			yāni
2s			yani
3s			ci
3's			yici
1p			yāhko
21			yahko
2p			yēko
3p			twāwi
3'p			yici

Animate Intransitive Verbs - Future Conditional			
person	preverb-	verb stem +	singular suffix
1s			yāni
2s			yani
3s			ci
3's			yici
1p			yāhko
21			yahko
2p			yēko
3p			twāwi
3'p			yici

* Do not use any part of the singular suffixes for plural object; use the plural suffixes only.

Verb Chart 7
Inverse-1 for VTA-1 & 4 (regular & "t" stems)

Inverse Independent Mode							
person	person indicator	connective	tense-	preverb-	verb stem +	singular suffix +	plural suffix
1s	ni					ik	wak
2s	ki					ik	wak
3s						ikow	∅
3's						ikoyiwa	∅
1p	ni					ikonān	ak
21	ki					ikonaw	ak
2p	ki					ikowāw	ak
3p						ikowak	∅
3'p						ikoyiwa	∅

Inverse Conjunct Mode						
person	ē-	tense-	preverb-	verb stem +	singular suffix +	plural suffix
1s	ē-				it*	cik
2s	ē-				isk	ik
3s	ē-				ikot	∅
3's	ē-				ikoyit	∅
1p	ē-				ikoyāhk	ik
21	ē-				ikoyahk	ik
2p	ē-				ikoyēk	ik
3p	ē-				ikocik	∅
3'p	ē-				ikoyit	∅

* Delete this "t" before adding the plural suffix for plural object.

Verb Chart 8
Inverse-2 for VTA-2 (Vw stem)

		Inverse Independent Mode					
person	person indicator	connective	tense-	preverb-	verb stem +	singular suffix +	plural suffix
1s	ni					āk	wak
2s	ki					āk	wak
3s						ākow	Ø
3's						ākoyiwa	Ø
1p	ni					ākonān	ak
21	ki					ākonaw	ak
2p	ki					ākowāw	ak
3p						ākwak	Ø
3'p						ākoyiwa	Ø

		Inverse Conjunct Mode				
person	ē-	tense-	preverb-	verb stem +	singular suffix +	plural suffix
1s	ē-				it*	cik
2s	ē-				āsk	ik
3s	ē-				ākot	Ø
3's	ē-				ākoyit	Ø
1p	ē-				ākoyāhk	ik
21	ē-				ākoyahk	ok
2p	ē-				ākoyēk	ok
3p	ē-				ākocik	Ø
3'p	ē-				ākoyit	Ø

* delete this "t" before adding the plural suffix for plural object.

Verb Chart 9
Inverse-3 for VTA-3 (Cw stem)

Inverse Independent Mode							
person	person indicator	connective	tense-	preverb-	verb stem +	singular suffix +	plural suffix
1s	ni					ok	wak
2s	ki					ok	wak
3s						okow	Ø
3's						okoyiwa	Ø
1p	ni					okonān	ak
21	ki					okonaw	ak
2p	ki					okowāw	ak
3p						okowak	Ø
3'p						okoyiwa	Ø

Inverse Conjunct Mode						
person	ē-	tense-	preverb	verb stem +	singular suffix +	plural suffix
1s	ē-				ot*	cik
2s	ē-				osk	ik
3s	ē-				okot	Ø
3's	ē-				okoyit	Ø
1p	ē-				okoyāhk	ik
21	ē-				okoyahk	ok
2p	ē-				okoyēk	ok
3p	ē-				okocik	Ø
3'p	ē-				okoyit	Ø

* Delete this "t" before adding the plural suffix for plural object.

Verb Chart 10
Unspecified Actor: VTA-1 & 4 (regular & "t" stems)

Unspecified Actor - Independent Mode						
person	person indicator	connective	tense-	preverb-	verb stem +	suffix
1s	ni					ikawin
2s	ki					ikawin
3s						āw
3's						imāwa
1p	ni					ikawinān
21	ki					ikawinaw
2p	ki					ikawināwāw
3p						āwak
3'p						imāwa

Unspecified Actor - Conjunct Mode					
person	ē-	tense-	preverb-	verb stem +	suffix
1s	ē-				ikawiyān
2s	ē-				ikawiyan
3s	ē-				iht
3's	ē-				imiht
1p	ē-				ikawiyāhk
21	ē-				ikawiyahk
2p	ē-				ikawiyēk
3p	ē-				ihcik
3'p	ē-				imiht

Verb Chart 11
Unspecified Actor: VTA-2 (Vw Stem)

		Unspecified Actor - Independent Mode				
person	person indicator	connective	tense-	preverb-	verb stem +	suffix
1s	ni					ākawin
2s	ki					ākawin
3s						āw
3's						āmimāwa
1p	ni					ākawinān
21	ki					ākawinaw
2p	ki					ākawināwāw
3p						āwak
3'p						āmimāwa

		Unspecified Actor - Conjunct Mode			
person	ē-	tense-	preverb-	verb stem +	suffix
1s	ē-				ākawiyān
2s	ē-				ākawiyan
3s	ē-				āht
3's	ē-				āmiht
1p	ē-				ākawiyāhk
21	ē-				ākawiyahk
2p	ē-				ākawiyēk
3p	ē-				āhcik
3'p	ē-				āmiht

Verb Chart 12
Unspecified Actor: VTA-3 (Cw stem)

person	person indicator	connective	tense-	preverb-	verb stem +	suffix
			**Unspecified Actor - Independent Mode**			

person	person indicator	connective	tense-	preverb-	verb stem +	suffix
1s	ni					okawin
2s	ki					okawin
3s						āw
3's						omāwa
1p	ni					okawinān
21	ki					okawinaw
2p	ki					okawināwāw
3p						āwak
3'p						omāwa

person	ē-	tense-	preverb-	verb stem +	suffix
		**Unspecified Actor - Conjunct Mode**			

person	ē-	tense-	preverb-	verb stem +	suffix
1s	ē-				okawiyān
2s	ē-				okawiyan
3s	ē-				oht
3's	ē-				omiht
1p	ē-				okawiyāhk
21	ē-				okawiyahk
2p	ē-				okawiyēk
3p	ē-				ohcik
3'p	ē-				omiht

Verb Chart 13
You–Me set for VTA-1 & 4 (regular, "t," Vw stems)

Immediate Imperative Mode- *Inverse - 1 & 2*				
person	preverb-	verb stem +	1s	1p
2s			in	∅
2s/2p			∅	inān
2p			ik	∅

Delayed Imperative Mode - *Inverse - 1 & 2*				
person	preverb-	verb stem +	1s	1p
2s			ihkan	∅
2s/2p			∅	ihkāhk
2p			ihkēk	∅

You–Me set for VTA-3 (Cw stems)

Immediate Imperative Mode - *Inverse - 3*				
person	preverb-	verb stem +	1s	1p
2s			on	∅
2s/2p			∅	onān
2p			ok	∅

Delayed Imperative Mode - *Inverse 3*				
person	preverb-	verb stem +	1s	1p
2s			ohkan	∅
2s/2p			∅	ohkāhk
2p			ohkēk	∅

Appendix B: Vocabulary
Cree to English

A

acāhkos (NA): star

acimosis (NA): little dog/puppy

ācimowasinahikan (NI): newspaper

ācimowin (NI): story/news

aciyaw (P): awhile

āh (P): oh

āha (P): yes

āhāsiw (NA): crow

āhcanis (NA): ring

āhcaniwicihcīs (NI): ring finger

ahcāpiy (NI): bow [as in bow & arrow]

āhkosiwikamik (NI): hospital

āhkosiwin (NI): illness/sickness

āhkwatihcikan (NI) freezer/fridge

ahpō (P): even/or

ahpō cī (Ph): or else

ahpō ētikwē (Ph): I suppose/perhaps/maybe/
     possibly

-āhtik (Sf): wooden

ākayāsīmowin (NI): English

akāmi-tipahaskān (NI)/ kihci-mōhkomānināhk (P):
United States

akāwāc (P): hardly

akihtāsona (NI): numbers

akimāw (refers to dates) (vP): it is counted

akocikan (NI): cupboard

akohp (NI): blanket

akwanān (NA): shawl

āmaciwēpicikan (NI): elevator/lift

āmaciwīspimowinihk (P): Stanley Mission, SK

amisk (NA): beaver

amiskowiyās (NI): beaver meat

āmōmēyi (NI): honey

āmōsīsipāskwat (NI): honey

āmōw (NA): bee

ana (Pr-A/sg) that one

anāskān (NI): sheet

anāskāsimon (NI): mattress

anihi (Pr-I/pl): those ones

aniki (Pr-A/pl): those ones

anikwacās (NA): gopher or squirrel

anima (Pr-I/sg): that one

anohc (P): today, now

anohc kā-kīsikāk (Ph): today

anōmin (NA): oatmeal

āpacihcikana (NI): appliances

āpahkwēwikamik (NI): big top (tent)

āpāpiskahikan (NI): key

apihkēsak (NA): Chinese people

āpihtā-kīsikāw (vP): midday/noon

āpihtā-tipiskāw (NI): midnight

āpihtaw (P): half

āpihtawikosisān (NA): Metis person

āpihtawikosisānak (NA): Metis people

apisci-kahkākīs (NA): magpie

apisimōsos (NA): deer

apisīs/apisis (P): a little bit

-āpisk (Sf): made of metal

apistacihkos (NA): antelope

apoy (NA): paddle

-āpoy (Sf): denotes liquid

asām (NA): snowshoe

asapāp (NA): thread

āsay (P): already

āsay mīna (Ph): over again

asicāyihk (P): against/along/beside

asici (P): with

asikan (NA): sock

asinīwipwātak/pwāsīmowak (NA): Assiniboine
     people

asinīwipwātināhk (P): Assiniboine country

asiniy (NA): stone/rock

asiskiy (NI): soil/mud

asiskīhkwān/kotawān (NI) fireplace

askīhk (P): reserve, (on the)

askihk (NA): pail

askihkos (NA): a pot

askipwāwa (NI): potatoes

askipwāwi (NI): potato

askīwin (NI): year

askīwisīwihtākan (NI): pepper

askiy (NI): earth/land

aspin (P): since

aspiskwēsimon (NI): pillow

āstam (P): Come!

āstam ōta (Ph): Come here

astis (NA): mitt

Appendix B Abbreviation Key

A - animate	P - particle	Pp - pre-particle	sg - singular
Cj - conjunction	Ph - particle phrase	Pr - pronoun	vP - verbal particle
I - inanimate	pl - plural	Pv - preverb	
N - noun	Pn - prenoun	Sf - suffix	

astisiy (NI): sinew
astotin (NI): hat
āta (P): although
atāmihk (P): bottom/under
atāmipīhk (P): underwater
atāmayiwinisa (NI): underclothes
atāwēwikamik (NI): store
ātayōhkēwin (NI): a legend/story
ati- (Pv): begin/start
atihkamēk (NA): whitefish
ātiht (P): some
atim (NA): dog
awa (Pr-A/sg): this one
awas! (P-sg): Go! get out of here!
awas! (P) Go on with you!
awasitik! (P-pl): Go! get out of here!
awasi- (Pp): before/after
awasi-otākosīhk (P): the day before yesterday
awasi-tipiskāki (P): the night after next
awasi-tipiskohk (P): the night before last
awasi-wāpahki (P): the day after tomorrow
awāsis (NA): child
awāsisak (NA): children
awāsisihkān (NA): doll
awīna (Pr): who (sg)
awīniki (Pr): who (pl)
awiyak (Pr): someone
awiyakak (Pr): some people
ayamihēwikīsikāw (vP): Sunday
ayamihēwiskwēw (NA): nun
ayamihēwiyiniw (NA): preacher/priest
ayapihkēsīs (NA): spider
ayapiy (NA): net
ayīki-pīsim (NA): Frog Moon/April
ayīkis (NA): frog
ayēnānēw (P): eight
ayēnānēwomitanaw (P): eighty
ayēnānēwosāp (P): eighteen
ayisiyiniw (NA): person, human being
ayisk (Cj): because/but
ayiwāk (P): more
ayiwinisa (NI): clothes
anōmin (NA): oatmeal
ayōskan (NA): raspberry

C

cahcahkāyow (NA): blackbird
cahcahkiw (NA): pelican
capasīs/capasis (P): below/under/lower

cēhcapiwinis (NI): little chair/baby chair
cēskwa (P): wait a minute/wait
cī (P): question marker
cīkahikan (NI): axe
cīkahikanāhtik (NI): axe handle
cikāstēpayihcikan (NI): television
cikēma (Cj): because/of course
cīki (P): near
cīmān (NI): canoe
cipahikanis (NI): minute
cīpotōn (NI): pointed lips
cīpwēyānak (NA): Chipweyan people
cīpwēyānināhk (P): Chipweyan country/region
cīstahāsēpon (NI): fork

E

ēha (P): yes
ēkā (P): don't
ēkāwiya (P): don't
-ēkin (Sf): made of cloth; fabric
ēkosi (P): enough, so
ēkos īsi (Ph): like that
ēkosi mīna (Ph): also; and also/then
ēkota (P): there (a specific place)
ēkotē (P): over there
ēkwa (P): and/now
ēkwa mīna (Ph): also
ēkwayikohk (P): that much
ēmihkwān (NA): a spoon
ēmihkwānis (NA): a little spoon
ēskwa (P): while
ētikwē (P): perhaps/I suppose
ēwako (Pr): that's the one
ēwak ōma (Pr-I/sg): this same one
ēwakw āna (Pr-A/sg): that same one
ēwakw ānihi (Pr-I/pl): those same ones
ēwakw āniki (Pr-A/pl): those same ones
ēwakw ānima (Pr-I/sg): that same one
ēwakw āwa (Pr-A/sg): this same one
-ēyāpiy (Sf) string/cord
ēyikos (NA): ant

I

ihkopiwi-pīsim/iyīkopiwi-pīsim (NA):
    Frost Moon/November
-imina (Sf): denotes berries
isi (P): denotes direction to/towards
isko (P): as far as/up to (distance)
iskonikan (NI): leftover/reservation/Indian Reserve

Appendix B Abbreviation Key

A - animate	P - particle	Pp - pre-particle	sg - singular
Cj - conjunction	Ph - particle phrase	Pr - pronoun	vP - verbal particle
I - inanimate	pl - plural	Pv - preverb	
N - noun	Pn - prenoun	Sf - suffix	

iskotēw (NI): fire
iskotēwāpoy (NI): liquor
iskotēwotāpānāsk (NA): train
iskwāhtēm (NI): door
iskwayāc (P): last time/one
iskwēcihcīs (NI): the little finger
iskwēsis (NA): little girl
iskwēsisāpoy (NI): beer
iskwēsisihkān (NA): doll
iskwēw (NA): woman
iskwēwasākay (NI): dress/woman's coat
ispatinaw (NI): hill
ispayiki (vP): when it happens/comes to be
ispī (P): when/at that time
ispīhk (P): when/at that time
ispimihk (P): up/upstairs
itē (P): denotes directions to/at
itēhkē isi (Ph): in that direction
itokē (P): perhaps
itwahikanicihcīs (NI): the index/pointer finger
iyīkopiwi-pīsim/ihkopiwi-pīsim (NA): Frost
    moon/November
iyikohk (P): that much
iyinimina (NI): blueberries
iyinīsiwin (NI): intelligence
iyinito-mostos (NA): buffalo
iyiniw (NA): First Nations person/Indian person
K
ka-/ta-/wī- (Pv): future tense markers
kahkiyaw (P): all
kahkiyaw awiyak (Pr): all [everybody]
kahkiyaw kīkway (Pr): all [everything]
kakēpātisiwin (NI): foolishness
kā-kihtwām (P): again and again
kākikē (P): always
kā-kīsikāk (vP): today
kākwa (NA): porcupine
kakwē- (Pv): try
kakwāhyaki (P): great, extremely
kakwēcihkēmowina (NI): questions
kamāmakos (NA): butterfly
kā-mihkwaskwāhki (vP): beets
kanātēyihtamowin (NI): clean thoughts
kapē-kīsik (P): all day
kapē-tipisk (P): all night
kā-piskatahastāhk (vP): province
kasīhkwēwiyākan (NI): sink/basin
kaskikwāsonāpisk (NA): thimble
kēhcinā (P): perhaps/maybe

kēhkēhk/sākwahtamow (NA): hawk
kēhtē-ayak (NA): Elders
kēkā- (Pp): almost
kēkāc (P): almost
kēkā-mitātaht (P): nine
kēkāc-mitātahtomitanaw-mitātahtosāp (P):
    ninety-nine
kēkāc-nīsitanaw (P): nineteen
kēsiskaw (P): quickly
kēsiskawihkasikan (NI): microwave
kēyāpic (P): still/yet
kīhcēkosīwināhtik (NI): ladder
kihci- (Pv/Pn): big/large/great
kihci-kīsik (NI): outer space
kihci-kiskinwahamātowikamik (NI): university
kihci-mēskanaw (NI) highway
kihci-mitātahtomitanaw (P): a thousand
kihci-mōhkomānināhk (P)/akāmi-tipahaskān (NI):
    United States
kihc-ōkimāskwēw (NA): queen
kihc-ōkimāw (NA): king
kihc-ōkiniy (NA): tomato
kihc-ōtēnaw (NI): city
kihciniskēhk (P): on/to the right
kihiw/mikisiw (NA): eagle
kīhkwētakāk (vP): corner
kihtwām (P): again/āsay mīna
kikāwīs (NA): your(sg) aunt (mother's sister)
kiki (NI): your home
kīkisēp (P): this morning
kīkisēpāki (vP): in the morning
kīkisēpāyāw (NI): morning
kīkway (Pr): something
kīkwāy? (Pr): what?
kīkwaya (Pr/NI): something, things (pl)
kīkwāya? (Pr):What?
kimis (NA): your(sg) older sister
kimisāhowinēkin (NI): toilet paper
kimiwanāpoy (NI): rain water
kimiwanasākay (NI): raincoat
kīmōc (P): secretly
kinēpik (NA): snake
kinikinik (NI): shrub bark mixture to smoke in a
pipe (red willow bark & green leaves)
kinosēskāw (vP): lots of fish
kinosēw (NA): fish [generic term]
kinosēwikamik (NI): fish plant
kipahikanihk (NI): jail, Fort Qu'Appelle, SK
kipatāhtāmowin (NI): faint [condition]/loss of

Appendix B Abbreviation Key

A - animate	P - particle	Pp - pre-particle	sg - singular
Cj - conjunction	Ph - particle phrase	Pr - pronoun	vP - verbal particle
I - inanimate	pl - plural	Pv - preverb	
N - noun	Pn - prenoun	Sf - suffix	

breath

kisāstēwāpoy/sīwāpoy (NI): pop

kiscikānis (NI): garden

kisē-manitowaskisina (NI): sandals

kisē-pīsim (NA):The Great Moon/January

kisīmis (NA): your younger brother/sister

kīsik (NI): the sky

kīsikāwi-pīsim (NA): sun

kisīmis (NA): your(sg) younger brother/sister

kisīmis (NA): your(sg) cousin

kisipanohk (P): edge, back, against the wall

kisipēkinikan (NI): soap

kisipēkini-mahkahk (NI): clothes-washer/tub

kisipēkinikēwimahkahk (NI): washtub

kisipēkistēwimahkahk (NI): bathtub

kisipēkiyākanikan (NI): dishwasher

kisisowin (NI): fever

kīskasākās (NI): little skirt

kīskasākay (NI): skirt

kīskimitās (NA): shorts

kiskinwahamātowikamik (NI): school

kiskinwahamawākan (NA): student

kīskipocikan (NI): a saw

kīsowahpison (NA): a warm scarf

kīspin/kīsāspin (P): if

kīsta (Pr): you (sg) too/also

kīstanaw (Pr): us (incl) also

kistapinānihk (P): Prince Albert, SK

kīstawāw (Pr): you (pl) too/also

kistikān (NI): field/farm

kistikāna/askipwāwa (NI) potatoes

kitānis (NA): your daughter

kitohcikan (NI): musical instrument

kitihtāwāw (NA) your co-in-law

kitohcikan kā-natohtamihk (NI): radio

kitohcikanēyāpiy: guitar string

kīwētinohk (P): in the north

kiya (Pr): you (sg)

kiyām (P): it's all right/okay

kiyām (P): nevermind, it's alright, doesn't matter, so what!

kiyānaw (Pr): we (incl)

kiyawāw (Pr): you (pl)

kīyipa (P): hurry up

kocawākanis (NI): match

kocawānis (NA): campfire

kōhkominānihk (P): Grandmother's Bay, SK

kohkōs (NA): pig, swine

kohkōsowiyās (NI): pork/ham

kohkōsowiyin (NI): bacon

kōna (NA): snow

kōniwāpoy (NI): snow water

kostācihkwāmiwin (NI): nightmare

kotak (Pr): other/another

kotakak (Pr): others

kotak mīna (Ph): yet another

kotawān/asiskīhkwān (NI) fireplace

kotawānāpisk (NA): stove

kwāskohcīsis (NA): grasshopper

kwayask (P): right/correct

kwēkwēkocīs (NA): firefly

M

macostēhamānakēwin (NI): offering [ceremony]

māci- (Pv): begin, start

maci- (Pv/Pn): bad, evil

mahkacāp (NA): one with big eyes

mahkatay (NI): a big belly

mahkahk (NI): barrel/tub

mahkēsīs (NA): fox

mahkihtawakay (NA): one with big ears

mahkikot (NI/NA): a big nose/one with a big nose

mahkisit (NI): a big foot

mahkisōkan (NI): large buttocks, large derriere

mahkitōn (NA) one with a big mouth

mahkwan (NI): heel

mahtāmin (NA): corn

mahti (P): let me see

māka (Cj): but

māka mīna (Ph): as usual/of course

mākohikēwin (NI): difficulty

mākwa (NA): loon

mākwēyimowin (NI): fear

māmaskāc: [exclamation indicating surprise, wonder/amazement]

māmawapiwin (NI): meeting

māmawi- (Pv): together

māmitonēyihcikana (NI): thoughts

māna (P): usually/used to

manahikan (NI): cream

manicōs (NA): bug

maniway (NI): a cheek

manōmin (NA): oatmeal/wild rice

masinahikan (NI): book

masinahikanāhcikos (NA/NI): pencil

masinahikanēkin (NI): paper

maskasiy (NA): finger/toe nail

maskēkōmina (NI): cranberries

Appendix B Abbreviation Key

A - animate	P - particle	Pp - pre-particle	sg - singular
Cj - conjunction	Ph - particle phrase	Pr - pronoun	vP - verbal particle
I - inanimate	pl - plural	Pv - preverb	
N - noun	Pn - prenoun	Sf - suffix	

maskihkīsa (NI): pills
maskihkīwāpoy (NI): herb tea/medicine
maskihkīwiskwēw (NA): nurse
maskihkīwiyiniw (NA): doctor
maskihkiy (NI): medicine
māskikan (NI): a chest
maskimocisak (NA): beans [little bags]
maskimot (NI): bag
maskisin (NI): shoe
maskisinēyāpiy (NI): shoelace
māskōc (P): perhaps/maybe
maskohkān (NA): teddy bear
maskosīminak (NA): wild rice
maskosiya (NI): grass/hay
maskwa/wākayōs (NA): brown/bear
mastaw (P): new, recent
matay (NI): stomach/belly
matwān cī (Ph): perhaps/I wonder
mawimoscikēwin (NI): prayer
māyatihk (NA): sheep
māyi- (Pv/Pn): bad, evil
mēkiwin (NI) gift/present
mēkwāc (P): presently
mēnikan (NI): fence
mēscakāsa (NI): hair
mēskanaw (NI) road
mēstacākanis (NA): coyote
mētawākan (NI): toy
mētoni (P): really, surely, very
micakisīsa (NI): sausages
micihciy (NI): hand
mīcimāpoy (NI): soup
mīcisowikamik (NI): cafe/dining room
mīcisowināhtik (NI): table
mīciwin (NI): food/groceries
mihcēt (P): many, lots
mihcētwāw (P): many times
mihcikwan (NI): knee
mihkināhk (NA): turtle
mihko (NI): blood
mihkokwaniy (NI): rose [flower]
mihko-piscipowin (NI): blood poison
mihkwāpēmakwa (NI): red willows
mihta (NI/pl): firewood
mihti (NI/sg): a piece of wood
mihtawakay (NI): ear
mīkis (NA): bead
mīkisistahikēwin (NI): beadwork
mikisiw/kihēw (NA): eagle

mikisiwi-pīsim (NA): Eagle Moon/February
mīkiwām (NI): home
mīkiwāhp (NI): tipi
mikot (NI): nose
mīkwan (NA): feather
mikwāskonēw (NI): chin
mikwayaw (NI): neck
mīna āpihtaw (Ph): half past
minihkwācikan (NI): cup
minihkwākan (NI): cup
mīnisa (NI): saskatoon berries
minōs/pōsīs (NA): cat
mīpit (NI): tooth
mipwām (NI): thigh
misacimosis (NA): a little horse/pony
misāskwatōmina (NI): saskatoon berries
misatim (NA): horse
misawāc (P): anyway
misi- (Pv/Pn): big, large; greatly
misicihcān (NI): thumb
misit (NI): foot
misiwē (P): all over/everywhere
mīsīwoyākan (NI): toilet bowl/bed pan
miskāhtik (NI): forehead
miskāt (NI): leg
miskīsik (NI): eye
miskīsikohkāna (NI): eye-glasses
miskiwan (NI): nose
miskotākay (NI): coat or dress
miskwamiy (NA): ice
misōkan(NI): buttocks
mispiskwan (NI): back [body part]
mispiton (NI): arm
mistahi (P): lots [quantity]
mistahkēsiw (NA): lion
mistanask (NA): badger
mistāpos (NA): a jackrabbit/big rabbit
mistik (NA): tree/log
mistik (NI): stick
mistikōsi (NI): wooden boat
mistikōsiwak (NA): [*French people, literally wood boat people*]
mistikowacis (NI):little/small box
mistikowat (NI): box
mistikwān (NI): head
mistikwaskihk/tēwēhikan (NA): drum
mistiyākan (NI): platter
mitāpiskan (NI): jaw
mitās (NA): pants/trousers

Appendix B Abbreviation Key

A - animate
Cj - conjunction
I - inanimate
N - noun

P - particle
Ph - particle phrase
pl - plural
Pn - prenoun

Pp - pre-particle   sg - singular
Pr - pronoun   vP - verbal particle
Pv - preverb
Sf - suffix

mitahtahkwan (NI): wing
mitātaht (P): ten
mitātahtomitanaw (P): one hundred
mitakikom (NA): mucus
mitēh (NI): heart
mitēhimin (NI): strawberry
mitīhikan (NI): shoulder blade
mitihtikon (NI): armpit
mitihtiman (NI): shoulder
mitohtōsim (NA): breast/teat
mitōn (NI): mouth
mītos (NA): tree
mitōskwan (NI): elbow
miyaw (NI): body
miyikowisiwin (NI): gift/blessed with a talent
miyo- (Pv/Pn): good/nice/well
miywātisiwin (NI): good naturedness
mohcihk (P): on the floor/ground
mohcihtakāhk (P): on the floor
mohcohkān (NA): a clown
mohkahasiw (NA): blue heron
mōhkomān (NI): knife
mohtēw (NA): caterpillar/worm
mōnahipān (NI): a well
mōniyās (NA): caucasian
mōniyāw (NA): caucasian
mōsowiyās (NI): moose meat
mostos (NA): cow
mostosowiyās (NI): beef
mōswa (NA): moose
mōswākan (NI): scissors
mōswaskāw (vP): lots of moose
mōswēkin (NI): moose hide
mōtēyāpisk (NI): jar
mōy wihkāc (Ph): never
mwāc (P): no
mwāc ahpō (Ph): not even/no
mwēstas (P): later, after

N
nah (P): here, take this
nahiyikohk (P): just right (amount)
nakahpēhanohk (P): to the west
nāha (Pr-A/sg): that yonder
nahkawiyinīnāhk (NA): Saulteaux region
nahkawiyiniw (NA): a Saulteaux/ person
nahkwan (NA): my heel
nakiskātowin (NI): meeting
namahcīhk (P): to/on the left

namēkōs (NA): lake trout
namōya/mwāc (P): no
nam āwiyak (Pr): nobody
namōya cēskwa (Ph): not yet
nama kīkway (Pr): nothing
nānapāwisk (P): used to express: [*Oh he's arriving now when he should have arrived earlier (like when was I moving the stove or some other more convenient time)*]
nānapēc (P): all of a sudden, suddenly
nānitaw/sisikwac (P): about (approximately)/ perhaps
naniway (NI): my cheek
napakitāpānāsk(wak) (NA): toboggan(s)
napakiyākan (NI): plate
nāpēsis (NA): boy
nāpēw (NA): man
nāpēwasākay (NI): a man's coat
napwahpison (NI): hobble
nasihkāc (P): slowly, carefully
nāskikan (NI): my chest
naskwēwasihtwēwina (NI): answers
naspāc (P): opposite
napatāk(wa) (NI): potato(es)
nāspic (P): continuous, forever
nawac (P): better/more
nāway (P): behind/at the back/end
nēhi (Pr-I/pl): those yonder
nēhiyānāhk (P): Cree country/region
nēhiyaw (NA): Cree person
nēhiyawēwin (P): Cree langugae
nēhiyaw-mawimoscikēwin (NI): Cree ceremony
nēma (Pr-I/sg): that yonder
nēmitanaw (P): forty
nēwāpēwak (vP): there are four brothers
nēwāpisk (P): four dollars
nēwāw (P): four times
nēwo (P): four
nēwo-kīsikāw (vP): Thursday
nēwosāp (P): fourteen
nicāhkos (NA): my sister-in-law [used by females only]
nicawāsimis(ak) (NA): my child(ren)
nicimos (NA): my boyfriend/cousin(s) [sweetheart]
nīhcāyihk (P): down/downstairs
nihtā- (Pv): ability to do something well/do stwell
nihtiy/maskihkīwāpoy (NI): tea
nikā (NA): Mom(voc)

Appendix B Abbreviation Key

A - animate	P - particle	Pp - pre-particle	sg - singular
Cj - conjunction	Ph - particle phrase	Pr - pronoun	vP - verbal particle
I - inanimate	pl - plural	Pv - preverb	
N - noun	Pn - prenoun	Sf - suffix	

nīkān (P): first/before ahead [*refers to position but may be used to refer to priority in time*]

nikāwīs (NA): my aunt [mother's sister]

nikāwiy (NA): my mother

nīki (NI): my home

nikik (NA): otter

nikiskwēyāwinihk (P): in my own foolishness

nikosis (NA): my son

nikotwāsik (P): six

nikotwāso-kīsikāw (vP): Saturday

nikotwāsomitanaw (P): sixty

nikotwāsosāp (P): sixteen

nikotwāswāpisk (P): six dollars

nimāmā (NA): my mother

nimis (NA): my older sister

nimosōm(ak) (NA): my grandfather/s

nināpēm/niwīkimākan (NA): my husband/man/my spouse

nipēwin (NI): bed

nīpimināna (NI): cranberries

nīpit (NI): my tooth

nipiy (NI): water

nīpiy (NI): leaf/leaves/grass/salad

nisikos (NA): my aunt/my mother-in-law [father's sister]

nisīmis (NA): my younger brother/sister

nisis(ak) (NA): my uncle [mother's brother/also father-in-law]

nīsitanaw (P): twenty

niskāt (NI): my leg

niska(k) (NA): goose/geese

niski-pīsim (NA): Goose Moon/March

nīso (P): two

nīso-kīsikāw (vP): Tuesday

nīsosāp (P): twelve

nīso sōniyās (NA): two quarters

nīsta (Pr): me too/also

nistam (P): first, before

nīstanān (Pr): us too/also

nistēs (NA): my older brother

nisto (P): three

nisto-kīsikāw (vP): Wednesday

nistomitanaw (P): thirty

nistosāp (P): thirteen

nisto sōniyās (NA): three quarters

nistwāpisk (P): three dollars

nistwāw (P): thrice/three times

nīswāpisk (P): two dollars

nīswāw (P): twice

nīswāw-mitātahtomitanaw (P): two hundred

nitānis (NA): my daughter

nitawāc (P): instead

nitawi- (Pv): to go and …

nitēm (NA): my dog

nitihtāwāw (NA): my co-in-law

nītisān(ak) (NA): my sibling/s

nitisiy (NI): my navel

nitiskwēm (NA): my woman/my wife

nitōsis (NA): my aunt [mother's sister]

nitōtēm(ak) (NA): my friend(s)

niwāhkōmākan (NA): my relative

niwīhowin (NI): my name

niwīkimākan (NA): my spouse/wife/husband

niya (Pr): me/I

niyā (P-sg): go

niyāk (P-pl): go

niyanān (Pr): us/we

niyānan (P): five

niyānanwāpisk (P): five dollars

niyāno-kīsikāw (vP): Friday

niyānomitanaw (P): fifty

niyānosāp (P): fifteen

nōcihitowi-pīsim (NA): Mating Moon/September

nōhcāwīs (NA): my uncle [father's brother]

nohcimihk (P): inland [on the other side]

nōhkom(ak) (NA): my grandmother(s)

nōhtāwiy (NA): my father

nōhtē- (Pv): to want

nōtokwēw (NA): an old lady

O

ocāhk (NA): crane

ōcēnās (NI): a small town

ōcēw (NA): fly

ocipitikowin (NI): seizures/cramps

ohci (P): from/for/out of

ohcitaw (P): purposely

ōhōw (NA): owl

ohpahowi-pīsim (NA): Flying Up Moon/August

ohpihkasikan (NA): yeast

okāw (NA): pickerel/walleye

okāwiya (NA): his/her mother

okimāhkān (NA): chief

okiniyak (NA): rose bush berries [rose hips]

omāciw (NA): hunter

omīkwanak (NA): feathers

omisīsi (P): this way

opāskwēyāhk (P): Le Pas, Manitoba

Appendix B Abbreviation Key

A - animate	P - particle	Pp - pre-particle	sg - singular
Cj - conjunction	Ph - particle phrase	Pr - pronoun	vP - verbal particle
I - inanimate	pl - plural	Pv - preverb	
N - noun	Pn - prenoun	Sf - suffix	

ōsa (NI): boats
osām (Cj): because
osāmitōn (NA): mouthy/gossipy/person who talks
   too much
osāwāpoy (NI): orange juice/pop
osāwās (NA): orange (fruit)
ōsi (NI): boat
oskan (NI): bone
oskana kā-asastēki (vP): pile-of-bones; Regina, SK
oskātāskw(ak) (NA): carrot(s)
osk-āyak (NA): young people/teenagers
oskinīkiskwēw (NA): young woman [adolescent]
oskinīkiw (NA): young man [adolescent]
ospwākan (NA): pipe
ostēsimāwasinahikan (NI): treaty/constitution
ostēsimāwiyasiwēwin (NI): constitution
otāhk (P): at the back/behind
otākosīhk (vP): yesterday
otāpān (NA): wagon
otāpānāsk (NA): sled/car
otāpiskākanēsis (NA): killdeer
otēhimin (NA): strawberry
ōtēnaw (NI): town
otisihkān (NI): turnip
otōnapiy (NA): tullabee
owanihikēw (NA): trapper
owīkihtow (NA): bridegroom
oyākan (NI): dish

P

pāhkahāhkwān (NA): chicken [domestic]
pahkahāhkwānowiyās (NI): chicken meat
pahkān (P): different kind
pahkēkin (NI): leather/hide
pahkwastēwinikan (NI): clothes dryer
pahkwēsikan (NA): bannock
pakahatowān (NA): ball
pakāhtowān (NA): ball
pakān (NA): nut
pakwahtēhon (NI): belt
pakwānikamik (NI): tent
pāmwayēs (Cj): before
panacāy (NA): Punnichy, SK
panacāyis: (NA) a newly-hatched bird
papakiwayān (NI): shirt/blouse
papakiwayānēkin (NI): cotton fabric
papayēkatōn/osāmitōn (NA): big mouth/mouthy
   person
papēyahtak (P): slowly/carefully

pāskac (P): besides
paskāwihowi-pīsim (NA): Hatching Moon/June
paskēwihitowin (NI): separation [re: marriage]
pāskisikan (NI): rifle/gun
paskowi-pīsim (NA): The Moulting Moon/July
paskwāmostos (NA): buffalo
paskwāmostosowiyās (NI): buffalo meat
paskwāwīhkwaskwa (NI): sage
paspaskiw (NA): birch grouse
pāstāmowin (NI): curse
pātos (P): later
pawācakinasīsi-pīsim (NA): Frost-Exploding
   Moon/December
pē- (Pv): come [action coming towards speaker]
pēci- (Pv): come [action coming towards speaker]
pēskōmina (NI): pepper
pēyak (P): one
pēyako- (Pv/Pn): alone/by oneself
pēyako-kīsikāw (vP): the first day/Monday
pēyak sōniyās (NA): a quarter/25 cents
pēyakosāp (P): eleven
pēyakwan (P): the same/similar
pēyakwāpisk (P): one dollar
pēyakwāw (P): once
pēyakwāw ēsa (Ph): once upon a time/one time
pēyakwāw-kihci-mitātahtomitanaw (P): one
   thousand
picikwās (NA): apple
pīhcāyihk (P): indoors/inside
pihēw (NA): grouse/partridge
pihkasikan (NA): toast
pihkahtēwāpoy (NI): coffee
pihpihciw/pihpihcēw (NA): robin
pīhtawētās (NI): undershorts
pīhtokamik (P): inside/indoors
pīhtowēskikanak/wīhkwēpānak (NA): long
   underwear/longjohns
pikiwaskisin (NI): rubber boot
piko (P): only
pimācihowin (NI): culture
pimicāskwēyāsihk (P): Lloydminster, SK
pimicāyihk (P): along
pimihākan (NI): aeroplane
pimihāwi-pīsim (NA): Migrating Moon/October
pimīhkān (NI): pemmican
pīminahkwān (NI): rope
pimipicēs (NA): motorized vehicle/car
pimiy (NI): lard/grease/oil/gas
pimiyākan (NI): aeroplane

Appendix B Abbreviation Key

A - animate	P - particle	Pp - pre-particle	sg - singular
Cj - conjunction	Ph - particle phrase	Pr - pronoun	vP - verbal particle
I - inanimate	pl - plural	Pv - preverb	
N - noun	Pn - prenoun	Sf - suffix	

pipikwan (NI): eagle-bone whistle
piponasākay (NI): winter coat
piponāsiw (NA) chicken hawk
piponāyis (NA): little chicken hawk
piscipowin (NI): poison
pīsim (NA): the moon/sun/month
pīsimohkān (NA): clock
pīsmohkānis (NA) watch
pisiskēs (NA): raccoon
pisiskiw (NA): animal
pīswēkasikan (NA): bread/yeast
pīswēkasikanisak (NA): buns
pīswēsākās (NI): sweater
pitamā (P): first [before doing something else]
pītatowēwak (NA): Europeans
pīwāpisk (NI): steel/iron
pīwāpiskos (NI): penny
pīwaya (NI): hair off a hide
piyēsīs (NA): bird
piyēsiw (NA): thunderbird
piyisk (P): finally
pokwītē (P): everywhere anywhere
pōni- (Pv): quit/stop
pōni-āpihtā-kīsikāw (vP): afternoon
pōsināpāsk (NA): bus
pōsīs (NA): cat
pōsiwat/pōsiwas (NI): suitcase
pōtācikēsis (NA): mole
pwāsimowak (NA): Assiniboine people
pwātak (NA): Sioux people
pwātināhk (P): Sioux reserve/country

S
sakahikan (NI): nail [for building]
sākahikan (NI): lake
sakimēs (NA): mosquito
sakimēskāw (vP): a lot of mosquitoes
sākipakāwi-pīsim (NA): The Budding Moon/ May
sākitawāhk (P): Buffalo Narrows, SK
sākwahtamow/kēhkēhk (NA): large hawk
sāpahcikanihk (P): tipi smoke opening
sāpo- (Pv): through
sāpōminak (NA): gooseberries
sāpwāpahcikan (NI): x-ray
sasakāwāpiskos (NA): chipmunk
sāsāpiskisikan (NA): frying pan
saskāwāpiskos (NA): striped gopher
sēhkēpayīs (NA): car
sēkowēpināpisk (NI): oven

sēmāk (P): immediately
sēnapān (NA): ribbon
sēnapānēkin (NI): satin/silk fabric
seskicēs (NI): head roach-regalia
sihkos (NA): weasel
sikāk (NA): skunk
sikopocikan (NI): grinder
sikopocikaniwiyās (NI): hamburger/ground meat
sīkwanāspinēwin (NI): spring fever
simākanis (NA): policeman
sīpāhk (P): under
sīpēkiskāwayān/sīpēkiskāwisākās(NI): sweater
sīpiy (NI): river
sisikoc/siskwac (P): suddenly/all of a sudden
sisikwac/sisikoc (P): all of a sudden/suddenly
sisikopicikaniwiyās (NI): hamburger/ground beef
sīsīp (NA): duck
sīsīp-askihk (NA): kettle
sīsipāskwat (NI): maple sugar
sisonē (P): along
siwāpoy (NI): juice/pop/kool aid
sīwās (NI): candy
sīwihkasikan/wīhkihkasikan (NA): cake/sweet
    baked goods
sīwihtākan (NI): salt
sīwinikan (NA): sugar
sīwinos (NI): candy
-skāw (Sf): denotes an abundance of
sōhkēsīs (P): little faster/harder [effort]
sōhki- (Pv): denotes great effort
sōminak (NA): raisins/grapes
sōmināpoy (NI): wine
sōminisak (NA): currants/raisins
sōniyās (NA): quarter
sōniyāw (NA): money
sōniyāwikimāw (NA): Indian Agent
sōskwahikan (NA): an iron [for ironing clothes]
sōsowatim (NA): mule

T
tahkascikan (NI): refrigerator
tahkohc (P): on top of
tahkopicikanēyāpiy (NI): string
tahtopipon (P): yearly
takōtāni (P): it is a good thing
takwahimināna (NI): chokecherries
takwāki-pīsim (NA): Autumn Moon/ September
tāna (Pr-A/sg): which one?
tānēhki (Pr): why?

Appendix B Abbreviation Key

A - animate	P - particle	Pp - pre-particle	sg - singular
Cj - conjunction	Ph - particle phrase	Pr - pronoun	vP - verbal particle
I - inanimate	pl - plural	Pv - preverb	
N - noun	Pn - prenoun	Sf - suffix	

tāniki (Pr-A/pl): which ones?
tānima (Pr-I/sg): which one?
tānimayikohk/tāniyikohk (Pr): how much?
   [quantity]
tānisi (Pr): how/how are you?
tānispīhk (Pr): when?
tānitahto (Pr): how many? [number]
tānitahtwāw (Pr): how many times?
tānitē (Pr): where?
tānitowahk (Pr): what kind?
tāniwā (Pr-A/sg): where is he/she?
tāniwē (Pr-I/sg): where is it?
tāniwēhā (Pr-I/pl): where are they?
tāniwēhkāk (Pr-A/pl): where are they?
tāniyikohk/tānimayikohk (Pr): how much?
   [quantity]
tāpisimin (NA): necklace [beads]
tāpakwān (NI): snare
tāpiskākan (NA): scarf/necktie
tāpiskākan (NI): collar [horse collar]
tāpiskōc (P): just like/similar
tāpitaw/kākikē (P): always
tāpwē (P): sure/truly
tāpwēhtamowin (NI): belief
tawāw (vP): there is room/come in
tāwicihcīs (NI): the middle finger
tēhtapiwin (NI): chair/saddle
tēpakohp (P): seven
tēpakohpomitanaw (P): seventy
tēpakohposāp (P): seventeen
tēpakohptahtomitanaw (P): seventy
tēpakohptahtosāp (P): seventeen
tēpiyāhk (P): as long as, just so, at least
tēwāpitēwin (P): tooth ache
tēwēhikan/mistikwaskihk (NA): drum
tipahaskān (NI): mile
tipahikan (NI): hour/measurement
tipiskāwi-pīsim (NA): moon
tipiskāki (vP): tonight
tipiskohk (P): last night
tohtōsāpōwipimiy (NI): butter
tohtōsāpoy (NI): milk
tohtōsim (NA): a breast/teat

W

wacask (NA): muskrat
wācistakāc (P): gee! [*exclamation*]
waciston (NI): nest
waciy (NI): hill

wahpamēk (NA): whale
wāhyaw (P): far
wāhyawēs (P): little further
wākās (NA): banana
wākayōs/maskwa (NA): bear
wanaskoc (P): at the end/tip
wāpahki (vP): tomorrow
wāpakosīs (NA): mouse
wāpamon (NI): glass/mirror
wāpicāhk (NA): whooping crane
wāpikwaniy (NI): flower
wāpisiw (NA): swan
wāpos (NA): rabbit
wāposwayān (NA): rabbit skin
wāsakām (P): around
wāsaskotēnikan (NI): lamp
wāsēnamān (NI): window
wāsēnikan (NI): window
wāskahikan (NI): house
wāskāhikan (NI): pliers/screwdriver
wāskahikanihk (P): Cumberland House, SK
wāskāsimowin (NI): Round Dance
waskitaskisin (NI): overshoe
waskwēyāhtik (NA): birch tree
wāwa (NI): eggs
wāwāsaskotēpayin/wāwāstēpayin (NI): lightning
wāwāskēsiw (NA): elk
wawētinahk (P): easily
wāwi (NI): egg
wā-wīpac (P): frequently
wāwīs (P): especially/more so
wayakayak (NA): fish scales
wayawītimihk (P): outside/outdoors
wēpināson (NI): ceremonial cloth
wīhcēkaskosīs (NA): onion
wīhcēkaskosīwi-mīcimāpoy (NI): onion soup
wihkāc (P): ever
wīhkaskwa (NI): sweetgrass
wīhkēs (NI): muskrat root
wīhkihkasikan (NA): cake
wīhkwaskwa/wīhkaskwa (NI): sweet grass
wīhkwēpanak (NA): long underwear/longjohns
wīhowin (NI): name
wīhtikohkāni-mīciwin (NI): popcorn
-wikamik (Sf): denotes buildings
wīnasakātihp (NA): groundhog
wīnimahkahk (NA): garbage/slop pail
wīpac (P): soon/early
wīpicīsis (NA): goldeye

Appendix B Abbreviation Key

A - animate	P - particle	Pp - pre-particle	sg - singular
Cj - conjunction	Ph - particle phrase	Pr - pronoun	vP - verbal particle
I - inanimate	pl - plural	Pv - preverb	
N - noun	Pn - prenoun	Sf - suffix	

wīsakat (NI): pepper
wiyakāc (P): that's too bad
wiyās (NI): meat
wiyitihp (NI): brain

Y
-yāpiy (Sf): denotes cords/strings/lines
yāyaw (P): rather/instead
yēkaw (NI): sand
yīwahikanak (NA): pounded meat/fish
yiyīkastis (NA): glove
yiyīkicihcīs (NI): finger
yiyīkisitān (NI): toe

Appendix B Abbreviation Key

A - animate	P - particle	Pp - pre-particle	sg - singular
Cj - conjunction	Ph - particle phrase	Pr - pronoun	vP - verbal particle
I - inanimate	pl - plural	Pv - preverb	
N - noun	Pn - prenoun	Sf - suffix	

Appendix C: Vocabulary
English to Cree

A

ability to do something: (Pv) nihtā-
about perhaps/maybe: (P) nānitaw/(P) māskōc
abundance of: (Sf) -skāw
aeroplane: (NI) pimihākan/(NI) pimiyākan
after/later: (P) mwēstas/pātos
afternoon: (vP) pōni-āpihtā-kīsikāw
again: (P) kihtwām/āsay mīna
again and again: (Ph) kā-kihtwām
against: (P) asicāyihk/asici
all: (P) kahkiyaw
all [everybody]: (Pr) kahkiyaw awiyak
all [everything]: (Pr) kahkiyaw kīkway
all day: (P) kapē-kīsik
all night: (P) kapē-tipisk
all of a sudden/suddenly: (P) nānapēc/sisikwac
all over/everywhere: (P) misiwē
almost: (P) kēkāc/kēkā
alone/by oneself: (Pv) pēyako-
along: (P) sisonē, pimicāyihk
already: (P) āsay
also: (Ph) ēkwa mīna/ēkosi mīna
although: (P) āta
always: (P) tāpitaw
always: (P) kākikē
and/also: (P) ēkwa/(P) mīna/ (Ph) ēkwa mīna
and/now: (P)ēkwa
animal: (NA) pisiskiw
another: (Pr) kotak, kotak mīna
answers: (NI) naskwēwasihtwēwina
antelope: (NA) apistacihkos
anyway: (P) misawāc
apple: (NA) picikwās
appliances: (NI) āpacihcikana
April/Frog Moon: (NA) ayīki-pīsim
arm: (NI) mispiton
armpit: (NA) mitihtikon
around an object: (P) wāsakām
as far as/up to [distance]: (P) isko
as long as: (P) tēpiyāhk
as usual/of course: (Ph) māka mīna
Assiniboine Country: (P) asinīwipwātināhk
Assiniboine people: (NA) asinīwipwātak/
    pwāsimowak

Assiniboine reserve: asinīwipwātināhk
at the end: (P) wanaskoc
August/Flying Up Moon: (NA) ohpahōwi-pīsim
aunt, my: (NA) nikāwīs/nitōsis
aunt, my/[also: my mother-in-law]: (NA) nisikos
Autumn Moon/September: (NA) takwāki-pīsim
awhile: (P) aciyaw
axe: (NI) cīkahikan
axe handle: (NI) cīkahikanāhtik

B

back [part of body]: (NI) mispiskwan
back [direction], at the: (P) nāway/otāhk
back [up against the wall]: (P) kisipanohk
bacon: (NI) kohkōsiwiyin
bad: (Pv) māyi-
bad/evil: (Pv) maci-
badger: (NA) mistanask
bag: (NI) maskimot
ball: (NA) pahkahtowān
banana: (NA) wākās
bannock: (NA) pahkwēsikan
barrel: (NI) mahkahk
bath tub: (NI) kisipēkistēwimahkahk
bead: (NA) mīkis
beadwork: (NI) mīkisistahikēwin
beans/little bags: (NA) maskimocisak
bear, brown (NA) maskwa/wākayōs
beaver: (NA) amisk
beaver meat: (NI) amiskowiyās
because/but: (Cj) ayisk
because: (Cj) cikēmā/osām
bed: (NI) nipēwin
bee: (NA) āmōw
bee, a little: (NA) āmōsis
beef: (NI) mostosowiyās
beer: (NI) iskwēsisāpoy
beets: (NI) kā-mihkwaskwāhki
before: (Cj) pāmwayēs
before: (Pp) awasi-
before/ahead: (P) nīkān [*used when referring to
    position, but may be used to refer to time*]
begin/start: (Pv) māci-, -ati
beginning to/in process of: (Pv) ati-

Appendix C Abbreviation Key

A - animate	P - particle	Pp - pre-particle	sg - singular
Cj - conjunction	Ph - particle phrase	Pr - pronoun	vP - verbal particle
I - inanimate	pl - plural	Pv - preverb	
N - noun	Pn - prenoun	Sf - suffix	

behind [at the back/end]: (P) nāway/otāhk
belief: (NI) tāpwēhtamowin
belly/stomach: (NI) matay
belly, a big: (NI) mahkatay
below/under/lower: (P) capasīs
belt: (NI) pakwahtēhon
beneath/under: (P) atāmihk
berries [denotes]: (Sf) -imina
berries, a large patch of: (vP) mahkiminakāw
berries, saskatoon: (NI) mīnisa
beside/along: (P) asicāyihk
besides: (P) pāskac
better/more: (P) nawac
between: (P) tastawāyihk
big mouth/a mouthy person: (NA) papayēkatōn/
    osāmitōn
big top tent: (NI) āpahkwēwikamik
big/large: (Pv/Pn) misi-
big/large/great: (Pv/Pn) kihci-
birch grouse: (NA) paspaskiw
birch tree: (NA) waskwēyāhtik
bird: (NA) piyēsis
blackbird: (NA) cahcahkāyow
blanket: (NI) akohp
blessed/gift: (NI) miyikowisiwin
blood: (NI) mihko
blood poison: (NI) mihkopiscipowin
blouse/shirt: (NI) papakiwayān
blue heron: (NA) mohkahasiw
blueberries: (NI) iyinimina
boat(s): (NI) ōsi/(ōsa)
body: (NI) miyaw
bone: (NI) oskan
book: (NI) masinahikan
boot, rubber: (NI) pikīwaskisin
bottom: (P) atāmihk
bow: (NA) ahcāpiy
box: (NI) mistikowat
box, a little: (NI) miscikowacis
boy: (NA) nāpēsis
boyfriend/cousin, my: (NA) nīcimos
brain: (NI) wīyitihp
bread: (NA) pīswēkasikan
breast/teat: (NA) mitohtōsim
bridegroom: (NA) owīkihtow
brother, older: (NA) nistēs
Budding Moon/May: (NA) sākipakāwi-pīsim
buffalo: (NA) paskwāmostos/(NA) iyinito-mostos
Buffalo Narrows, SK: (P) sākitawāhk

bug: (NA) manicōs
building: (Sf) -wikamik
building nail: (NI) sakahikan
buns: (NA) pīswēkasikanisak
bus: (NA) pōsināpāsk
but: (Cj) māka/cikēmā
but/because: (Cj) ayisk
butter: (NI) tohtōsāpōwipimiy
butterfly: (NA) kamāmakos
buttocks: (NI) misōkan
buttocks, large(NI) mahkisōkan

C
cafe/dining room: (NI) mīcisowikamik
cake: (NA) sīwihkasikan wihkihkasikan
campfire: (NI) kotawān/kocawānis
candy: (NI) sīwinos/sīwās
canoe: (NI) cīmān
car: (NA) sēhkēpayīs/otāpānāsk/pimipicēs
carefully: (P) nasihkāc
carefully: (P) pēyahtak
carrot: (NA) oskātāskw
cat: (NA) minōs/pōsīs
caterpillar: (NA) mohtew
caucasian: (NA) mōniyāw/mōniyās
ceremonial cloth: (NI) wēpināson
chair: (NI) tēhtapiwin
chair, a little: (NI) cēhcapiwinis
cheek, a: (NI) maniway
cheek, my: (NI) naniway
chest, a: (NI) māskikan
chest, my: (NI) nāskikan
chicken, domestic: (NA) pāhkahāhkwān
chicken hawk: (NA) piponāyis
chief: (NA) okimāhkān
child: (NA) awāsis
child, your: (NA) kicawāsimis
child(ren), my: (NA) nicawāsimis(ak)
children: (NA) awāsisak
child(ren), your: (NA) kicawāsimis(ak)
chin: (NI) mikwaskonēw
Chinese people: (NA) apihkēsak/ sēkipwacāskwak
chipmunk: (NA) sāsakāwāpiskos
Chipweyan country/region: (NI) cīpwēyānināhk
Chipweyan people: (NA) cīpwēyānak
chokecherries: (NI) takwahimināna
chokecherry tree: (NA) takwahimināhtik
city: (NI) kihci-ōtēnaw
clean thoughts: (NI) kanātēyihtamowin

Appendix C Abbreviation Key

A - animate	P - particle	Pp - pre-particle	sg - singular
Cj - conjunction	Ph - particle phrase	Pr - pronoun	vP - verbal particle
I - inanimate	pl - plural	Pv - preverb	
N - noun	Pn - prenoun	Sf - suffix	

clock: (NA) pīsimohkān
watch, a: (NA) pīsimohkānis
cloth/fabric: (NI) papakiwēyānēhkin
cloth, made of: (Sf) -ēkin
clothes: (NI) ayiwinisa
clothes dryer: (NI) pahkwāstēwinikan
clown: (NA) mohcohkān
coat: (NI) miskotākay
coat, man's: (NI) nāpēwasākay
coat, woman's: (NI) iskwēwasākay
coffee: (NI) pihkahtēwāpoy
co-in-law, my: (NA) nitihtāwāw
co-in-law, your: (NA) kitihtāwāw
collar: (NI) tāpiskākan
come: (P) āstam
come here.(Ph) āstam ōta
come: (Pv) pē-/pēci-
come in: (Ph) tawāw
constitution: (NI) ostēsimāwiyasiwēwin
continuous (P): nāspic
cord/string: (Sf) -ēyāpiy/-yāpiy
corn: (NA) mahtāmin
corner: (vP) kīhkwētakāk
correct/right: (P) kwayask
cotton [fabric]: (NI) papakōwayānēkin
counted, it is: (vP) akimāw
cow: (NA) mostos
coyote: (NA) mēstacākanis
cramps: (NI) ocipitikowin
cranberries: (NI) maskēkōmina/nīpimināna
crane: (NA) ocāhk
cream: (NI) manihikan
Cree language: (NI) nēhiyawēwin
Cree, a person: (NA) nēhiyaw
Cree ceremony: (NI) nēhiyaw-mawimoscikēwin
Cree region/country: (P) nēhiyānāhk
crow: (NA) āhāsiw
culture: (NI) pimācihowin
Cumberland House, SK: (P) wāskahikanihk
cup: (NI) minihkwākan/(NI) minihkwācikan
cupboard: (NI) akocikan
currants/raisins: (NA) sōminis
curse: (NI) pāstāmowin

D

daughter, my: (NA) nitānis
daughter, your: (NA) kitānis
dawn, approaching: (NI) pētāpan
day after tomorrow: (vP) awasi-wāpahki

day before/yesterday: (vP) awasi-otākosīhk
day, all: (P) kapē-kīsik
December/Frost-Exploding Moon: (NA)
    pawācakinasīsi-pīsim
deer: (NA) apisimōsos
derriere, a big: (NI) mahkisōkan
difficulty: (NI) mākohikēwin
dining room: (NI) mīcisowikamik
direction [denotes to/at]: (P) itē
direction, in that: (Ph) itēhkē isi
direction to/towards: (P) isi
dish: (NI) oyākan
dish washer: (NI) kisīpēyākanikan
doctor: (NA) maskihkīwiyiniw
dog: (NA) atim
dog, my: (NA) nitēm
doll: (NA) awāsisihkān
dollar, one: (P) pēyakwāpisk
dollars, two: (P) nīswāpisk
dollars, three: (P) nistwāpisk
dollars, five: (P) niyānwāpisk
dollars, four: (P) nēwāpisk
dollars,six: (P) nikotwāswāpisk
dollars, seven: (P) tēpakohptahtwāpisk
don't: [Imperative only] ēkāwiya/ēkā
door: (NI) iskwāhtēm
down/downstairs: (P) nīhcāyihk
down/on ground: (P) mohcihk
down lower: (P) capasīs
dress: (NI) miskotākay
dress, woman's: (NI) iskwēwasākay
drum: (NA) mistikwaskihk
drum: (NA) tēwēhikan
duck: (NA) sīsīp

E

eagle: (NA) mikisiw/kihēw
Eagle Moon/February: (NA) mikisiwi-pīsim
eagle-bone whistle: (NI) pipikwan
ear: (NI) mihtawakay
ears, one with big: (NI) mahkihtawakay
early: (P) wīpac
earth: (NI) askiy
easily: (P) wawētinahk
east, to the: (P) sākāstēnohk
effort, great: (Pv) sōhki-
egg: (NI) wāwi
eggs: (NI) wāwa
eight: (P) ayēnānēw

Appendix C Abbreviation Key

A - animate	P - particle	Pp - pre-particle	sg - singular
Cj - conjunction	Ph - particle phrase	Pr - pronoun	vP - verbal particle
I - inanimate	pl - plural	Pv - preverb	
N - noun	Pn - prenoun	Sf - suffix	

eighteen: (P) ayēnānēwosāp

eighty: (P) ayēnānēwomitanaw

elbow: (NI) mitōskwan

Elders: (NA) kēhtē-ayak

elevator: (NI) āmaciwēpicikan

eleven: (P) pēyakosāp

elk: (NA) wāwāskēsiw

English: (NI) ākayāsimowin

enough: (P) ēkosi

especially: (P) wāwis

Europeans: (NA) pītatowēwak

even: (P) ahpō

ever: (P) wihkāc

everybody: (Pr) kahkiyaw awiyak

everyone/anyone: (Pr) pikw āwiyak

everything: (Pr) kahkiyaw kīkway

everything: (Pr) piko kīkway

everywhere: (P) pokwītē/(Ph) misiwē ita

evil: (Pv) maci-

eye: (NI) miskīsik

eyes, one with big: (NA) mahkacāp

F

fabric: (Sf) -ēkin

faint [condition]: (NI) kipatāhtāmowin

far: (P) wāhyaw

farm/field: (NI) kistikān

farther, a little: (P) wāhyawēs

faster: (P) sohkēsīs

father, my: (NA) nōhtāwiy

father, your: (NA) kōhtāwiy

father-in-law/uncle: (NA) nisis

fear: (NA) mākwēyimowin

feather: (NA) mīkwan

February/Eagle Moon: (NA) mikisiwi-pīsim

fence: (NI) mēnikan

fever: (NI) kisisowin

field/farm: (NI) kistikān

fifteen: (P) niyānosāp

fifty: (P) niyānomitanaw

finally: (P) piyisk

finger: (NI) yiyīkicihcīs

finger, index/pointer: (NI) itwahikanicihcīs

finger, middle: (NI) tāwicihcīs

finger, ring: (NI) āhcaniwicihcīs

finger, the little: (NI) iskwēcihcīs

finger/toe nail: (NA) maskasiy

fire, there is a: (NI) iskotēw

firefly: (NA) kwēkwēkocīs

fireplace: (NI) kotawān/asiskihkwān

firewood: (NI) mihta

first before doing something: (P) pitamā

first/before/ahead: (P) nīkān: [*referring to position but may be used to refer to priority in time*]

fish [generic term]: (NA) kinosēw

fish, lots of: (vP) kinosēskāw

fish plant: (NI) kinosēwikamik

five: (P) niyānan

five dollars: (P) niyānanwāpisk

floor, on the: (P) mohcihtakāhk

flower: (NI) wāpikwaniy

fly: (NA) ōcēw

Flying Up Moon/August: (NA) ohpahōwi-pīsim

food/groceries: (NI) mīciwin

fool, a: (NA) okakēpātis

foolishness: (NI) kakēpātisiwin

foolishness, in my own: (P) nikīskwēyāwinihk

foot: (NI) misit

foot, a big: (NI) mahkisit

forehead: (NI) miskahtik

fork: (NI) cīstahāsēpon

Fort Qu'Appelle, SK: (P) kipahikanihk

forty: (P) nēmitanaw

four: (P) nēwo

four brothers: (vP) nēwāpēwak

four times: (P) nēwāw

fourteen: (P) nēwosāp

fox: (NA) mahkēsīs

freezer, a: (NI) āhkwatihcikan

French people/wood boat people: (NA) mistikōsiwak

frequently: (P) wā-wīpac

Friday: (vP) niyāno-kīsikāw

fridge: (NI) tahkascikan

friend(s), my: (NA) nitōtēm(ak)

friend/partner: (NA) wīcēwākan

frog: (NA) ayīkis

Frog Moon/April: (NA) ayīki-pīsim

from/for: (P) ohci

Frost Moon/November: (NA) ihkopiwi-pīsim

Frost-Exploding Moon/ December: (NA) pawācak-inasīsipīsim

frying pan: (NA) sāsāpiskisikan

G

garbage/slop pail: (NA) wīnimahkahk

garden: (NI) kistcikānis

gee!: (P) wācistakāc

geese: (NA) niskak

Appendix C Abbreviation Key

A - animate	P - particle	Pp - pre-particle	sg - singular
Cj - conjunction	Ph - particle phrase	Pr - pronoun	vP - verbal particle
I - inanimate	pl - plural	Pv - preverb	
N - noun	Pn - prenoun	Sf - suffix	

gift/blessed: (NI) miyikowisiwin
girl, a little: (NA) iskwēsis
girl, young: (NA) oskinīkiskwēw
girlfriend/cousin: (NA) nīcimos
glass/mirror: (NI) wāpamon
glasses, eye: (NI) miskīsikohkāna
glove: (NI) yiyīkastis
go! Get out of here: (P-sg) awas!
go! Get out of here: (P-pl) awasitik!
go: (P-sg) niyā
go: (P-pl) niyāk
go and: (Pv) nitawi-
go away!: (P-sg) awas!
go on with you!: (P-sg) awas!
goldeye: (NA) wīpicīsis
good: (Pv) miyo-
good naturedness: (NI) miywātisiwin
goose/(geese): (NA) niska(k)
Goose Month/March: (NA) niski-pīsim
gooseberries: (NA) sāpōminak
gopher/squirrel: (NA) anikwacas
grandfather(s), my: (NA) nimosōm(ak)
grandmother(s), my: (NA) nōhkom(ak)
Grandmother's Bay, SK: (NI) kōhkominānihk
grapes/raisins: (NA) sōminak
grass/hay: (NI) maskosiya/ nīpiya
grass dance: (NI) pwātisimowin
grasshopper: (NA) kwāskohcīsis
grease: (NI) pimiy
Great Moon/January: (NA) kisē-pīsim
great/big/large: (Pv/Pn) kihci-
great/extremely: (Pv) kakwāhyaki
grinder: (NI) sikopocikan
groundhog: (NA) winasakātēhp
grouse: (NA) pihēw
grouse, a birch: (NA) papaskiw
guitar string: (NI) kitohcikanēyāpiy
gum: (NA) pikiw
gum, a bit: (NA) pikīs
gymnasium: (NI) mētawēwikamik

H
hair: (NI) mēscakāsa
hair off a hide: (NI) pīwaya
half: (P) āpihtaw
half past: (Ph) mīna āpihtaw
ham/pork: (NI) kohkōsiwiyās
hamburger/ground meat: (NI) sikopicikaniwiyās
hand: (NI) micihciy

hard: (Pv) sōhki-
hardly: (P) akāwāc
hat/cap: (NI) astotin
Hatching Moon/June: (NA) paskāwihowi-pīsim
hawk, a large: (NA) sākwahtamo
hawk: (NA) kēhkēk
hay: (NI) maskosiya
head: (NI) mistikwān
head roach-regalia: (NI) sēskicēs
heart: (NI) mitēh
herb tea: (NI) maskihkīwāpoy
here take this: [Imperative only] nah
heel, a: (NI) mahkwan
heel, my : (NI) nahkwan
hide, a: (NI) pāhkēkin
highway: (NI) kihci-mēskanaw
hill: (NI) ispatinaw/waciy
him/her: (Pr) wiya
him/her too: (Pr) wīsta
home: (NI) mīkiwām
home, my: (NI) nīki
home, your: (NI) kīki
honey: (NI) amōmēyi/(NI) amōsīsipāskwat
hopple: (NI) napwapison
horse: (NA) misatim/mistatim
horse, a little: (NA) miscacimosis
horse collar: (NI) tāpiskākan
hospital: (NI) āhkosiwikamik
hour/measurement: (NI) tipahikan
house: (NI) wāskahikan
how?: (Pr) tānisi?
how?: (Pr) tānis īsi
how are you?: (Pr) tānisi?
how many? [numbers]: (Pr) tānitahto?
how many times?: (Pr) tānitahtwāw?
how much? [quantity]: (Pr) tāniyikohk?
how much? [quantity]: (Pr) tānimayikohk?
hunter: (NA) omācīw
hurry up: (P) kiyipa
husband, my: (NA) nināpēm/niwīkimākan

I
I/me: (Pr) niya
I suppose/maybe: (Ph) āhpō ētikwē
ice: (NA) miskwamiy
if: (P) kīspin/kīsāpin
illness/sickness: (NI) āhkosiwin
immediately: (P) sēmāk
in the morning [tomorrow]: (vP) kīkisēpāki

Appendix C Abbreviation Key

A - animate	P - particle	Pp - pre-particle	sg - singular
Cj - conjunction	Ph - particle phrase	Pr - pronoun	vP - verbal particle
I - inanimate	pl - plural	Pv - preverb	
N - noun	Pn - prenoun	Sf - suffix	

index finger/pointer: (NI) itwahikanicihcīs
Indian agent: (NA) sōniyāwikimāw
Indian person: (NA) iyiniw
indicates a question: (P) cī
indoors/inside: (P) pīhcāyihk
inland [on the inside]: (P) nohcimihk
inside/indoors: (P) pīhtokamik
inside/indoors: (P) pīhcāyihk
instead: (P) nitawāc
intelligence: (P) iyīnisiwin
iron: (NI) pīwāpisk
iron, an [clothes]: (NA) sōskwahikan
it is all right/okay/never mind: (P) kiyām
it is a good thing: (P) takōtāni

J

jackrabbit: (NA) mistāpos
jail/Fort Qu'Appelle: (P) kipahikanihk
January/Great Moon: (NA) kisē-pīsim
jar: (NI) mōtēyāpisk
jaw: (NI) mitāpiskan
juice/pop/kool aid: (NI) sīwāpoy/kisāstewāpoy
July/Moulting Moon: (NA) paskowi-pīsim
June/Hatching Moon: (NA) paskāwihowi-pīsim
just like/similar: (P) tāpiskōc
just right amount: (P) nahiyikohk

K

kettle: (NA) sīsip-askihk
key: (NI) āpāpiskahikan
killdeer: (NA) otāpiskākanēsīs
kindergarten pupils: (NA) okāsīcihkomēsak
kindness: (NI) kisēwātisiwin
king: (NA) kihc-ōkimāw
kinikinik: (NI) mixture of tree bark and leaves
knee: (NI) mihcikwan
knife: (NI) mōhkamān
kool aid: (NI) sīwāpoy

L

lace, shoe: (NI) maskisinēyāpiy
ladder: (NI) kīhcēkosīwināhtik
lady, old: (NA) nōtokwēw
lake: (NI) sākahikan
lake trout: (NA) namēkōs
lamp: (NI) wāsasotēnikan
land: (NI) askiy
lard: (NI) pimiy
large/great/greatly: (Pn/Pv) kihci-

large/big/greatly: (Pn/Pv) misi-
lasso: (NI) tāpakwēwēpinikan
last night: (P) tipiskohk
last/one time: (P) iskwayāc
later: (P) pātos
later: (P) mwēstas
Le Pas, Manitoba: (P) opāskwēyāhk
leaf: (NI) nīpiy
leather: (NI) pahkēkin
left, to the : (P); namahcīhk
leftover/Reserve: (NI) iskonikan
leg: (NI) miskāt
leg, my: (NI) niskāt
legend/story: (NI) ātayōhkēwin
Let me see: (P) mahti
lettuce: (NI) nīpiya
lift [elevator], a: (NI) āmaciwēpicikan
lightning: (NI) wāwāsaskotēpayin
like that: (Ph) ēkosi isi
line/cord/string: (Sf) -yāpiy/-ēyāpiy
lion: (NA) mistahkēsiw
liquids: (Sf) -āpoy
liquor: (NI) iskotēwāpoy
little bit, a: (P) apisīs
Lloydminister, SK: (P) pimicāskwēyāsihk
log, a: (NA) mistik
long underwear/longjohns: (NI)
pīhtowēskikanak/wīhkwēpāna
loon: (NA) mākwa
loss of breath: (NI) kipatāhtāmowin
lots [number]: (P) mihcēt
lots [quantity]: (P) mistahi
love: (NI) sākihitowin
lower: (P) capasīs

M

made of metal: (Sf) -āpisk
magpie: (NA) apisci-kahkākīs
man/men: (NA) nāpēw
man, my: (NA) nināpēm
many/lots: (P) mihcēt
many times: (P) mihcētwāw
maple sugar: (NI) sīsipāskwat
March/Goose Moon: (NA) niski-pīsim
match: (NI) kocawākanis
Mating Moon/September: (NA) nōcihitowi-pīsim
mattress: (NI) anāskāsimon
May/Budding Moon: (NA) sākipakāwi-pīsim
maybe: (P) māskōc/(Ph) ahpō ētikwē nānitaw

Appendix C Abbreviation Key

A - animate	P - particle	Pp - pre-particle	sg - singular
Cj - conjunction	Ph - particle phrase	Pr - pronoun	vP - verbal particle
I - inanimate	pl - plural	Pv - preverb	
N - noun	Pn - prenoun	Sf - suffix	

measurement: (NI) tipahikan
meat: (NI) wiyās
medicine: (NI) maskihkiy
medicine: (NI) maskihkīwāpoy
me: (Pr) niya
me too: (Pr) nīsta
meeting: (NI) nakiskātowin
meeting [conference]: (NI) māmawapiwin
metal, made of: (Sf) -āpisk
Metis people: (NA) āpihtawikosisānak
Metis person: (NA) āpihtawikosisān
microwave: (NI) kēsiskawihkasikan
midday/noon: (vP) āpihtā-kīsikāw
midnight: (vP) āpihtā-tipiskāw
middle, in the: (Pp) tāwāyihk
Migrating Moon/October: (NA) pimihāwi-pīsim
mile: (NI/P) tipahikan/tipahaskān
milk: (NI) tohtōsāpoy
minute: (NI) cipahikanis
mirror: (NI) wāpamon
mitt: (NA) astis
mole: (NA) pōtācikēsīs
Mom: [Vocative only] nikā
Monday/the first day: (vP) pēyako-kīsikāw
money: (NA) sōniyāw
month: (NA) pīsim
moon: (NA) tipiskāwi-pīsim
moose: (NA) mōswa
moose hide: (NI) mōswēkin
moose, lots of : (vP) mōswaskāw
moose meat: (NI) mōswowiyās
more: (P) ayiwāk/nawāc
morning, it is: (vP) kikisēpāyāw
morning, it is: (vP) wāpan
mosquito: (NA) sakimēs
mosquitoes, lots of: (NA) sakimēskāw
mother, his/her: (NA) okāwīya
mother, my: (NA) nikāwiy
mother, my: (NA) nimāmā
motorized vehicle: (NA) pimipicēs
Moulting Moon/July: (NA) paskowi-pīsim
mouse: (NA) wāpakosīs
mouth: (NI) mitōn
mouth, (person with) a big: (NA) mahkitōn
much, that: (P) ēwakwayikohk
much/lots: (P) mistahi
mucus: (NA) mitatikom
mud/soil: (NI) asiskiy
mule: (NA) sōsowatim

musical instrument: (NI) kitohcikan
muskrat: (NA) wacask
muskrat root: (NI) wīhkēs

N

nail [building]: (NI) sakahikan
nail, finger/toe: (NA) maskasiy
name: (NI) wīhowin
name, my: (NI) niwīhowin
navel, my: (NI) nitisiy
near: (P) cīki
neck: (NI) mikwayaw
necklace [beads]: (NA) tahpisiminak
necktie: (NA) tāpiskākan
nest: (NI) waciston
net: (NA) ayapiy
never: (Ph) mōy wihkāc
never mind: (P) kiyām
new/recent: (P) mastaw
news: (NI) ācimowin
newspaper: (NI) ācimowasinahikan
nice: (Pv) miyo-
night: (vP) tipiskāw
night after next: (vP) awasi-tipiskāki
night before last: (P) awasi-tipiskohk
nightmare: (NI) kostācihkwāmiwin
nine: (P) kēkā-mitātaht
nineteen: (P) kēkāc-nīsitanaw
ninety: (P) kēkāc-mitātaht-omitanaw
ninety-nine: (P) kēkac-mitātahtomitanaw-
    mitātahtosāp
no: (P) namōya/mwāc/mōy
nobody: (Pr) nam āwiyak
north, in the: (P) kīwētinohk
nose: (NI) mikot
nose: (NI) miskiwan
nose, big: (NI) mahkikot
not even: (Ph) mwāc ahpō
not yet: (Ph) namōya cēskwa
nothing: (Pr) nama kīkway
November/Frost Moon: (NA) iyīkopiwi-pīsim
now: (P) ēkwa/mēkwāc
numbers: (NI) akihtāsona
nun: (NA) ayamihēwiskwēw
nurse: (NA) maskihkīwiskwēw
nut: (NA) pakān

O

oatmeal: (NA) anōmin

Appendix C Abbreviation Key

A - animate
Cj - conjunction
I - inanimate
N - noun

P - particle
Ph - particle phrase
pl - plural
Pn - prenoun

Pp - pre-particle
Pr - pronoun
Pv - preverb
Sf - suffix

sg - singular
vP - verbal particle

October/Migrating Moon: (NA) pimihāwi-pīsim
of course: (Ph) māka mīna/(P) cikēmā
offering: (NI) macostēhamānakēwin
oh: (P) āh
oil: (NI) pimiy
Ojibway reserve/region: (P) nahkawiyinīnāhk
Ojibway, Saulteaux person/people: (NA)
    nahkawiyiniw
old lady: (NA) nōtikwēw
on top of: (P) tahkohc
once: (P) pēyakwāw
once upon a time/one time: (Ph) pēyakwāw ēsa
one: (P) pēyak
one dollar: (P) pēyakwāpisk
one hundred: (P) mitātahtomitanaw
one thousand: (P) pēyakwāw-kihci-
    mitātahtomitanaw
onion: (NA) wīhcēkaskosīs
onion soup: (NA) wīhcēkaskosīs-mīcimāpoy
only: (P) piko/tēpiyāhk
opposite: (P) naspāc
or: (Cj) ahpō
or else: (Cj) kēmā/ahpō cī
orange: (NA) osāwās
orange juice/pop: (NI) osāwāpoy
other: (Pr) kotak
others: (Pr) kotakak
otter: (NA) nikik
out of: (P) ohci
outer space: (NI) kihci-kīsik
outside/outdoors: (P) wayawītimihk
oven: (NA) sēkowēpināpisk
over again: (Ph) āsay mīna
over there: (P) ēkotē
overshoe: (NI) waskitaskisin
owl: (NA) ōhōw

P

paddle: (NA) apoy
pail: (NA) askihk
pants: (NA) mitās
paper: (NI) masinahikanēkin
park, at the [Creeized word]: (P) parkihk
partner/friend: (NA) wīcēwākan
partridge: (NA) pihēw
pelican: (NA) cahcahkiw
pemmican: (NI) pimīhkān
pencil: (NA/NI) masinahikanāhcikos

penny: (NA) pīwāpiskos
pepper: (NI) askīwi-sīwihtākan/pēskōmina/wīsakat
perhaps: (P) ētokē
perhaps/I wonder: (Ph) matwān cī
perhaps/maybe: (Ph) ahpō ētikwē/(P) māskōc/(P)
    nānitaw
perhaps: (P) kēhcināc
person: (NA) ayisiyiniw
person who talks too much: (NA) osāmitōn
pig: (NA) kohkōs
pile of bones/Regina, SK: (vP) oskana kā-asastēki
pillow: (NI) aspiskwēsimon
pills: (NI) maskihkīsa
pipe: (NA) ospwākan
plate: (NI) napakiyākan
platter: (NI) mistiyākan
please/let's see: (P) mahti
pliers/screwdriver: (NI) wāskāhikan
pointed-lips: (NI) cīpotōn
poison: (NI) piscipowin
policeman: (NA) simākanis
pony: (NA) miscacimosis
pop/orange juice: (NI) osāwāpoy/sīwāpoy/
    kisāstēwāpoy
popcorn: (NI) wihtikohkānimīciwin
porcupine: (NA) kākwa
pork: (NI) kohkōsiwiyās
pot: (NA) askihkos
potato(es): (NI) napatāk(wa)
potatoes: (NI) askipwāwa/kistikāna
pounded meat/fish: (NA) yīwahikanak
prairie chicken: (NA) pihēw
prayer: (NI) mawimoscikēwin
preacher/priest: (NA) ayamihēwiyiniw
presently: (P) mēkwāc
pretend: (Sf) -kāso
Prince Albert, SK: (P) kistapinānihk
province: (vP) kā-piskatahastāhk
Punnichy, SK: (P) panicāyisihk
puppy/little dog: (NA) acimosis
purposely: (P) ohcitaw

Q

quarter: (NA) pēyak sōniyās
quarters, two: (NA) nīso sōniyās
quarters, three: (NA) nisto sōniyās
queen: (NA) kihci-okimāskwēw
question marker: (P) cī

Appendix C Abbreviation Key

A - animate	P - particle	Pp - pre-particle	sg - singular
Cj - conjunction	Ph - particle phrase	Pr - pronoun	vP - verbal particle
I - inanimate	pl - plural	Pv - preverb	
N - noun	Pn - prenoun	Sf - suffix	

questions: (NI) kakwēcihkēmowina
quickly: (P) kēsiskaw
quit/stop: (Pv) pōni-

R
rabbit: (NA) wāpos
rabbit, a big: (NA) mistāpos
rabbitskin: (NA) wāposwayān
raccoon: (NA) pisiskēs
radio: (NI) kitohcikan kā-natohtamihk
raincoat: (NI) kimiwanasākay
rainwater: (NI) kimiwanāpoy
raisins: (NA) sōminak
raspberry: (NA) ayōskan
rather/instead: (P) yāyaw
really/true: (P) tāpwē
really/surely/very: (P) mētoni
red willows: (NI) mihkopēmakwa
refrigerator: (NI) tahkascikan
Regina, SK: (vP) oskana kā-asastēki
relative, my: (NA) niwāhkōmākan
Reserve, Indian: (NI) iskonikan/askīhk
ribbon: (NA) sēnapān
rice: (NA) wāpinōmin
rifle: (NI) pāskisikan
right now: (P) sēmāk
right, to/on the: (P) kihcīniskēhk
right/true/correct: (P) kwayask
ring: (NA) āhcanis
ring finger: (NI) āhcaniwicihcīs
river: (NI) sīpiy
road: (NI) mēskanaw
robin: (NA) pihpihciw
rock/stone: (NA) asiniy
rope: (NI) pīminahkwān
rose: (NI) mihkokwaniy
rose hips: (NA) okiniyak
round dance: wāskāsimowin
rubber boot: (NI) pikīwaskisin

S
saddle: (NA) tēhtapiwin
sage: (NI) paskwāwīhkwaskwa
salad [literally leaves]: (NI) nīpiya
salt: (NI) sīwihtākan
same: (P) pēyakwan
sand: (NI) yēkaw
sandals: (NI) kisē-manitowaskisina

satin/silk fabric: (NI) sēnapānēkin
Saturday: (vP) nikotwāso-kīsikāw
sausages: (NI) micakisīsa
Saulteaux reserve: (P) nahkawiyinīnāhk
Saulteaux person: (P) nahkawiyiniw
saw, a: (NI) kīskipocikan
scarf, a warm: (NA) kīsowahpison
scarf/necktie: (NA) tāpiskākan
school: (NI) kiskinwahamātowikamik
scissors: (NI) mōswākan
screwdriver: (NI) wāskāhikan
secretly: (P) kīmōc
separation [re: marriage]: (NI) paskēwihitowin
September/Autumn Moon: (NA) takwāki-pīsim
seven: (P) tēpakohp
seventeen: (P) tēpakohposāp
seventy: (P) tēpakohpomitanaw
shawl: (NA) akwanān
sheep: (NA) māyatihk
sheet: (NI) anāskān
shirt/blouse: (NI) papakiwayān
shoe: (NI) maskisin
shorts: (NA) kīskimitās
shoulder: (NI) mitihtiman
shoulder blade: (NI) mitīhikan
shrub mixture [red willow bark & green leaves]:
    (NI) kinikinik
sibling, my: (NA) nītisān
similar: (P) tāpiskōc
since: (P) aspin
sinew: (NI) astisiy
sink: (NI) kasīhkwēwiyākan
Sioux people: (NA) pwātak
Sioux reserve: (P) pwātināhk
sister, your: (NA) kimis
sister [my older]: (NA) nimis
sister-in-law, my [used by female only]: (NA)
    nicāhkos
six: (P) nikotwāsik
sixteen: (P) nikotwāsosāp
sixty: (P) nikotwāsomitanaw
skirt: (NI) kīskasākay/kīskasākās
skunk: (NA) sikāk
skunk, a little: (NA) sikākos
sky: (NI) kīsik
sled/car: (NA) otāpanāsk
slowly: (P) nasihkāc/papēyahtak
smokey, a haze: (NI) osāpahtēw

Appendix C Abbreviation Key

A - animate	P - particle	Pp - pre-particle	sg - singular
Cj - conjunction	Ph - particle phrase	Pr - pronoun	vP - verbal particle
I - inanimate	pl - plural	Pv - preverb	
N - noun	Pn - prenoun	Sf - suffix	

snake: (NA) kinēpik
snare: (NI) tāpakwān
snow: (NA) kōna
snow water: (NI) kōniwāpoy
snowshoe: (NA) asām
so: (P) ēkosi
soap: (NI) kisīpēkinikan
sock: (NA) asikan
soft: (Pv) yōski-
soil/mud: (NI) asiskiy
soldier: (NA) simākanis
some: (P) ātiht
something: (Pr-sg) kīkway
some things: (Pr-pl): kīkwaya
someone: (Pr-sg) awiyak
some people: (Pr-pl) awiyakak
son, my: (NA) nikosis
soon: (P) wīpac
soot: (NI) pihko
soup: (NI) mīcimāpoy
south, in the: (P) sāwanohk
spider: (NA) ayapihkēsīs
spittle: (NI) sihkowin
spoon: (NA) ēmihkwān
spoon, a little: (NA) ēmihkwānis
spring fever: (NI) sīkwanāspinēwin
squirrel: (NA) anikwacās
Stanley Mission, SK: (P) āmaciwīspimowinihk
star: (NA) acāhkos
start/begin: (Pv) ati-
still/yet: (P) kēyāpic
stocking: (NA) asikan
stomach/belly: (NI) matay
stone: (NA) asiniy
stop: (Pv) pōni-
store: (NI) atāwēwikamik
story: (NI) ātayōhkēwin/ācimowin
stove: (NA) kotawānāpisk
strawberry: (NI) mitēhimin
string, violin/guitar: (NI) kitohcikanēyāpiy
string: (NI) tahkopicikanēyāpiy
string: (Sf) -yāpiy/-ēyāpiy
striped gopher: (NA) sasakawāpiskos
student: (NA) kiskinwahamawākan
sturgeon, a fish: (NA) namēw
suckerfish, a: (NA) namēpin
suddenly: (P) sisikoc
sugar: (NA) sīwinikan

suitcase: (NI) pōsiyiwat
sun: (NA) kīsikāw-pīsim
Sunday: (vP) ayamihēwi-kīsikāw
surely/true: (P) tāpwē
surprise/wonder [exclamation]: (P) māmaskāc
swan: (NA) wāpisiw
sweater: (NI)
pīswēsākas/sīpēkiskāwayān/sīpēkiskāwisākās
sweet baked goods: (NA) sīwihkasikanak
sweetgrass: (NI) wīhkwaskwa
swine: (NA) kohkōs
T
table: (NI) mīcisowināhtik
tea: (NI) nihtiy
tea, herbal(NI) maskihkīwāpoy
teddy bear: (NA) maskohkān
television: (NI) cikāstēpayihcikan
ten: (P) mitātaht
tent: (NI) pakwānikamik
that much: (P) ēkwayikohk
that one: (Pr-A/sg) ana
that one: (Pr-I/sg) anima
that same one: (Pr-I/sg) ēwakw ānima
that same one: (Pr-A/sg) ēwakw āna
that's enough/right/all: (P) ēkosi
that's the one: (Pr) ēwako
that's too bad: (P) wiyakāc
that yonder: (Pr-A/sg) nāha
that yonder: (Pr-I/sg) nēma
then: (Ph) ēkosi mīna/(P) ēkosi
them: (Pr) wiyawāw
them too: (Pr) wīstawāw
there, a specific place: (P) ēkota
there are four brothers: (vP) nēwāpēwak
there is room/come in: (vP) tawāw
these: (Pr-A/pl) ōki
these: (Pr-I/pl) ōhi
they too: (Pr) wīstawāw
thigh: (NI) mipwām
things: (NI) kīkwaya
thimble: (NA) kaskikwāsonāpisk
thirteen: (P) nistosāp
thirty: (P) nistomitanaw
this: (Pr-A/sg) awa
this: (Pr-I/sg) ōma
this morning: (P) kīkisēp
this same one: (Pr-A/sg) ēwakw āwa
this same one: (Pr-I-/sg) ēwakw ōma

Appendix C Abbreviation Key

A - animate	P - particle	Pp - pre-particle	sg - singular
Cj - conjunction	Ph - particle phrase	Pr - pronoun	vP - verbal particle
I - inanimate	pl - plural	Pv - preverb	
N - noun	Pn - prenoun	Sf - suffix	

this way: (P) omisīsi
those: (Pr-A/pl) aniki
those: (Pr-I/pl) anihi
those same ones: (Pr-A/pl) ēwakw āniki
those same ones: (Pr-I/pl) ēwakw ānihi
those yonder: (Pr-A/pl) nēki
those yonder: (Pr-I/pl) nēhi
thoughts: (NI) māmitonēyihcikana
thousand: (P) kihci-mitātahtomitanaw
thread: (NA) asapāp
three: (P) nisto
three dollars: (P) nistawāpisk
three times/thrice: (P) nistwāw
through: (Pv/Pn) sāpo-
thumb: (NI) misicihcān
thunderbird: (NA) piyēsiw
Thursday: (vP) nēwo-kīsikāw
tipi: (NI) mīkiwāhp
tipi smoke opening: (P) sāpahcikanihk
today: (P) anohc
today: (Ph) anohc kā-kīsikāk
to go and: (Pv) nitawi-
to want: (Pv) nohtē
toast: (NA) pihkasikan
toboggan(s): (NA) napakitāpānāsk(wak)
toe: (NI) yiyīkisitān
toe nail/finger nail: (NA) maskasiy
together: (Pv) māmawi-
toilet bowl/bed pan: (NI) mīsiwoyākan
toilet paper: (NI) kimisāhowinēkin
tomato: (NA) kihc-ōkiniy
tomorrow: (vP) wāpahki
tonight: (vP) tipiskāki
tooth: (NI) mīpit
tooth, my: (NI) nīpit
toothache: (NI) tēwāpitēwin
top of, on: (P) tahkohc
town: (NI) ōcēnās
toy: (NI) mētawākan
train: (NA) iskotēwotāpānāsk
trapper: (NA) owanihikēw
treaty/constitution: (NI) ostēsimāwasinahikēwin
tree: (NA) mitōs
tree, chokecherry: (NA) takwahiminānāhtik
trousers, a pair: (NA) mitās
trout, lake: (NA) namēkōs
town: (NI) ōtēnaw
true: (P) tāpwē/kwayask

truly: (P) tāpwē
try: (Pv) kakwē-
Tuesday: (vP) nīso-kīsikāw
tullabee: (NA) otōnapiy
turnip: (NA) otisihkān
turtle: (NA) mihkināhk
twelve: (P) nīsosāp
twenty: (P) nīstanaw
twice: (P) nīswāw
two: (P) nīso
two hundred: (P) nīswāw mitātahtomitanaw

U

uncle, my [also father-in-law]: (NA) nisis
uncle [father's brother]: (NA) nōhcāwīs
under: (P) atāmihk/sīpāhk
underclothes: (NI) atāmayiwinisa
undershorts: (NA) pīhtawētās
underwater: (P) atāmipīhk
underwear, long/longjohns: (NA) pīh-
towēskikanak/wīhkwēpānak
United States: (P) kihci-mōhkomānināhk/(NI)
akāmi-tipahaskān
university: (NI) kihci-kiskinwahamātowikamik
until: (Cj) ispī
up to a distance: (P) isko
up/upstairs: (P) ispimihk
us (inclusive) too/also: (Pr) kīstanaw
us (exclusive) too/also: (Pr) nīstanān
us/we: (Pr) niyanān
usually/used to: (P) māna

W

wait a minute/wait: (P) cēskwa
want to/to: (Pv) nōhtē-
washer [clothes]: (NI) kisīpēkinimahkahk
water: (NI) nipiy
we/us (exclusive) too/also: (Pr) nīstanān
we/us (inclusive) too/also: (Pr) kīstanaw
we/us (exclusive): (Pr) niyanān
we/us (inclusive): (Pr) kiyānaw
weasel: (NA) sihkos
Wednesday: (vP) nisto-kīsikāw
well, a: (NI) mōnahipān
well, do it: (Pv) nihtā-/miyo-
west, to the: (P) nakahpēhanohk
west, to the: (P) pahkisimotāhk
whale: (NA) wahpamēk

Appendix C Abbreviation Key

A - animate	P - particle	Pp - pre-particle	sg - singular
Cj - conjunction	Ph - particle phrase	Pr - pronoun	vP - verbal particle
I - inanimate	pl - plural	Pv - preverb	
N - noun	Pn - prenoun	Sf - suffix	

what?: (Pr-sg) kīkwāy?
what?: (Pr-I/pl) kīkwāya?
what kind?: (Pr) tānitowahk?
when/at that time?: (Pr) ispīhk/ispī
when?: (Pr) tānispīhk?
when it happens/comes to be: (vP) ispayiki
where?: (Pr) tānitē?
where are they?: (Pr-I/pl) tāniwēhā?
where are they?: (Pr-A/pl) tāniwēhkāk?
where is he/she?: (Pr-A/sg) tāniwā?
where is it?: (Pr-I/sg) tāniwē?
which one?: (Pr-A/sg) tāna?
which one?: (Pr-I/sg) tānima?
which ones?: (Pr-I/pl) tānihi?
which ones?: (Pr-A/pl) tāniki?
while: (P) ēskwa, mēkwāc
whitefish: (NA) atihkamēk
who?: (Pr-A/sg) awīna?
who?: (Pr-A/pl) awīniki?
whooping crane: (NA) wāpicāhk
why?: (Pr) tānēhki
wife, my: (NA) niwīkimākan
wild rice: (NA) manōmin/maskosīminak
window: (NI) wāsēnamān/wāsēnikan
wine: (NI) sōmināpoy
wings: (NI) mitahtahkwan
winter coat: (NI) piponasākay
with: (P) asici
woman: (NA) iskwēw
woman, my: (NA) nitiskwēm
woman's coat: (NI) iskwēwasākay
wood, a piece of/stick: (NI) mihti
wood [fire]: (NI) mihta
wooden: (Sf) -āhtik
wooden boat: (NI) mistikōsi
worm: (NA) mohtēw

X
x-ray: (NI) sāpwāpahcikan

Y
year: (NI) askīwin
yearly: (P) tahto-pipon
yeast: (NA) ohpihkasikan
yes: (P) ēha/āha
yesterday: (P) otākosīhk
yet another: (Ph) kotak mīna
yet/still: (P) kēyāpic
you (pl): (Pr-pl) kiyawāw
you (sg): (Pr-sg) kiya
you/too/also: (Pr-sg) kīsta
you/too/also: (Pr-pl) kīstawāw
young man: (NA) oskinīkiw
young woman: (NA) oskinīkiskwēw
younger brother/sister: (NA) nisīmis
your aunt [mother's sister]: (NA) kikāwīs
your brother: (NA) kisīmis
your cousin: (NA) kisīmis
your home: (NI) kīki
your older sister: (NA) kimis
youth/young people: (NA) osk-āyak

Appendix C Abbreviation Key

A - animate	P - particle	Pp - pre-particle	sg - singular
Cj - conjunction	Ph - particle phrase	Pr - pronoun	vP - verbal particle
I - inanimate	pl - plural	Pv - preverb	
N - noun	Pn - prenoun	Sf - suffix	

Appendix D: Verbs
Cree to English

A

ācimo VAI: tell a story/inform

ācimostaw VTA-2: tell him/her a story/inform him/her

āhcipici VAI: move camp

ahi VTA-1 (irreg): place him/her/it

ahkamēyimo VAI: persevere/keep trying

āhkosi VAI: be sick

āhkwaci VAI: freeze

āhkwatihtā VTI-2: freeze it

āhkwakihtēw VII-2: it is expensive

āhkwakiso VAI: (be) expensive

āhkwatisim VTA-1: freeze it

āhkwakiso VAI: be expensive

āhkwatin VII-2: frozen

akāwāt VTA-4: desire him/her/it

akāwāta VTI-1: desire it, wish for it

ākayāsimo VAI: speak English

ākayasimototaw VTA-2: speak English to him/her

akihcikē VAI: count

akihta VTI-1: count them

akimik VTA-1: count them

akot VTA-4: hang it

akotā VTI-2: hang it

akwātaskinēw VII-2: it is overfilled

āmaciwē VAI: climb up/walk up

āmaciwēpahtā VAI: run up

ānwēhta VTI-1: doubt it/reject it/deny it

ānwēhtaw VTA-2: doubt him/her/reject him

āpacih VTA-1: use it

āpacihtā VTI-2: use it

api VAI: sit/be at home

apisīsisi VAI: little, (be)

āpocikwānī VAI: somersault

apwē VAI: roast over a fire [spit]

apwēpahtā VAI: sweat as you run

apwēsi VAI: sweat, perspire

asam VTA-1: feed him/her/it

asamiso VAI: feed yourself

asawēyihta VTI-1: be careful of it

asēhtē VAI: walk backwards

asēn VTA-1: refuse him/her

asēnamaw VTA-1: return it to him/her

asēpayi VAI: drive backwards

askihtakonākosiw VAI: it appears green

askihtakosiw VAI: it is green

askihtakwāw VII-2: it is green

askowēh VTA-1: follow him/her

āsowaha VTI-1: cross over [by water]

āsōwihtamaw VTA-2: pass a message to him/her

astā VTI-2: put it here/there

āstam [Imperative only]: come here

āstawēha VTI-1: extinguish the fire

āstawēhikē VAI: extinguish the fire

āstawēnikē VAI: extinguish the light

āstēpayi VAI: feel better

āstēsini VAI (irreg): rest

atamiskaw VTA-2: shake his/her hand/ greet him/her

atāwē VAI: buy

atāwēstamaw VTA-2: buy it for him/her

atimikāpawi VAI: stand with your back to me

atimipahtā VAI: run [away from speaker]

atisa VTI-1: tan it

atiso VAI: be tanned

atisw VTA-3: tan it

atoho VAI: choke on food/liquid

atoskah VTA-1: hire him/her

atoskāta VTI-1: work at it

atoskaw VTA-2: work for him/her

atoskē VAI: work

atot VTA-4: hire him/her

ātota VTI-1: tell about it

awas (Imperative only): go away!

awih VTA-1: loan it to him/her

ayā VAI: be

ayā VTI-2: have it

ayamihā VAI: pray

ayamihcikē VAI: read

ayamihēstamaw VTA-2: pray for him

ayamihtā VTI-3: read it

ayapinikē VAI: turn everything upside down

ayāsīhta VTI-2: respond to it [statement, letter]

ayāw VTA-1: have it

ayēskosi VAI: be exhausted/tired

āyiman VII-2: it is difficult

ayiwēpi VAI stop and have a rest

C

canawī VAI: be busy

cāstapī VAI: hurry up

cēcēmipahtā VAI: trot

cīhcīkwanapi VAI: kneel

cīhkēyihta VTI-1: like it

cīhkēyim VTA-1: like him/her

cīkaha VTI-1: chop it

cīkahikē VAI: chop

cīkahw VTA-3: chop him/her/it

ciposa VTI-1: sharpen it [stick]

cīstaha VTI-1: pierce it

cīstahw VTA-3: pierce him/her

I

isitisaha VTI-1 send it
isitisahw VTA-4: send him/her
isiyihkāso VAI: be named/called
iskwāhtawī VAI: climb
ispahtā VAI: run over there [yonder]
ispākonakāw VII-1: the snow is deep
ispayi VAI: ride to/drive to
ispīhtisī VAI: reach a certain age [he is—years old]
itācim VTA: talk about him/her so
itahtopiponē VAI: be a certain age [he is—years old]
itakihtēw VII-2: cost [so much]
itakisow VAI: cost [so much]
itakocini VAI (irreg): travel to
itamahciho VAI: feel [as in health]
itāmo VAI: flee towards a specific direction/place
itāpi VAI: look over there
itēyihta VTI-1: think so about it [assess]
itēyim VTA-1: think so about him/her [assess]
itīhtākwan VII-2: it sounds like so
itisaha VTI-1: send it
itisahw VTA-4: send him/her/it
itasināso VAI: be colored so
itasinātēw VII-2: it is colored so
itohtah VTA-1: take him there
itohtatā VTI-2: take it there
itohtatamaw VTA-2: take it there for him/her
itōta VTI-1: do it
itōtamaw VTA-2: do [it for him]
itwahamaw VTA-2: point it out to him
itwē VAI: say it
itwēstamākē VAI: interpret

K

kāhcitin VTA-1: catch hold of him/her/it
kāhcitina VTI-1: catch it
kāhcitiniwē VAI: catch, be the one to
kahkwēyihta VTI-1: jealous, (be)
kahkwēyim VTA-1: jealous of him/her, (be)
kakāyawisī VAI: industrious, (be)
kakēpātisi VAI: foolish, (be)
kakēskim VTA-1: preach/counsel to him
kakēskimāwaso VAI: counsel your children
kakēskimiwē VAI: preach/counsel
kakwātakih VTA-1: distress/torment him/her
kakwātakihtā VAI: distressed, (be)
kakwēcihkēmo VAI: ask
kakwēcim VTA-1: ask him/her
kakwēciyāho VAI: hurry
kakwēyācih VTA-1: get him/her/it ready
kakwēyācihtā VTI-2: get it ready
kanācih VTA-1: clean him/her/it
kanācihtā VTI-2: clean it
kanātan VII-2: it is clean

kanawāpahta VTI-1: look at it/watch it
kanawāpam VTA-2: look at him/her/it; watch him/her
kanawēyihta VTI-1: keep it
kanawēyihtamaw VTI-1: keep it for him/her
kanawēyim VTA-1 keep him/her/it
kanawēyimāwaso VAI: keep the children/ babysit
kapā VAI: go ashore
kapēsi VAI: camp
kapēsīstaw VTA-2: camp with him/her
kāsāpitē VAI: have sharp teeth
kāsīcihcē VAI: wash [hands]
kāsīha VTI-1: wipe it
kāsīhkwē VAI: wash [face]
kāsīhw VTA-3: wipe him/her/it
kāsīyākanē VAI: wipe dishes
kaskaniwipēscāsin VII-1: it is drizzling
kaskaniwipētāw VII-1: it is drizzling
kaskāpahtēw VII-2: it is smoking [as smoke emitting from a chimney]
kaskēyihta VTI-1: be lonesome
kaskēyim VTA-1: miss/yearn for him/her
kaskiho VAI: escape
kaskihtā VTI-2: be able to do it
kaskikwāso VAI: sew
kaskikwāt VTA-4: sew it
kaskikwāta VTI-1: sew it
kaskikwātamaw VTA-2: sew it for him/her
kakitēsiw VAI: s/he/it is black
kaskitēwāw VII-2: it is black
kaskitēwinākosiw VAI: s/he/it appears black
kaskitēwinākwan VII-2: it appears black
kāskipāso VAI: shave
kāsō VAI: hide
kāsōstaw VTA-2: hide [from him]
kaspāhcikē VAI: chew [with a crunching noise]
kāt VTA-4: hide him/her
kātā VTI-2: hide it
kātamaw VTA-2: hide it for him/her
kawaci VAI: cold, (be)
kawacihkwāmi VAI: be cold as you sleep
kawāhkatoso VAI: be skinny
kawāso VAI: be blown down(e.g.: a tree)
kawatim VTA-1: cold [make him/her]
kawatin VII-2): cold [it is]
kawihkwasi VAI: doze off
kawisimo VAI: bed down/go to bed
kēcikon VTA-1: take it off
kēcikona VTI-1: take it off
kēcikoska VTI-1: take it off (clothing)
kēhcināho VAI: make sure
kēsiyākē VAI: cheat
kēsiyohw VTA-3: cheat him/her
kētasākē VAI: take off your coat, undress
kētasikanē VAI: take off your socks

kētaskisinē VAI: take off your shoes
kētastisē VAI: take off your mitts
kētastotinē VAI: take off your hat/cap
kēyakicēn VTA-1: tickle him/her
kēyakicihcē VAI: itchy [hands] have
kēyakihtawakē VAI: itchy [ear] have an
kēyakisī VAI: itch
kēyakisitē VAI: itchy [feet], have
kēyakistikwānē VAI: itchy [head], have an
kīhcēkosī VAI: climb [on horse or other object]
kihcēyihta VTI-1: think highly of it; be proud of it
kihcēyim VTA-1: think highly of him/her
kihtimi VAI: be lazy
kīkisēpāyāw VII-1: it is morning
kimiwan VII-1: it is raining
kimiwasin VII-1: it is drizzling
kimwē VAI: whisper
kinosi VAI: tall, (be)
kinwāniskwē VAI: have long hair
kinwāw VII-2: it is long
kipaha VTI-1: close it
kipahw VTA-3: imprison him
kipahw VTA-3: close him/her in
kipāpiskaha VTI-1: lock it
kipāpiskahikē VAI: lock up
kipotēkāta VTI-1: knock it over
kisākamisa VTI-1: heat the water/liquid
kisākamisikē VAI: heat water to make tea
kisākamitēw VII-2: the liquid is hot
kisapwēyāw VII-1: it is hot weather
kisāstēw VII-1: it is hot [weather]
kisāta VTI-1: stay put/stay with it
kisēwātisi VAI: be kind
kīsih VTA-1: finish it
kīsihtā VTI-2: finish it
kisikāyāstēw VII-1: it is moonlight
kisināw VII-1: it is cold
kisīpēkihtakinikē VAI: wash [floor]
kisīpēkikwayawē VAI: wash [neck]
kisīpēkin VTA-1: bathe/wash him/her/it
kisīpēkina VTI-1: wash it
kisīpēkinamaw VTA-2: wash it for him/her
kisīpēkinikē VAI: wash clothes
kisīpēkiniso VAI: bathe/wash yourself
kisīpēkistikwānē VAI: wash [head/hair]
kisīpēkisitē VAI: wash [feet]
kisīpēkiyākanē VAI: wash dishes
kīsisa VTI-1: cook it
kisiso VAI: have a fever
kīsisw VTA-3: cook it
kīsitēpo VAI: cook [finished]
kisitēw VII-1: it is hot [temperature]
kisiwāsi VAI: angry, (be)
kisiwāsīstaw VTA-2: angry at him/her
kisiwaskatē VAI: have indigestion

kisīwē VAI: speak loudly
kiskēyihta VTI-1: know it
kiskēyihtākwan VII-2: it is known
kiskēyim VTA-1: know him
kiskim VTA-1: make appointment with him/remind him/her
kiskimo VAI: make an appointment
kiskinohamaw VTA-2: show him/her how
kiskinohtah VTA-1: show him the way [direction]
kiskinwahamākē VAI: teach/educate
kiskinwahamaw VTA-2: teach him/her
kiskisi VAI: remember it
kīskosī VAI: whistle
kīskwē VAI: be mad (insane)
kīskwēpē VAI: be drunk
kīsowākamin VII-1: the liquid is warm
kīsowāw VII-1: it is warm
kīsowēyāw VII-1: it is warm weather
kisowikanawāpahta VTI-1: frown at it
kisowikanawāpam VTA-1: frown at him/her
kisowinākosi VAI: frown
kispakāw VII-2: it is thick
kīspo VAI: be full from eating
kistikē VAI: farm/seed
kitā VTI-3: eat all of it
kitamw VTA-3: eat all of it
kitānawē VAI: eat all your food
kitāpahta VTI: look at it
kitāpam VTA-1 look at him/her
kitimākēyim VTA-1: have pity on him/her
kitimākim VTA-1: belittle him/her
kitimākinaw VTA-2: have pity on him/her
kitimākisi VAI: poor/unfortunate, (be)
kitohcikē VAI: make music
kīwē VAI: go home
kīwēhtah VTA-1: take him/her home
kīwēhtatā VTI-2: take it home
kīwēpahtā VAI: run home [towards home]
kīwētacikē VTI-2: take/bring things home
kiyāmapi VAI: quiet, (be)
kiyāski VAI: lie [falsehood]
kiyāskīm VTA-1: lie to him/her
kiyāskīstaw VTA-2: lie to him/her
kiyokaw VTA-2: visit him/her
kiyokē VAI: visit
kocihtā VTI-2: try it
kocispit VTA-4: taste it
kocispita VTI-2: taste it
kohcipayihtā VTI-1: swallow it
kōkī VAI: dive
kosikwati VAI: be heavy
koskon VTA-1: awaken him/her
koskowātapi VAI: sit still
koskwēyihta VTI-1: be surprised about it
koskwēyim VTA-1: be surprised about him/ her

kosokwan VII-2: it is heavy
kost VTA-4: be afraid of him
kosta VTI-1: be afraid of it
kostāci VAI: afraid/scared, (be)
kotikosini VAI (irreg): sprain [joint]
kwahtohtē VAI: to wander far away
kwāskohti VAI: jump
kwāskwēpicikē VAI: fish [with a rod/angle]
kwatapiska VTI-1: knock it over
kwatapiskaw VTA-2: knock it over
kwēskātisi VAI: repent
kwēskī VAI: turn
kwēskin VTA-1: turn him/her/it
kwēskina VTI-1: turn it
kwēyakon VTA-1: take him/her/it out
kwēyakona VTI-1: take it out
kwēyakopit VTA-4: pull him/her out
kwēyakopita VTI-1: pull it out
kwēyaskokāpawi VAI: stand straight
kwēyātapi VAI: be ready
kwēyātisi VAI: be ready
kwihtawēyihta VTI-1: miss/yearn for
kwihtawēyim VTA-1: miss/yearn for

M
macātisi VAI: be bad/evil
macēyihtākosi VAI: be mean/difficult/nasty
māci VAI: hunt
mācihtā VTI-2: start doing it
maci-kīsikāw VII: it is a nasty day
macispakosiw VAI: it tastes bad
macispakwan VII-2: it tastes bad
macipīkiskwē VAI: speak evil
macastawēha VTI-1: set it on fire
macastawēpayi VAI: fall [into the fire]
macastawēpin VTA-1: throw him/her in the fire
macastawēpina VTI-1: throw it in the fire
mahkāpitē VAI: have big teeth
māhtin VTA-1: move him/her/it
māhtina VTI-1: move it
mākwahcikē VAI: chew
mākwahta VTI-1: chew it
mākwam VTA-1: chew it
mamāhpinē VAI: moan
māmaskātēyihtākwan VII: it is amazing
mamāyī VAI: inefficient, (be)
mamēhcikāpahta VTI-1: stare in awe
mamihcimiso VAI: brag about yourself
mamihcimo VAI: brag
mamisim VTA-1: to tell on/to rat on him/her
māmitonēyihta VTI-1: ponder [think about it]
māmitonēyim VTA-1: ponder/think of him/her
manisa VTI-1: cut it
manisw VTA-3: cut it
mānokē VAI: camp [make/set up camp]

māsīh VTA-1: fight/wrestle someone
masinaha VTI-1: write it
masinahamaw VTA-2: owe him/her, write it for him/her
masinahikē VAI: owe/write
masinahikēh VTA-1: hire him/her
masināstēw VII-2: it is striped
maskam VTA-1: take it away from him/her
maskawāw VII-2: it is strong
maskawisī VAI: be strong
māskih VTA-1: maim him/her
māskikātē VAI: have a lame [leg]
māskipayi VAI: limp
māskisi VAI: be lame
maskisinihkē VAI: make moccasins
māskisitē VAI: lame foot, (have a)
māto VAI: cry
matwēhkwāmi VAI: snore
māwasakon VTA-1 gather them
māwasakona VTI-1: gather them [things]
māwasakonamāso VAI: gather them for yourself
mawihkāt VTA-4: cry for him/her
mawihkāta VTI-1: cry for it
mawinēskom VTA-1: challenge him/her
mawiso VAI: pick berries
māyātan VII: it is bad/ugly
māyātisi VAI: bad/ugly in appearance, (be)
māyi-kīsikāw VII: it is not a nice day
māyimahciho VAI: feel poorly
māyispakosiw VII-2: it tastes bad
māyispakwan VII-2: it tastes bad
mēki VAI: give [away]
mēscih: VTA-1: annihilate [them]
mēscipita VTI-2: use all/exhaust all sources
mēskoci VAI: changes clothes
mēskotāsiyānēh VTA-1: change his/her diaper
mēskotayowinisē VAI: change clothes
mēskwacipayan VII-2: it changes
mēstawihikawi VAI: be exhausted of one's own sources
mētawē VAI: play
mīci VTI-3: eat
mīcimāpohkē VAI: make soup
mīciso VAI: eat
mihkawakī VAI: be a fast runner
mihkosiw VAI: it is red
mihkonākosiw VAI: it appears red
mihkonākwan VII-2: it appears red
mihkwāw VII-2: it is red
mihtāt VTA-4: mourn/feel sorry/grieve for him/her/it
mihtāta VTI-1: mourn/feel sorry/grieve
mīkisīstahikē VAI: beadwork [do]
mikisimo VAI: bark [like a dog]
mikoskācih VTA-1: bother him/her

mikoskācihtā VTI-2: bother it
mikoskātisi VAI: bothersome, (be)
minah VTA-1: drink [give him a]
minihkwē VAI: drink
misāw VII-2: it is large/big
misikiti VAI: be big/large
miska VTI-1: find it
miskaw VTA-1: find him/her
mīskon VTA-1: feel/examine him/her/it
mīskona VTI-1: feel/examine it
mīskoniso VAI: feel/examine yourself
mīskotāsiyānēh VTA: change his/her diaper
miskwamiy pahkisin VAI (irreg): it is hailing
mispon VII-1 it is snowing
mistakihtēw VII-2: it is expensive
mistakiso VAI: expensive, (be)
miy VTA-1: give it to him
miyāhta VTI-1: smell it
miyākwan VII-2: it smells
miyām VTA-1: smell him/her/it
miyāska VTI-1: pass it by
miyāskaw VTA-1: pass him/her/it
miyawēsi VAI: be hairy
miyēstawē VAI: have a beard
miyo-kīsikāw VII-2: it is a nice day
miyohtwā VAI: be kind
miyohkwāmi VAI: sleep well
miyomahciho VAI: feel well
miyonākosi VAI: be beautiful
miyonākwan VII: it is beautiful
miyopayin (sg) VII-2: it works/runs well
miyopayinwa (pl) VII-2: they work/run well
miyopayi VAI: it works well
miyosi VAI: be nice
miyosisi VAI: be nice
miyoskaminVII-1: it is spring
miyospakosiw VAI: it tastes nice
miyospakwan VII-2: it tastes nice
miywāsin VII-2: it is nice
miywasinahikē VAI: write well
miywatoskē VAI: work well
miyw-āyā VAI: well, (be)
miywēyihta VTI-1: like it/be happy
miywēyihtākwan VII-2: it is enjoyable
miywēyihtamih VTA-1: please him/her
miywēyim VTA-1: like him/her
mōcikihtā VAI: have fun
mōh VTA-1: cry [make someone]
mohcohkāso VAI: foolish [act]
mōhkiciwanipēw VII-2: spring [water]
mōminē VAI: eat berries while picking
mōsahkin VTA-1: gather [up]
mōsahkina VTI-1: gather [up]
mōsāpēwi VAI: bachelor, (be a)
mōsiskwēwi VAI: single lady, (be a)

mōskom VTA-1: move him/her to tears
mostāpēkasē VAI: be bare/naked/nude
mostohtē VAI: go [but walk rather than riding]
mōw VTA-1: eat it
mwēstasisini VAI: late, (be)

N
nah : here take this
nahapi VAI: sit down
nahascikē VAI: tidy up
nahastā VTI-2: place/put it in order
nahēyihta VTI-1: be satisfied with it
nahihta VTI-1: listen/heed
nakat VTA-4: leave him/her
nakata VTI-1: leave it
nākatēyim VTA-1: be careful with him/her/ it
nākatēyihta VTI-1: be careful with it
nakī VAI: stop
nakin VTA-1: stop him/her
nakiska VTI-1: meet it
nakiskamohtaw VTA-1: introduce him/her
nakiskaw VTA-2: meet him/her/it
nakwāt VTA-4: snare it
nanamaci VAI: shiver
nanamiskwēyi VAI: nod/shake your head
nanāskomo VAI: be grateful
nanātawih VTA-1: heal him/her/it
nanōyacih VTA-1: tease him/her/it
napācihtā VTI-2: fix/repair it
nāpēhkāso VAI: act brave
napwahpit VTA-4: hobble it [usually horse]
nat VTA-4: fetch/get him/her/it
nāta VTI-1: fetch/get it
nātamaw VTA-2: fetch [for him]
nātāmostaw VTA-1: seek advice from him/ her
nātāmototaw VTA-2: seek help, advice from
   him/her
nitawēyihta VTI-1: want it
nitawēyim VTA-1: want him
nātisaha VTI-1: send/order for it
nātisahw VTA-1: send for him/her
natohta VTI-1: listen to it
natohtaw VTA-2: listen to him/her/it
natona VTI-1: look for it
natonaw VTA-2: look for him/her/it
nawacī VAI: bake/cook
nawakī VAI: bend over
nawaswāt VTA-4 : run after/chase him/her
nawaswāsiwē VAI: chase
nawaswāta VTI-1: run after/chase it
nawatin VTA-1: grab him/her/it
nawatina VTI-1: grab it
nēhiyawē VAI: speak Cree
nēhpēmastā VTI-2: place it nearby
nēsowisi VAI: weak, (be)

nēstosi VAI: tired, (be)
nīhtaciwē VAI: climb down/walk down
nīhtaciwēpahtā VAI: run down [stairs/hill]
nīhtāhtawī VAI: climb [off of something]
nīhtin VTA-1: take him/her down/off
nīhtina VTI-1: take/lift it off/down
nikamo VAI: sing
nikamoski VAI: sing [habitually]
nikohtē VAI: get wood
nimā VAI: carry a lunch
nīmi VAI: dance
nīmihito VAI: dance
nīminikē VAI: pray over the food [as in a feast]
nipā VAI: sleep
nipah VTA-1: kill him/her/it
nipahāhkatē VAI: be extremely hungry/perish from
      hunger
nipahāskwaci VAI: freeze to death
nipahipāwanī VAI: be skinny/lean
nipāhkāso VAI: pretend to sleep
nipākwēsimo VAI: dance [Rain Dance]
nipāski VAI: sleeps, (likes to)
nipātwēwita VAI: talk constantly
nīpāmāyatan VII-2: it is purple
nīpāmāyātisiw VAI: it is purple
nīpāyāstēw VII-1: it is moonlight
nipēpayi VAI: doze off
nīpēpi VAI: be at a wake
nīpin VII-1: it is summer
nisitawēyihta VTI-1: recognize it
nisitawēyim VTA-1: recognize him/her/it
nisitohta VTI-1: understand it
nisitohtaw VTA-1: understand him/ her/it
nisiwanācih VTA-1: ruin him/her/it
nisiwanācihtā VTI-2: ruin it
nisiwanātisi VAI: perish/die
nitawēyihta VTI-1: want it
nitawēyim VTA-1: want it/him/her
nitom VTA-1: invite him/her
niyā [Imperative only]: go!
nōcih VTA-1: hunt it
nōcikinosēwē VAI: fish
nōcisipē VAI: hunt ducks
nōh VTA-1: breastfeed him/her
nōhtēhkatē VAI: hungry, (be)
nōhtēhkwasi VAI: sleepy, (be)
nōhtēpayi VAI: run out of it [as in food]
nōhtēsini VAI: exhausted, (be)
nōhtēyāpākwē VAI: thirsty, (be)
nōkosi VAI: appear/come into view
nōkwan VAI: it appears/comes into view
nōni VAI: nursing/breast feeding
nōtin VTA-1: fight [him]
nōtinikē VAI: fight
nōtinikēski VAI: be always wanting to fight

O

ocēhta VTI-1: kiss it
ocēm VTA-1: kiss him/her/it
ocipit VTA-4: pull him/her
ocipita VTI-1: pull it
ocipohkasa VTI-1: shrivel it [with heat]
ōhōsimo VAI: dance [Owl Dance]
ohpiki VAI: grow
ohpikihtā VTA-2: grow it
ohpin VTA-1: lift him/her/it
ohpina VTI-1: lift it
onāpēmi VAI: have a husband
osāmakocini VAI (irreg): drive past destination
osāmitōni VAI: gossip, (be a)
osīh VTA-1: make it
osīhtā VTI-2: make it
osīhtamaw VTA-2: make it for him/her
osipēha VTI-1: write it
oskāyiwi VAI: young, (be)
ostostota VTI-1: cough
otākosin VII-1: it is evening
otāpāso VAI: ride a vehicle (i.e. wagon)
otin VTA-1: take him
otina VTI-1: take it
oyascikē VAI: set the table
oyōyo VAI: howl [like a coyote]

P

pacipayi VAI: miss [e.g. chair]
pacisīkina VTI-1: miss when pouring liquid
pahkihtin VII-2: it falls
pahkipēstāw VII-1: big drops of rain are falling
pahkisimon VII-2: sunset
pahkisini VAI (irreg): fall
pahkon VTA-1: skin it
pahkonikē VAI: be skinning
pahkwēpayin VII-1: a piece breaks off
pahkwēpit VTA-4: break a piece off
pahkwēpita VTI-1: break a piece off
pahkwēsikanihkē VAI: make bannock
pāhpi VAI: laugh
pāhpih VTA-1: laugh at him/her/it
pāhpihkwē VAI: smile
pāhpinākosi VAI: smile
pāhpihtā VTI-2: laugh at it
pāhkwaha VTI-1: dry it
pāhkwahw VTA-3: dry/wipe him/her/it
pakahatowē VAI: play ball
pakāhta VTI-2: boil it
pakamaha VTI-1: hit it
pakamahw VTA-3: hit him/her/it
pakāsim VTA-1: boil it
pakāsimo VAI: bathe/swim
pakastawēpin VTA-1: throw him/her/it in the water
pakastawēpina VTI-1: throw into the water

pakastawēpayi VAI: fall into the water
pakitahwā VAI: fish [with a net]
pakitin VTA-1: allow/let go of [him/her]
pakitina VTI-1: allow/let go/put it down
pakosēyimo VAI: have expectation/desire
pakwāt VTA-4: hate/dislike him/her
pakwāta VTI-1: hate it
pakwātamaw VTA-2: hate/dislike it for him/her
pamihcikē VAI: drive
paminawaso VAI: cook/prepare a meal
papakāsin VII-2: it is thin
papāmipahtā VAI: run around/about
papāmipayi VAI: ride around
papāmitisahw VTA-3: run/follow after someone
papāmohtē VAI: walk around/about
papāsi VAI: hurry
papēcī VAI: slow, (be)
papēskwatāstan VII-1: the snow is drifting
papimohtē VAI: walk along
pāsa VTI-1: dry it
pasakwāpi VAI: close your eyes
pasastēhw VTA-3: strap/whip someone
pasīhkwētahw VTA-3: slap his/her face
pasikō VAI: arise/stand up
pāskisa VTI-1: shoot it
pāskisw VTA-3: shoot him
paskostikwānē VAI: be bald
pāsoso VAI: dry oneself
paspāpi VAI: look out the window
paspī VAI: escape
pāstām VTA-1: curse him/her
pāstāmiso VAI: bring a curse on self
pāstāmo VAI: bring a curse on self
pāsw VTA-1: dry him/her/it
pataha VTI-1: miss a/your target
patahw VTA-3: miss a/your target
pawāt VTA-4: dream about him/ her
pawāta VTI-1: dream about it
pēh VTA-1: wait for him/her/it
pēho VAI: wait
pēhta VTI-1: hear it
pēhtākwan VII: it is audible
pēhtaw VTA-2: hear him/her/it
pēsiw VTA-1: bring him/her
pētā VTI-2: bring it
pētamaw VTA-2: bring it for him
pētāpan VII-1: it is (coming) daylight
pīcicī VAI: dance [Round Dance]
pīhcipayi VAI: fall [into]
pihkohkē VAI: make ashes/cinders
pihkwan VII-2: it is coarse
pīhtokwē VAI: come in/enter/go in
pīhtokwēyāmo VAI: flee/run into building
pīhtwā VAI: smoke [cigarette]
pīhtwāh VTA-1: give [him a smoke]

pīkiskāta VTI-1: feel sad
pīkiskwē VAI: speak/talk
pīkon VTA-1: break it
pīkona VTI-1: break it
pīkwēyihta VTI-1: be distressed
pīkwēyihtamih VTA-1: distress him/her
pimācih VTA-1: save him
pimāsi VAI: sail
pimātakā VAI: swim [making a "v"]
pimātisi VAI: alive, (be)
pimihā VAI: fly
piminawaso VAI: cook a meal
piminawat VTA-4: cook/prepare a meal for him/her
pimipahcāsi VAI: trot
pimipahtā VAI: run
pimipayihtā VTI-2: run or drive something
pimisini VAI (irreg): lie [down]
pimitisaha VTI-1: follow it
pimitisahw VTA-3: follow him/her/it
pimohtah VTA-1: take [along]
pimohtatā VTI-2: take [along]
pimohtē VAI: walk
pimohtēho VAI: travel
pimowitā VTA-2: take it along
pimowih VTA-1: take him/her along
pipon VII-2: it is winter
piscipo VAI: be poisoned
piscipoh VTA-1: poisin him/her/it
pisiskēyihcikē VAI: regard/look after it
pīskatahikē VAI: make kindling
piskwāw VII-2: it is lumpy
pisosini VAI (irreg): stumble/trip
pistisa VTI-1: cut it [accidentally]
pistisoso VAI: cut oneself [accidentally]
pistisw VTA-3: cut him/her [accidentally]
pīswēhkasikanihkē VAI: make bread
pīwan VII-1: it is drifting [snow]
pōmē VAI: be discouraged
pōmēh VTA-1: discourage him/her
pōnēyihta VTI-1: forget it
pōnēyihtamaw VTA-2: forgive him
pōnēyim VTA-1: forget him/her
pōnih VTA-1: leave [him alone]
pōnihtā VTI-2: leave it be/quit
pōnipayin VII-2: it stops/quits
pōnwēwita VTI-1: quit talking
poscitāsē VAI: put pants on
pōsi VAI: board
pōsih VTA-1: put him/her/it on board
pōsihtā VTI-2: put it on board
postasākē VAI: put on clothes/coat
postasikanē VAI: put socks on
postaskisinē VAI: put on shoes
postastisē VAI: put mitts on
postastotinē VAI: put on a hat

postayiwinisē VAI: put on clothes
postiska VTI-1: put it on
postiskaw VTA-1: put it on
pōtācikē VAI: blow
pōtāt VTA-4: blow on him/her/it
pōtāta VTI-1: blow it
pōyo VAI: quit
pwākamo VAI: vomit
pwātisimo VAI: dance [Sioux dance]
pwēkito VAI: fart

S
sakahpit VTA-4: tie him/her/it
sakahpita VTI-1: tie it
sakapwē VAI: roast over a fire [hang]
sākaskinah VTA-1: fill it
sākaskinahtā VTI-2: fill it
sākaskinahtamaw VTA-2: fill [it for him]
sakicīhcēn VTA-1: shake hands with him/ her
sākih VTA-1: love him/her
sākihtā VTI-2: love it
sākihtā VTI-2: be stingy/selfish of it
sākohcim VTA-1: convince him/her
sakwāskwaha VTI-1: fasten/zipper it up
samatapi VAI: sit up
sāpohkwāmi VAI: sleep in/over sleep
sāpohtē VAI: walk through it
sasākisi VAI: be stingy
sasāpiskisa VTI-1: fry it
sasāpiskisw VTA-3: fry it
sasīpihta VTI-1: disobedient, (be)
sasīpihtawakē VAI: disobedient, (be)
sāsāpiskisikē VAI: fry
sāsisa VTI-1: fry it
sāsisw VTA-3: fry it
saskaha VTI-1: kindle [ignite] it
saskahw VTA-3: kindle [ignite] it
saskan VII-1: it is melting/spring breakup
sawahamaw VTA-2: spread it for him/her
sawēyim VTA-1: love him/her
sēkih VTA-1: scare him/her
sēkisi VAI: scared, (be)
sēsāwipahtā VAI: jog
sīhkiskaw VTA-1: incite/encourage
sīhtahpit VTA-4: tie him/her/it tightly
sīhtahpita VTI-1: tie it tightly
sīhtatoskāta VTI-1: work hard at something
sīkahāhtaw VTA-2: splash/sprinkle someone
sīkaho VAI: comb your hair
sīkahoso VAI: comb your hair for yourself
sīkahw VTA-3: comb his/her hair
sīkina VTI-1: pour it
sīkipita VTI-1: pour/spill it
sikohkina VTI-1: empty it
sikwan VII-2: it is spring

sīpihkonākosiw VII-2: it appears blue
sīpihkosiw VII-2: it is blue
sīpihkonākwan VII-2: it appears blue
sīpihkwāw VII-2: it is blue
sipwēhtē VAI: start to leave
sipwēpahtā VAI: start to run
sipwēyāmo VAI: flee
sisikwacih VTA-1: startle him/her/it
sōhkan VII-2: it is strong
sōhkēpahtā VAI: run fast
sōhkēyimo VAI: brave, (be)
sōhkisi VAI: be strong
sōniskwātahikē VAI: ski
sōskopayi VAI: to slip
sōskoyāpawi VAI: ski
sōskwaciwē VAI: slide down hill
sōskwaha VTI-1: iron [clothing]
sōskwahikē VAI: iron [clothing]
sōskwahw VTA-3: iron [clothing]
sōskwātahikē VAI: skate

T
tāhcipo VAI: fat, (become)
tahkākamin VII-2: it is cold [liquid]
tahkāyāw/kisināw VII-1: it is cold
tahkipēstāw VII-1: cold rain
tahkiska VTI-1: kick it
tahkiskācikē VAI: kick
tahkiskaw VTA-2: kick him/her
tahkohtastā VTI-2: put it on top of
tahkohtastēw VII-2: it sits on top of something
tahkopit VTA-4: tie him/her/it
tahkopita VTI-1: tie it
tahkoskāta VTI-1: step on it
tahkoskaw VTA-2: step on him/her/it
takohtē VAI: arrive
takona VTI-1: include it/add it to st
takopahtā VAI: arrive running
takopayi VAI: arrive by vehicle/horse
takosini VAI (irreg): arrive
takwaha VTI-1: crush it
takwahw VTA-3: crush it
takwākin VII-2: it is fall
tāpakwē VAI: set a snare
tapasī VAI: run away
tāpwēski VAI: speak the truth always
tāpwēhta VTI-1: believe it/agree with it
tāpwēhtaw VTA-2: believe him/her/it/agree
tāstapī VAI: hurry up
taswēkastā VTI-2: spread them around/ spread it
   out [sheet]
tāwati VAI: open your mouth
tēhcipayiho VAI: jump on top of
tēpakēyimo VAI: be willing
tēpēyimo VAI: agree

tēpwāt VTA-4: call him/her
tēpwē VAI: call/yell/shout
tēwāpitē VAI: ache [tooth], (have an)
tēwihtawakē VAI: ache [ear] (have an)
tēwikanē VAI: ache [bones] (have an)
tēwikotē VAI: ache [nose] (have an)
tēwipitonē VAI: ache [arms] (have an)
tēwisitē VAI: ache [feet] (have an)
tēwistikwanē VAI: ache [head] (have an)
tihkisa VTI-1: melt it
tihkisw VTA-3: melt it
tihkitēw VII-2-1: it is melting
timikoniw VII-1: it is deep snow
tipaha VTI-1: measure/pay for it
tipahamaw VTA-2: pay him/pay it for him/her
tipahikē VAI: pay
tipahw VTA-3: measure it/pay it for him/her
tipātiskwēyi VAI: put your head down
tipēyimiso VAI: independent, (be)
tipiskāw VII-1: it is dark/night
tohkāpi VAI: open your eyes wide
tōmin VTA-1: grease it
tōmina VTI-1: grease it
twēho VAI: to land
twēhōmakan VII-2: land [the plane lands]

W
wākin VTA-1: bend it
wākina VTI-1: bend it
wākipayin VII-2: it bends
wanām VTA-1: interrupt & confuse
wanāmo VAI: lose train of thought while speaking
wanascikē VAI: misplace things
wanastā VTI-2: misplace it
wanih VTA-1: lose him/her/it
wanihikē VAI: trap [muskrats]
wanihitōta VAI: sin
wanihkē VAI: forget
waniho VAI: lost, (be)
wanihtā VTI-3: lose him/her/it
wanikiskisi VAI: faint/forget
waninē VAI: mad/delirious [disoriented]
waniskā VAI: arise from bed
wanitipiskāw VII-1: it is very dark/night
wāpahta VTI-1: see it
wāpahtah VTA-1: show it to him/her
wāpam VTA-1: see him/her/it
wāpan VII-1: it is daylight/it is morning
wāpi VAI: see [to have sight]
wāpinākwān VII-2: it appears white
wāpiskāw VII-2: it is white
wāpiskisiw VII-2: it is white
wāsakāmē VAI: go around an object
wāsakāmēpahtā VAI: run around an object
wāsakāmēpihā VAI: fly in circle

wāsaskotēnikē VTI-2: turn the lights on
wāsēskwan VII-1 it is sunny/clear
waskawin VTA-1: arouse/move [into motion]
waskawina VTI-1: arouse/move [into motion]
wātīhkē VAI: dig a hole
wawēyī VAI: get dressed
wawēyihtākwan VII-2: it is amusing
wawīpitāpiskanēpayi VAI: chattering teeth, (have)
wawiyatēyihtākosi VAI: amusing, (be)
wawiyēsim VTA-1: smooth-talk him/her
wayawī VAI: go outside
wayawīkocini VAI (irreg): fly out
wayawīkotin VII-2: it flies out as in being thrown out
wayawīpahtā VAI: run out of building
wayawītisahw VTA-3: as in send someone out
wayawīyāmo VAI: flee outdoors
wāyinōhtah VTA-1: take him/her back [to a place]
wāyinōhtatā VTI-1: take it back [to a place]
wēhcasin VII-2: it is easy
wēhtan VII-2: it is easy
wēpin VTA-1: throw him away
wēpina VTI-1: throw it away
wīcēw VTA-1: go with him/her
wīcih VTA-1: help him/her
wīcihiso VAI: help yourself
wīcisimōm VTA-1: dance with him/her
wīcisimōmiso VAI: dance by/with yourself
wīcihtāso VAI: be helpful
wīhkipw VTA-3: like the taste of
wīhkista VTI-1: like the taste of
wīhkohkē VAI: feast, (make a)
wīhkwaciho VAI: escape
wīhta VTI-1: tell/inform about it
wīhtamaw VTA-2: tell/inform him/her
wīkihto VAI: married, (be)
wīkim VTA-1: marry [him/her]
wīnēyihta VTI-1: loathe it
wīnēyim VTA-1: loathe him/her because of uncleanliness
wīpācikīsikāw VII-1: it is wet weather
wīsakahw VTA-3: hurt him/her/it
wīsakatahw VTA-3: hurt him by a blow
wīsakastēhw VTA-3: strap/whip him/her harshly
wīsakēyihta VTI-1: be sore
wīsakisini VAI (irreg): be injured by a fall
wīsakistikwānē VAI: have a hurting head
wīsām VTA-1: invite him/her
wītapim VTA-1: sit with/by him/her
wītisānīhito VAI: related to one another as family [genealogy/ bloodline]
wīwi VAI: married [have a wife], (be)
wiyatēyihta VTI-1: be amused by something
wiyino VAI: fat, (be)
wiyipātan VII-2: it is dirty

Y

yāhkasin VII-2: it is light in weight
yīkowan VII-1: it is foggy
yiyīkwatin VII-1: there is hoar frost
yōhtēna VTI-1: open it
yōhtēnamaw VTA-1: open to him
yōhtēkotā VTI-2: leave it ajar
yōskātisi VAI: gentle/meek, (be)
yōskāw VII-2: it is soft
yōskisi VAI: be soft
yōtin VII-1: it is windy

Appendix E: Verbs
English to Cree

A

able to do it, (be) VTI-2: kaskihtā

accompany/go with him/her VTA-2: wīcēw

ache [arms] VAI: tēwipitonē

[bones] VAI: tēwikanē

[ear] VAI: tēwihtawakē

[feet] VAI: tēwisitē

[head] VAI: tēwistikwānē

[nose] VAI: tēwikotē

[tooth] VAI: tēwāpitē

act brave VAI : nāpēhkāso

afraid, (be) VAI: kostāci

afraid of him/her, (be) VTA-4: kost

afraid of it, (be) VTI-1: kosta

age, be a certain [he is —- years old] VAI:
itahtopiponē

age, reach a certain [he is —- years old] VAI:
ispihtisī

agree VAI: tēpēyimo

alive, (be) VAI: pimātisi

allow/let go of him/her VTA-1: pakitin

allow/let it go VTI-1: pakitina

amazing VII-2: māmaskātēyihtākwan

amusing, (be) VAI: wawiyatēyihtākosi

amusing, consider it VTI-1: wiyatēyihta

amusing, it is VII-2: wawēyihtākwan

angle [fishing] VAI: kwāskwēpicikē

angry, (be) VAI: kisiwāsi

angry at him/her, (be) VTA-2: kisiwāsīstaw

annihilate them VTA-1: mēscih

appear [come into view] VAI: nōkosi

appears/comes into view, it VII-2: nōkwan

appointment, make an VAI: kiskimo

appointment, make with him/her VTA-1: kiskim

arise/stand up VAI: pasikō

arise [from bed] VAI: waniskā

arrive VAI (irreg): takosini

arrive [by foot] VAI: takohtē

arrive by vehicle/horse VAI: takopayi

arrive running VAI: takopahtā

arouse/move him/her VTA-1: waskawin

arouse/move it VTI-1: waskawina

ask VAI: kakwēcihkēmo

ask him/her VTA-1: kakwēcim

audible, it is VII-2: pēhtākwan

awaken him/her VTA-1: koskon

B

babble/be mouthy VAI: osāmitoni

baby-sit VAI: kanawēyimāwaso

bachelor, (be a) VAI: mōsāpēwi

bad/evil, (be) VAI: macātisi

bad/ugly [in appearance] VAI: māyātisi

bad/ugly, it is VII-2: māyātan

bake/cook VAI: nawacī

bald, (be) VAI: paskostikwānē

bathe/swim VAI: pakāsimo

bathe/wash him/her VTA-1: kisīpēkin

bathe/wash oneself VAI: kisīpēkiniso

be [there] VAI: ayā

beadwork, do VAI: mīkisistahikē

bearded, (be) VAI: miyēstawē

beautiful, (be) VAI: miyonākosi

bed down VAI: kawisimo

believe/agree with him/her VTA-2: tāpwēhtaw

believe/agree with it VTI-1: tāpwēhta

belittle him/her VTA-1: kitimākim

bend it VTA-1: wākin

bend it VTI-1: wākina

bend over VAI: nawakī

bends, it VII-2: wākipayin

big, (be) VAI: misikiti

big, it is VII-2: misāw

black, it appears VAI: kaskitēwinākosiw

black, it appears VII-2: kaskitēwinākwan

black, it is VAI: kaskitēsiw

black, it is VII-2: kaskitēwāw

blow VAI: pōtācikē

blow on him/her/it VTA-4: pōtāt

blow on it VTI-1: pōtāta

blown down, (be) VAI: kawāso

blue, it appears VAI: sīpihkonākosiw

blue, it appears VII-2: sīpihkonākwan

blue, it is VAI: sīpihkosiw

blue, it is VII-2: sīpihkwāw

board VAI: pōsi

board, put him/her on VTA-1: pōsih

board, put it on VTI-1: pōsihtā

boil it VTI-2: pakāhtā

boil it VTA-1: pakāsim

bother him/her VTA-1: mikoskācih

bother it VTI-2: mikoskācihtā

bothersome, (be) VAI: mikoskātisi

brag VAI: mamihcimo

brag about oneself VAI: mamihcimiso

brave, (be) VAI: sōhkēyimo

break into pieces VTA-4: pahkwēpit

break it VTA-1: pīkon

break it VTI-1: pīkona

break it into pieces VTI-1: pahkwēpita

breaks into pieces, it VII-2: pahkwēpayin

bring it VTI-2: pētā

bring it/him/her VTA-2: pēsiw
bring it for him VTA-2: pētamaw
busy, (be) VAI: canawī
buy VAI: atāwē
buy it for him VTA-2: atāwēstamaw

C

call/yell/shout VAI: tēpwē
call him/her VTA-4: tēpwāt
camp VAI: kapēsi
camp [make camp] VAI: mānokē
camp with him/her VTA-2: kapēsīstaw
careful of it, (be) VTI-1: asawēyihta
careful with him/her, (be) VTA-1: nākatēyim
careful with it, (be) VTI-1: nākatēyihta
catch, be the one to VAI: kāhcitiniwē
catch him/her VTA-1: kāhcitin
catch it VTI-1: kāhcitina
carry a lunch VAI: nīmā
carry him/her/it VTA-1: pimohtah
carry it VTI-2: pimohtatā
carry it with you VTA-1: pimowih
challenge him/her VTA-1: mawinēskom
change clothes VAI: mēskocī
change clothes VAI: mēskotayawinisē
change his/her diapers VTA-1: mīskotāsiyānēh
changes, it VII-2: mēskwacipayin
chase VAI: nawaswāsiwē
chase him/her/it VTA-4: nawaswāt
chase it VTI-1: nawaswāta
chattering teeth, (have) VAI: wawīpitāpiskanēpayi
cheat VAI: kēsiyākē
cheat him/her VTA-3: kēsiyohw
cherish/love him/her VTA-1: sawēyim
chew VAI: mākwacikē
chew [with a crunching noise] VAI: kaspāhcikē
chew it VTI-1: mākwahta
chew it VTA-1 mākwam
choke on food/liquid VAI: atoho
chop VAI: cīkahikē
chop him/her VTA-3: cīkahw
chop it VTI-1: cīkaha
clean, it is VII-2: kanātan
clean it VTI-2: kanācihtā
clean it/him/her VTA-1: kanācih
climb VAI: iskwāhtawī
climb [off of an something] VAI: nīhtāhtawī
climb [on horse or other object] VAI: kīhcēkosī
climb/walk up VAI: āmaciwē
close him/her in VTA-3: kipahw
close it VTI-1: kipaha
close your eyes VAI: pasakwāpi
coarse, it is VII-2: pihkwan
cold, (be) VAI: kawaci
cold, have a VAI: otakikomi

cold, it is VII-2: kawatin
cold, it is VII-1: kisināw/tahkāyāw
cold, make him/her VTA-1: kawatim
cold as you sleep, (be) VAI: kawacihkwāmi
colored so, (be) VAI: itasināso
colored so, it is VII-2: itasināstēw
comb one's hair VAI: sīkaho
comb someone's hair VTA-3: sīkahw
comb your hair for yourself VAI: sīkahoso
come here [Imperative only]: āstam
come in VAI: pīhtokwē
convince him/her VTA-1: sākohcim
cook VAI: paminawaso/ piminawaso
cook for someone VTA-4: piminawat
cook it VTA-3: kīsisw
cook it VTI-1: kīsisa
cook [finished] VAI: kīsitēpo
cost [so much] VAI: itakiso
costs [so much], it VII-2: itakihtēw
cough VTI-1: ostostota
counsel VAI: kakēskimiwē
counsel your child/ren VAI: kakēskimāwaso
counsel him/her VTA-1: kakēskim
count VAI: akihcikē
count them VTA-1: akim
count them VTI-1: akihta
crush it VTA-3: takwahw
crush it VTI-1: takwaha
cry VAI: māto
cry, make someone VTA-1: mōh
cry for him/her/it VTA-4: mawihkāt
cry for it VTI-1: mawihkāta
curse him/her VTA-1: pāstām
curse [bring curse on self] VAI: pāstāmiso
curse [bring a curse on self] VAI: pāstāmo
cut him/her [accidentally] VTA-3: pistisw
cut oneself [accidentally] VAI: pistisoso
cut it [accidentally] VTI-1: pistisa
cut it VTA-3: manisw
cut it VTI-1: manisa
cross over [by water] VTI-1: āsowaha

D

dance VAI: nīmihito/nīmi
dance [Owl dance] VAI: ōhōsimo
dance [Rain dance] VAI: nipākwēsimo
dance [Round dance] VAI: pīcicī
dance [Sioux dance] VAI: pwātisimo
dance by yourself VAI: wīcisimōmiso
dance with him/her VTA-1: wīcisimōm
dark/night, it is VII-1: tipiskāw
dark/night, it is a very VII-1: wanitipiskāw
dawn, it is VII-1: pētāpan
daylight, it is VII-1: wāpan
deep, the snow is VII-1: timikoniw/ ispāhkonakāw

deny him/her VTA-2: ānwēhtaw
deny it VTI-1: ānwēhta
desire him/her VTA-4: akāwāt
desire it VTI-1: akāwāta
difficult, it is VII-2: āyiman
dig a hole VAI: wātihkē
dirty, it is VII-2: wiyipātan
discourage him/her VTA-1: pōmēh
discouraged, (be) VAI: pōmē
dislike someone VTA-4: pakwāt
dislike it VTI-1: pakwāta
dislike it for someone VTA-2: pakwātamaw
disobedient, (be) VAI: sasīpihtawakē
disobedient, (be) VTI-1: sasīpihta
distressed about something, (be) VTI-1: pīkwēyihta
distress him/her VTA-1: kakwātakih
distress him/her VTA-1: pīkwēyihtamih
distressed, (be) VAI: kakwātakihtā
dive VAI: kōkī
do it VTI-1: itōta
do it for him VTA-2: itōtamaw
doubt/reject him/her VTA-2: ānwēhtaw
doubt it VTI-1: ānwēhta
doze off VAI: kawihkwasi
doze off VAI: nipēpayi
dream about him/her VTA-4: pawāt
dream about it VTI-1: pawāta
dressed, get VAI: wawēyī
drifting, it is (snow) VII-1: pīwan
drifting into snowbanks, it is VII-1: papēskwatāstan
drink VAI: minihkwē
drink, give him a VTA-1: minah
drive VAI: pamihcikē
drive backwards VAI: āsēpayi
drive past destination VAI (irreg): osāmakocini
drunk, (be) VAI: kīskwēpē
dry [yourself] VAI: pāsoso
dry him/her VTA-3: pāsw
dry it VTI-1: pāsa
dry/wipe him/her/it VTA-3: pāhkwahw
dry/wipe it VTI-1: pāhkwaha
drizzling, it is VII-1: kaskaniwipēscāsin
drizzling, it is VII-1: kaskaniwipēstāw
drizzling, it is VII-1: kimiwasin

E

earache, have an VAI: tēwihtawakē
easy, it is VII-2: wēhcasin/wēhtan
eat VAI: mīciso
eat [all of it] VTI-2: kitā
eat [all of it] VTA: kitamw
eat all your food VAI: kitāniwē
eat berries while picking VAI: mōminē
eat it VTA-1: mōw
eat it VTI-3: mīci

educate/teach VAI: kiskinwahamākē
educate/teach him/her VTA-2: kiskinwahamaw
empty it VTI-1: sīkohkina
enjoyable, it is VII-2: miywēyihtākwan
enter VAI: pīhtokwē
escape VAI: paspī
escape VAI: wīhkwaciho
escape VAI: kaskiho
evening, it is VII-1: otākosin
exhaust own resources VAI: mēstawihikē
exhausted, (be) VAI: nōhtēsini
exhausted, (be) VAI: ayēskosi
expensive, (be) VAI: āhkwakiso
expensive, it is VII-2: āhkwakihtēw
extinguish the fire VTI-1: āstawēha
extinguish the fire/light VAI: āstawēhikē
extinguish the light VAI: āstawēnikē

F

fall VAI (irreg) : pahkisini
fall [into] VAI: pīhcipayi
fall [into the fire] VAI: macostawēpayi
fall [into the water] VAI: pakastawēpayi
fall, it is VII-1: takwākin
falls, it VII-2: pahkihtin
farm/seed VAI: kistikē
fart VAI: pwēkito
fast runner, (be a) VAI: mihkawakī
fasten/zipper it VTI-1: sakwāskwaha
fat, (be) VAI: wiyino
fat, (become) VAI: tāhcipo
feast, make a VAI: wīhkohkē
feed him/her VTA-1: asam
feed oneself VAI: asamiso
feel [as in health] VAI: itamahciho
feel better VAI: āstēpayi
feel/examine him/her/it VTA-1: mīskon
feel/examine it VTI-1: mīskona
feel/examine oneself VAI: mīskoniso
feel poorly/ill VAI: māyimahciho
feel sad VTI-1: pīkiskāta
feel well VAI: miyomahciho
fetch him/her VTA-4 nāt
fetch it VTI-1: nāta
fetch it for him VTA-2 nātamaw
fever, (have a) VAI: kisiso
fight VAI: nōtinikē
fight, s/he always wants to VAI: nōtinikēski
fight him/her VTA-1: nōtin
fill it VTA-1: sākaskinah
fill it VTI-2: sākaskinahtā
fill it for him VTA-2: sākaskinahtamaw
find him/her VTA-2: miskaw
find it VTI-1: miska
finish it VTA-1: kīsih

finish it VTI-1: kīsihtā
fish VAI: nōcikinosēwē
fish [with a net] VAI: pakitahwā
fish [with a rod] VAI: kwāskwēpicikē
fix/repair it VTI-2: napācihtā
flee VAI: sipwēyāmo
flee VAI: tapasī
flee indoors VAI: pīhtokwēyāmo
flee outdoors VAI: wayawīyāmo
flee towards a specific area VAI: itāmo
flies out, it [as in being thrown out] VII-2:
wayawīkotin
fly VAI: pimihā
fly in a circle VAI: wāsakāmēpihā
fly out VAI (irreg): wayawīkocini
foggy, it is VII-1: yīkowan
follow him/her VTA-3: pimitisahw
follow him/her VTA-1: askowēh
follow him/her around VTA-3: papāmitisahw
follow it VTI-1: pimitisaha
foolish, act VAI: mohcohkāso
foolish, (be) VAI: kakēpātisi
forget VAI: wanihkē/wanikiskisi
forget it VTI-1: pōnēyihta
forget him/her VTA-1: pōnēyim
forgive him VTA-2: pōnēyihtamaw
freeze VAI: āhkwaci
freeze it VTI-2: āhkwatihtā
freeze it VTA-1: āhkwatisim
freeze to death (colloq) VAI: nipahāskwaci
from [some place], (be) VAI: ohcī
frown VAI: kisowinākosi
frown at him/her VTA-1: kisowikanawāpam
frown at it VTI-1: kisowikanawāpahta
frozen, it is VII-2: āhkwatin
fry VAI: sāsāpiskisikē
fry it VTI-1: sāsisa
fry it VTA-3: sāsisw
fry it VTI-1: sāsāpiskisa
fry it VTA-3: sāsāpiskisw
full from eating, (be) VAI: kīspo
fun, have VTI-2: mōcikihtā

G

gather for oneself VAI: māwasakonamāso
gather things VTA-1: māwasakon
gather things VTI-1: māwasakona
gentle, (be) VAI: yōskātisi
get dressed VAI: wawēyī
get firewood VAI: nikohtē
get him/her VTA-4: nāt
get him/her ready VTA-1: kakwēyācih
get it VTI-1: nāta
get it ready VTI-2: kakwēyācihtā
get up [from bed] VAI: waniskā

give him/her a smoke VTA-1: pīhtwāh
give it away VAI: mēki
give it to him VTA-1: miy
glad, (be) VTI-1: miywēyihta
go [Imperative only]: niyā
go [around an object] VAI: wāsakāmē
go [but walk rather than ride] VAI: mostohtē
go ashore VAI: kapā
go away [Imperative only]: awas
go down a hill/stairs VAI: nīhtaciwē
go home VAI: kīwē
go in VAI: pīhtokwē
go outside VAI: wayawī
go through [bush, door, hall] VAI: sāpohtē
go with him/her VTA-2: wīcēw
gossip/talk too much VAI: osāmitōni
grab him/her/it VTA-1: nawatin
grab it VTI-1: nawatina
grateful, (be) VAI: nanāskomo
grease it VTA-1: tōmin
grease it VTI-1: tōmina
green, it appears VAI: askihtakonākosiw
green, it is VAI: askihtakosiw
green, it is VII-2: askihtakwāw
grieve for someone VTA-4: mihtāt
grieve/long/sorry for it VTI-1: mihtāta
grow VAI: ohpiki
grow him/her [as in raise] VTA-1: ohpikih
grow it VTI-2: ohpikihtā

H

hailing, it is VAI (irreg): miskwamiy pahkisin
hairy, (be) VAI: miyawēsi
hang it/him/her VTA-4: akot
hang it VTI-2: akotā
hate him/her VTA-4: pakwāt
hate it VTI-2: pakwāta
have big teeth VAI: mahkāpitē
have expectation/desire VAI: pakosēyimo
have him/her/it VTA-1: ayāw
have a husband VAI: onāpēmi
have it VTI-2: ayā
have sharp teeth VAI: kāsāpitē
heal VTA-1: nanātawih
hear him/her VTA-2: pēhtaw
hear it VTI-1: pēhta
heat the liquid VTI-1: kisākamisa
heat the water to make tea VAI: kisākamisikē
heavy, (be) VAI: kosikwati
heavy, it is VII-2: kosikwan
help him/her VTA-1: wīcih
help oneself VAI: wīcihiso
helpful, (be) VAI: wīcihtāso
here, take this [Imperative only] nah
hide VAI: kāsō

hide from him/her VTA-2: kāsōstaw
hide him/her/it VTA-4 : kāt
hide it VTI-2: kātā
hide it from/for him/her VTA-2: kātamaw
hire him/her VTA-1: atoskah
hire him/her VTA-4: atot
hire him/her VTA-1: masinahikēh
hit him/her/it VTA-3: pakamahw
hit it VTI-1: pakamaha
hoar-frost, (there is) VII-1: yiyīkwatin
hobble it [horse] VTA-4: napwahpit
hot liquid, it is VII-2: kisākamitēw
hot, it is [temperature] VII-1: kisitēw
hot, it is [weather] VII-1: kisāstēw
hot weather, it is VII-1: kīsapwēyāw
howl like a coyote VAI: oyōyo
hungry, (be) VAI: nōhtēhkatē
hunt VAI: mācī
hunt ducks VAI: nōcisipē
hunt it VTA-1: nōcih
hurt him/her VTA-3: wīsakahw
hurt him/her [with a blow] VTA-3: wīsakatahw
hurting head, (have a) VAI: wīsakistikwānē
hurry VAI: kakwēciyāho
hurry VAI: papāsī
hurry up VAI: tāstapī
hurry up VAI: cāstapī

I
imprison VTA-3: kipahw
incite him/her VTA-2: sīhkiskaw
include/add it VTI-1: takona
independent, (be) VAI: tipēyimiso
indigestion, (have) VAI: kisiwaskatē
industrious, (be) VAI: kakāyawisī
inefficient, (be) VAI: mamāyī
inform/tell about it VTI-1: wīhta
inform/tell him/her VTA-2: wīhtamaw
injured [by a fall], (be) VAI (irreg): wīsakisini
interpret VAI: itwēstamākē
interrupt/confuse him/her VTA-1: wanām
introduce him/her VTA-2: nakiskamohtaw
invite him/her VTA-1: nitom
invite him/her VTA-1: wīsām
iron [clothing] VAI: sōskwahikē
iron it VTA-3: sōskwahw
iron it VTI-1: sōskwaha
itch VAI: kēyakisi
itchy [ear] VAI: kēyakihtawakē
  [feet] VAI: kēyakisitē
  [hands] VAI: kēyakicihcē
  [head] VAI: kēyakistikwānē

J
jealous of him/her, (be) VTA-1: kahkwēyim

jealous of it, (be) VTI-1: kahkwēyihta
jog VAI: sēsāwipahtā
jump VAI: kwāskohti
jump on top of VAI: tēhcipayiho

K
keep him/her/it VTA-1: kanawēyim
keep it for him VTA-2: kanawēyihtamaw
keep it VTI-1: kanawēyihta
keep the children/babysit VAI: kanawēyimāwaso
kick VAI: tahkiskācikē
kick him/her VTA-2: tahkiskaw
kick it VTI-1: tahkiska
kill him/her/it VTA-1: nipah
kind, (be) VAI: kisēwātisi
kind, (be) VAI: miyohtwā
kindle [ignite] VTA-3: saskahw
kindle/ignite it VTI-1: saskaha
kindling, make VAI: pīskatahikē
kiss him/her VTA-1: ocēm
kiss it VTI-1: ocēhta
kneel VAI: cīhcikwanapi
knock it over VTI-1: kipotēkāta
knock it over VTI-1: kwatapiska
knock him/her/it over VTA-2: kwatapiskaw
know him VTA-1: kiskēyim
know it VTI-1: kiskēyihta
known, it is VII-2: kiskēyihtākwan

L
lame VAI: māskisi
  [foot] VAI: māskisitē
  [leg] VAI: māskikātē
land VAI: twēho
lands, it VII-2: twēhōmakan
large, it is VII-2: misāw
late, (be) VAI: mwēstasisini
laugh VAI: pāhpi
laugh at him/her VTA-1: pāhpih
laugh at it VTI-2: pāhpihtā
lazy, (be) VAI: kihtimi
leave/depart VAI: sipwēhtē
leave him VTA-4: nakat
leave him be VTA-1: pōnih
leave it VTI-1: nakata
leave it ajar VTI-2: yohtēkotā
leave it be VTI-2: pōnihtā
let go of him/her VTA-1: pakitin
let it go VTI-1: pakitina
lie [falsehood] VAI: kiyāski
lie to him/her VTA-1: kiyāskīm
lie [to him] VTA-2: kiyāskīstaw
lie down VAI (irreg): pimisini
lift him/her VTA-1: ohpin
lift it VTI-1: ohpina

light [in weight], (it is) VII-2: yāhkasin
like him/her VTA-1: miywēyim
like him/her VTA-1: cīhkēyim
like it VTI-1: miywēyihta
like it VTI-1: cīhkēyihta
like the taste of it VTA-1: wīhkipw
like the taste of it VTI-1: wīhkista
limp, [to] VAI: māskipayi
listen to him/her VTA-2: natohtaw
listen to it VTI-1: natohta
listen well/heed VTI-1: nahīhta
little, (be) VAI: apisīsisi
loan it to him/her VTA-1: awih
loathe him/her [because of uncleanliness] VTA-1:
    winēyim
loathe it VTI-1: wīnēyihta
lock it VTI-1: kipāpiskaha
lock up VAI: kipāpiskahikē
lonesome, (be) VAI: kaskēyihta
long hair, (have) VAI: kinwāniskwē
long, it is VII-2: kinwāw
look at him/her VTA-1: kitāpam
look at him/her VTA-1: kanawāpam
look at it VTI-1: kitāpahta
look at it VTI-1: kanawāpahta
look for him/her VTA-2: natonaw
look for it VTI-1: natona
look [out of window] VAI: paspāpi
look over there VAI: itāpi
lose it VTI-2: wanihtā
lose it/her/him VTA-1: wanih
lose train of thought VAI: wanāmo
lost, (be) VAI: waniho
love him/her VTA-1: sākih
love it VTI-2: sākihtā
love him/her VTA-1: sawēyim
lumpy, it is VII-2: piskwāw

M

mad, (be) VAI: kīskwē
mad/delirious [because of illness] VAI: waninē
maim VTA-1: māskih
make [bannock] VAI: pahkwēsikanihkē
    [bread] VAI: pīswēhkasikanihkē
    [moccasins] VAI: maskisinihkē
    [music] VAI: kitohcikē
make an appointment VAI: kiskimo
make appointment with him VTA-1: kiskim
make ashes VAI: pihkohkē
make it VTA-1: osīh
make it VTI-2: osīhtā
make it for him] VTA-2: osīhtamaw
make soup VAI: mīcimāpōhkē
make sure VAI: kēhcināho
married, (be) VAI: wīkihto

married [to have a husband] VAI: onāpēmi
married [to have a wife] VAI: wīwi
marry him/her VTA-1: wīkim
mean/nasty/difficult, (be) VAI: macēyihtākosi
measure it VTA-3: tipahw
measure it VTI-1: tipaha
meek, (be) VAI: yōskātisi
meet him/her VTA-2: nakiskaw
meet it VTI-1: nakiska
melt it VTA-3: tihkisw
melt it VTI-1: tihkisa
melting, it is VII-2: tihkitēw
melting, it is [spring] VII-1: saskan
misplace it VTI-2: wanastā
misplace things VAI: wanascikē
miss [as in target] VTA-3: patahw
miss [chair] VAI: pascipayi
miss it VTI-1: pataha
miss target [when pouring liquid] VTI-1: pacisīkina
miss/yearn for him/her VTA-1: kaskēyim
miss/yearn for him/her VTA-1: kwihtawēyim
miss/yearn for it VTI-1: kwihtawēyihta/ kaskēyihta
moan VAI: mamāhpinē
moonlight, it is VII-1: nīpāyāstēw/ kīsikāyāstēw
morning, (it is) VII-1: kīkisēpāyāw
morning/daylight, (it is) VII-1: wāpan
mourn/cry for him/her VTA-4: mawihkāt
mourn/cry for it VTI-1: mawihkāta
mournful/sorry about it VTI-1: mihtāta
mournful/sorry for him/her, (be) VTA-4: mihtāt
move camp VAI: āhcipici
move him/her VTA-1: māhtin
move him/her VTA-1: waskawin
move it VTI-1: waskawina/māhtina
move to tears VTA-1: mōskom

N

naked/nude, (be) VAI: mostāpēkasē
named/called, (be) VAI: isiyihkāso
nasty day, (be a) VII-1: maci-kīsikāw
nice, (be [in appearance]) VAI: miyosisi
nice, (be) VAI: miyosi
nice, it is VII-2: miywāsin
nice day, it is a VII-1: miyo-kīsikāw
night, it is VII-1: tipiskāw
nod/[shake your head] VAI: nanamiskwēyi
not a nice day, it is VII-1: māyi-kīsikāw
nurse/breast feed him/her/it VTA-1: nōh
nurse/breast feed VAI: nōni

O

open it for him/her VTA-2: yōhtēnamaw
open it VTI-1: yōhtēna
open your eyes VAI: tōhkāpi
open your mouth VAI: tāwati

orange, it appears VAI: osāwinākosiw
orange, it appears VII-2: osāwinākwan
orange, it is VAI: osāwisiw
orange, it is VII-2: osāwāw
overfilled, it is VII-2: akwātaskinēw
owe VAI: masinahikē
owe him/her VTA-2: masinahamaw

P

pass a message to him/her VTA-2: āsōwīhtamaw
pass him/her VTA-2: miyāskaw
pass it VTI-1: miyāska
pay him/her VTA-2: tipahamaw
pay for it VTI-1: tipaha
pay VAI: tipahikē
perish/die VAI: nisiwanātisi
perish from hunger/be extremely hungry VAI:
nipahāhkatē
persevere VAI: ahkamēyimo
pick berries VAI: mawiso
pick thing/s up VTA-1: mōsahkin
pick thing/s up VTI-1: mōsahkina
pierce him/her [with sharp object] VTA-3 : cīstahw
pierce it VTI-1: cīstaha
pity him/her VTA-1: kitimākēyim
pity on him/her, (have) VTA-2: kitimākinaw
place him/her/it VTA-1 (irreg): ahi
place it in order VTI-2: nahastā
place it nearby VTI-2: nēhpēmastā
play VAI: mētawē
play ball VAI: pakahatowē
please him/her VTA-1: miywēyihtamih
point out to him/her VTA-2: itwahamaw
poison him/her VTA-1: piscipoh
poisoned, (be) VAI: piscipo
ponder/think of him/her VTA-1: māmitonēyim
ponder [think about it] VTI-1: māmitonēyihta
poor/unfortunate, (be) VAI: kitimākisi
pour it VTI-1: sīkina
pour/spill it VTI-1: sīkipita
pow-wow [dance] VAI: pwātisimo
pray VAI: ayamihā
pray for him VTA-2: ayamihēstamaw
pray over the food [feast] VAI: nīminikē
preach VAI: kakēskimiwē
preach to him VTA-1: kakēskim
preach to own children VAI: kakēskimāwaso
prepare/cook a meal VAI: paminawaso
pretend to sleep VAI: nipāhkāso
proud of it, (be) VTI-1: kihcēyihta
pull him/her VTA-4: ocipit
pull him/her out VTA-4: kwēyakopit
pull it VTI-1: ocipita
pull it out VTI-1: kwēyakopita
purple, it is VII-2: nīpāmāyātan

purple, it is VAI: nīpāmāyātisiw
put it [here/there] VTA-1 (irreg): āhi
put it [here/there] VTI-2: astā
put it on VTI-1: postiska
put it on VTA-2: postiskaw
put it on top of VTI-2: tahkohtastā
put on clothes VAI: postayiwinisē
put on coat/clothes VAI: postasākē
put on hat VAI: postastotinē
put on mitts VAI: postastisē
put on pants VAI: poscitāsē
put on shoes VAI: postaskisinē
put on socks VAI: postasikanē
put your head down VAI: tipātiskwēyi

Q

quiet, (be) VAI: kiyāmapi
quit VAI: pōyo
quit bothering/doing that VTI-2: pōnihtā
quit talking VAI: pōnwēwita

R

rain, large drops of VII-1: pahkipēstāw
rain, cold VII-1: tahkipēstāw
raining, it is VII-1: kimiwan
read VAI: ayamihcikē
read it VTI-2: ayamihtā
ready, (be) VAI: kwēyātapi/kwēyātisi
ready, get him/her VTA-1: kakwēyācih
ready, (get it) VTI-1: kakwēyācihtā
recognize him/her VTA-1: nisitawēyim
recognize it VTI-1: nisitawēyihta
red, it appears VAI: mihkonākosiw
red, it appears VII-2: mihkonākwan
red, it is VAI: mihkosiw
red, it is VII-2: mihkwāw
refuse him/her VTA-2: asēnamaw
regard/look after it VAI: pisiskēyihcikē
reject/deny him VTA-2: ānwēhtaw
reject/deny it VTI-1: ānwēhta
related to one another as family [genealogy/ blood-
line] VAI: wītisānīhito
remember it VAI: kiskisi
repent VAI: kwēskātisi
respond to it [statement, letter] VTI-1: ayāsīhta
rest VAI (irreg): āstēsini
rest VAI: aywēpi
return it to him/her VTA-2: asēnamaw
rid of them, get VTA-1: mēscih
ride a vehicle VAI: otāpāso
ride around VAI: pāmipayi
ride to/drive to VAI: ispayi
roast it over a fire [hang] VAI: sakapwē
roast over a fire [spit] VAI: apwē
ruin it VTI-2: nisiwanācihtā

ruin it/him/her VTA-1: nisiwanācih
run VAI: pimipahtā
run/drive it VTI-2: pimipayihtā
run/flee VAI: tapasī
run after/chase him/her VTA-4: nawaswāt
run after/chase it VTI-1: nawaswāta
run around VAI: papāmipahtā
run around an object VAI: wāsakāmēpahtā
run [away from speaker] VAI: atimipahtā
run down [stairs/hill] VAI: nīhtaciwēpahtā
run fast VAI: sōhkēpahtā
run home [towards home] VAI: kīwēpahtā
run into building in fear VAI: pīhtokwēyāmo
run out of building VAI: wayawīpahtā
run out of it [be in need] VAI: nōhtēpayi
run over there [yonder]VAI: ispahtā
run up [hill/stairs] VAI: āmaciwēpahtā
run when you go home VAI: ati-kīwēpahtā
runner, (be) a fast VAI: mihkawakī

S
sail VAI: pimāsi
satisfied with it, (be) VTI-1: nahēyihta
save him VTA-1: pimācih
say it VTI-3: itwē
scare him/her VTA-1: sēkih
scared, (be) VAI: sēkisi
scared of him/her, (be) VTA-4: kost
scared of it, (be) VTI-1: kosta
scared/afraid, (be) VAI: kostāci
see [to have sight] VAI: wāpi
see him VTA-1: wāpam
see it VTI-1: wāpahta
seed VAI: kistikē
seek advice from him/her VTA-2: nātāmostaw
seek help, advice from him/her VTA-2:
    nātāmototaw
send/order for it VTI-1: nātisaha
send for him/her/it VTA-3: nātisahw
send him/her/it VTA-3: itisahw
send him/her out of building VTA-3: wayawītisahw
send it VTI-1: itisaha
send it VTI-1: isitisaha
send him/her/it VTA-3: isitisahw
set it on fire VTI-1: macastawēha
set the table VAI: oyascikē
sew VAI: kaskikwāso
sew it for him/her VTA-2: kaskikwātamaw
sew it VTA-4: kaskikwāt
sew it VTI-1: kaskikwāta
shake his hand/greet him/her VTA-2: atamiskaw
shake/nod your head VAI: nanamiskwēyi
sharpen it [stick] VTI-1: cīposa
shave VAI: kāskipāso
shiver VAI: nanamaci

shrivel [with heat] VTI-1: ocipohkasa
shoot him/her VTA-3: pāskisw
shoot it VTI-1: pāskisa
show him/her directions VTA-1: kiskinohtah
show it to him/her VTA-1: wāpahtah
show him/her how VTA-2: kiskinohamaw
sick, (be) VAI: āhkosi
sin VAI: wanihitōta
sing VAI: nikamo
sing habitually VAI: nikamoski
single lady, (be a) VAI: mōsiskwēwi
sit/be at home VAI: api
sit down VAI: nahapi
sit on top of VII-2: tahkohtastēw
sit still VAI: koskowātapi
sit up VAI: samatapi
sit with/by him VTA-1: wītapim
skate VAI: sōskwātahikē
ski VAI: sōskoyāpawi
skin VAI: pahkonikē
skin it VTA-1: pahkon
skinny, (be) VAI: kawāhkatoso
skinny, (be) VAI: nipahipawanī
slap him/her on the face VTA-3: pasihkwētahw
sleep VAI: nipā
sleep, (like to) VAI: nipāski
sleep, pretend to VAI: nipāhkāso
sleep in VAI: sāpohkwāmi
sleep in/oversleep VAI: osāmihkwāmi
sleep well VAI: miyohkwāmi
sleepy, (be) VAI: nōhtēhkwasi
slide [downhill] VAI: sōskwaciwē
slip VAI: sōskopayi
slow, (be) VAI: papēcī
smell him/her VTA-1: miyām
smell it VTI-1: miyāhta
smells [it] VII-2: miyākwan
smile VAI: pāhpinākosi
smile VAI: pāhpihkwē
smoke [cigarette] VAI: pīhtwā
smoke, give him/her a VTA-1: pīhtwāh
smokes, it [chimney] VII-2: kaskāpahtēw
smooth-talk him/her VTA-1 wawiyēsim
snare, set a VAI: tāpakwē
snare him/her/it VTA-4: nakwāt
snore VAI: matwēhkwāmi
snow is deep, (the) VII-2: ispākonakāw
snowing, it is VII-1: mispon
soft, it is VII-2: yōskāw
soft, (be) VAI: yōskisi
somersault VAI: āpocikwānī
sore, (be) VTI-1: wīsakēyihta
sounds like so, it VII-2: itihtākwan
speak VAI: pīkiskwē
speak Cree VAI: nēhiyawē

speak English VAI: ākayāsimo
speak English to him/her VTA-2: ākayāsimototaw
speak evil VAI: macipīkiskwē
speak loudly VAI: kisīwē
speak the truth always VAI: tāpwēski
splash/sprinkle him/her VTA-2: sīkahāhtaw
sprain [joint] VAI (irreg): kotikosini
spread it [i.e. blanket] VTI-2: taswēkastā
spread it for him/her [i.e., butter] VTA-2:
    sawahamaw
spring, it is VII-1: miyoskamin
spring, it is VII-1: sīkwan
spring [as in spring-water] VII-2: mohkiciwanipēw
stand straight VAI: kwēyaskokāpawi
stand up VAI: nīpawi/pasikō
stand with your back to me VAI: atimikāpawi
stare in awe VTI-2: mamēhcikāpahta
start doing it VTI-2: mācihtā
start to leave VAI: sipwēhtē
start to run away VAI: sipwēpahtā
startle him/her VTA-1: sisikwacih
stay put/with it VTI-1: kisāta
step on him/her/it VTA-2: tahkoskaw
step on it VTI-1: tahkoskāta
stingy, (be) VAI: sasākisī
stop VAI: nakī
stop him VTA-1: nakin
stops, it VII-2: pōnipayin
strap/whip him/her harshly VTA-3: wīsakastēhw
striped, (be) VAI: masināso
striped, it is VII-2: masināstēw
storming/nasty, it is VII-1: maci-kīsikāw
strike him/her/it VTA-3: pakamahw
strong, (be) VAI: maskawisī
strong, (be) VAI: sōhkisi
strong, it is VII-2: maskawāw
strong, it is VII-2: sōhkan
stumble/trip VAI: pisosini
summer, it is VII-1: nīpin
sunny, it is VII-1: wāsēskwan
sunset VII-1: pahkisimon
sure, (be) VAI: kēhcināho
surprised about him/her, (be) VTA-1: koskwēyim
surprised about it, (be) VTI-1: koskwēyihta
swallow it VTI-2: kohcipayihtā
sweat VAI: apwēsi
sweat as you run VAI: apwēpahtā
swim VTI-1: yāhyāna
swim [making a "v"] VAI: pimātakā
swim/have a bath VAI: pakāsimo

T
take/carry it with you VTA-1: pimowih
take/carry it with you VTI-2: pimowitā
take him/her along VTA-1: pimohtah

take him/her down/off of VTA-1 : nīhtin
take him/her home VTA-1: kīwēhtah
take him/her out VTA -1: kwēyakon
take him/her/it VTA-1: otin
take him/her/it back VTA-1: wayinohtah
take him/her there VTA-1: itohtah
take it VTI-1: otina
take it along VTI-2: pimohtatā
take it away from him/her VTA-1: maskam
take it back VTI-2: wayinohtatā
take it home VTI-2: kīwēhtatā
take it off VTA-1: kēcikon
take it off VTI-1: kēcikona
take it off VTI-1: kēcikoska
take it off/down VTI-1: nīhtina
take it out VII-1: kwēyakona
take it there VTI-2: itohtatā
take it there for him VTA-2: itohtatamaw
take off your coat/clothes [undress] VAI: kētasākē
take off your hat/cap VAI: kētastotinē
take off your mitts VAI: kētastisē
take off your shoes VAI: kētaskisinē
take off your socks VAI: kētasikanē
take things home VAI: kīwēhtacikē
take this/here [Imperative only]: nah
tall, (be) VAI: kinosi
tall/long VII-2: kinwāw
talk VAI: ayami
talk VAI: pīkiskwē
talk about him/her so VTA-1: itācim
talk constantly VTI-1: nipātwēwita
tan it VTA-3: atisw
tan it VTI-1: atisa
tanned, (be) VAI: atiso
taste it VTI-1: kocispita
taste it VTA-4 : kocispit
tastes bad, it VII-2: macispakwan/ macispakosiw
tastes nice, it VII-2: miyospakwan/ miyospakosiw
tattle on him/her VTA-1: mamisim
teach VAI: kiskinwahamākē
teach him/her VTA-2: kiskinwahamaw
tear it VTA-4: yāyikipit
tear it VTI-1: yāyikipita
tease him VTA-1: nanōyacih
tell about it VTI-1: wīhta
tell about it VTI-1: ātota
tell him/her VTA-2: wīhtamaw
tell a story/inform VAI: ācimo
tell him/her a story/inform him/her VTA-2:
    ācimostaw
thick, it is VII-2: kispakāw
thin, it is VII-2: papakāsin
think about him VTA-1: māmitonēyim
think about it/ponder VAI: māmitonēyihta
think highly of him/her VTA-1: kihcēyim

think highly of it VTI-1: kihcēyihta
think of him VTA-1: māmitonēyim
think of it VTI-1: māmitonēyihta
think so about him [assess] VTA-1: itēyim
think so about it [assess] VTI-1: itēyihta
thirsty, (be) VAI: nōhtēyāpākwē
throw him/her/it away VTA-1: wēpin
throw him/her in the fire VTA-1: macastawēpin
throw him/her/it in the water VTA-1: pakastawēpin
throw it away VTI-1: wēpina
throw it in the fire VTI-1: macastawēpina
throw it in the water VTI-1: pakastawēpina
tickle him/her VTA-1: kēyakicēn
tidy up VAI: nahascikē
tie him/her VTA-4: tahkopit
tie it VTA-4: sakahpit
tie it VTI-1: sakahpita/tahkopita
tie him/her/it tightly VTA-4: sīhtahpit
tie it tightly VTI-1: sīhtahpita
tired/exhausted, (be) VAI: nēstosi
tired/exhausted, (be) VAI: ayēskosi
trap VAI: wanihikē
travel VAI: pimohtēho
travel to VAI (irreg): itakocini
trot VAI: pimipahcāsi
trot VAI: cēcēmipahtā
try it VTI-2: kocihtā
turn VAI: kwēskī
turn everything upside down VAI: ayapinikē
turn him/her/it VTA-1: kwēskin
turn it VTI-1: kwēskina
turn on the lights VTI-2: wāsaskotēnikē

U
ugly, (be) [in appearance] VAI: māyātisi
ugly, it is VII-1: māyātan
understand him/her VTA-2: nisitohtaw
understand it VTI-1: nisitohta
unfortunate/poor, (be) VAI: kitimākisi
use all/exhaust sources VTI-1: mēscipita
use it VTA-1: āpacih
use it VTI-2: āpacihtā

V
visit VAI: kiyokē
visit him VTA-2: kiyokaw
vomit VAI: pwākamo

W
wait VAI: pēho
wait for him VTA-1: pēh
wake, (be at a) VAI: nīpēpi
walk VAI: pimohtē
walk [rather than riding] VAI: mostohtē
walk about VAI: papāmohtē

walk along VAI: pa-pimohtē
walk backwards VAI: asēhtē
walk through it VAI: sāpohtē
walk up VAI: āmaciwē
wander far away VAI: kwāhtohtē
want him VTA-1: nitawēyim
want it VTI-1: nitawēyihta
warm VII-1: kīsowēyāw
warm, it is VII-1: kīsapwēyāw
warm, it is VII-2: kīsowāw
warm liquid, it is a VII-2: kīsowākamin
wash clothes VAI: kisīpēkinikē
wash dishes VAI: kisīpēkiyākinē
wash/bathe him/he/it VTA-1: kisīpēkin
wash it for him/her VTA-2: kisīpēkinamaw
wash the floor VAI: kisīpēkihtakinikē
wash your face VAI: kāsīhkwē
wash your feet VAI: kisīpēkisitē
wash your hands VAI: kāsīcihcē
wash your head/hair VAI: kisīpēkistikwānē
wash your neck VAI: kisīpēkikwayawē
watch him/her VTA-1: kanawāpam
watch it VTI-1: kanawāpahta
weak, (be) VAI: nēsowisī
well, (be) VAI: miywāyā
wet weather VII-1: wīpācikīsikāw
whisper VAI: kīmwē
whistle VAI: kīskosī
white, it appears VII -2: wāpinākwan
white, it is VAI: wāpikiskisiw
white, it is VII-2: wāpiskāw
whip him VTA-3: pasastēhw
whip/strap him/her harshly VTA-3: wīsakastēhw
willing, (be) VAI: tēpakēyimo
win VAI: otahowē
windy, it is VII-1: yōtin
winter, it is VII-1: pipon
wipe him/her VTA-3: kāsīhw
wipe it VTI-1: kāsīha
wipe the dishes VAI: kāsīyākanē
work VAI: atoskē
work at/on it VTI-1: atoskāta
work for him/her VTA-2: atoskaw
work hard at VTI-1: sīhtatoskāta
work well VAI: miywatoskē
work well, they VII-2: miyopayinwa
works well, it VII-2: miyopayin
works well, it VAI: miyopayiw
wrestle him VTA-1: māsīh
write VAI: masinahikē
write it VTI-1: masinaha/osipēha
write to/for him VTA-2: masinahamaw
write well VAI: miywasinahikē

Y
yell/shout VAI: tēpwē
yellow, it appears VAI: wāposāwinākosiw
yellow, it appears VII-2: wāposāwinākwan
yellow, it is VAI: wāposāwisiw
yellow, it is VII-2: wāposāwāw
young, (be) VAI: oskāyiwi